IMAGES
of America

EATONTOWN AND FORT MONMOUTH

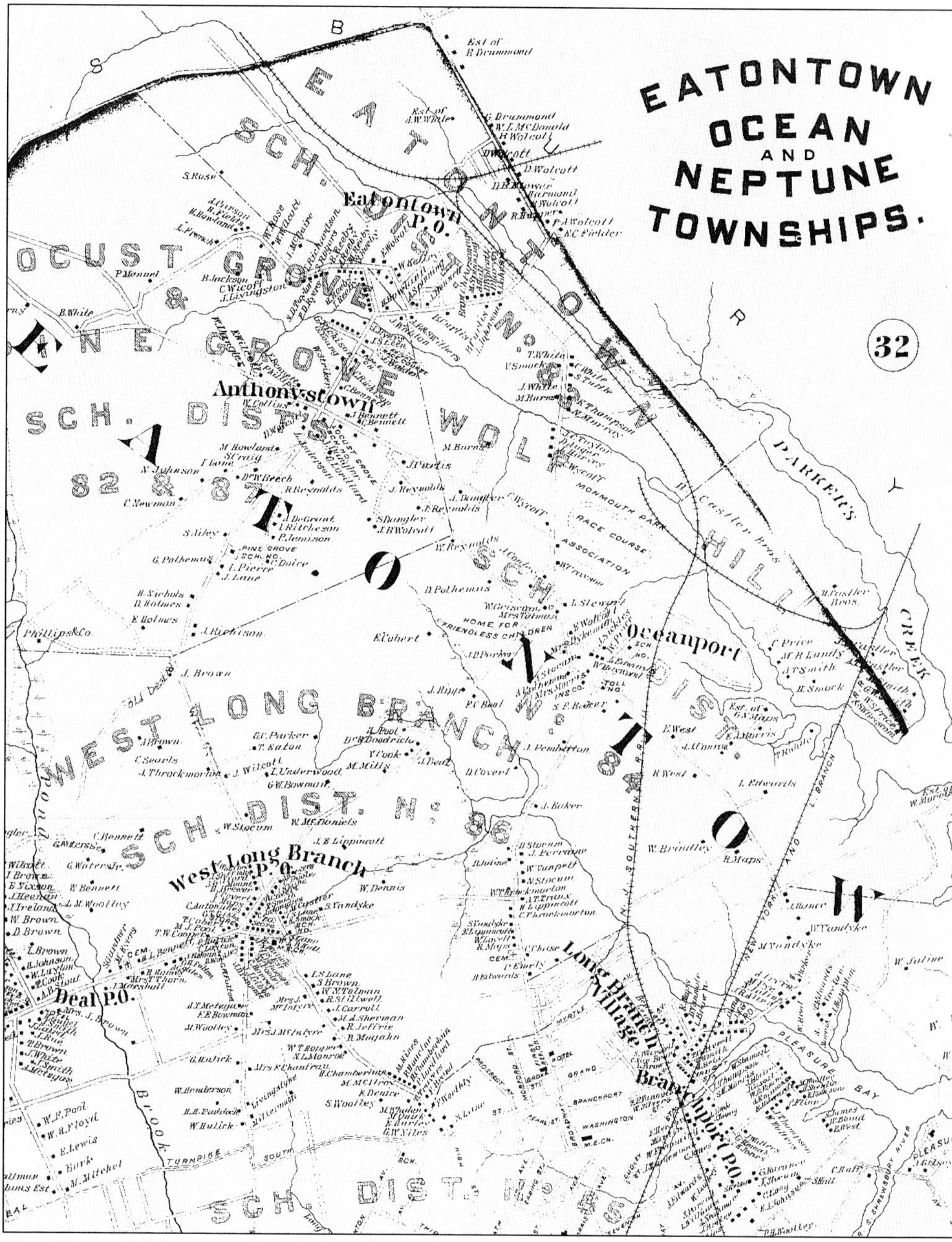

The *Chester Wolverton Atlas of 1889* shows the township's three villages: Eatontown, Oceanport, and West Long Branch.

IMAGES
of America

EATONTOWN AND FORT MONMOUTH

Helen C. Pike and Glenn D. Vogel

ARCADIA
PUBLISHING

ISBN 978-0-7385-5697-0

Published by Arcadia Publishing
Charleston, South Carolina

Printed in the United States of America

Library of Congress Control Number: 2008922468

For all general information, please contact Arcadia Publishing:
Telephone 843-853-2070
Fax 843-853-0044
E-mail sales@arcadiapublishing.com
For customer service and orders:
Toll-Free 1-888-313-2665

Visit us on the Internet at www.arcadiapublishing.com

We would like to dedicate this book
to the people who have inspired and encouraged us
from our earliest beginnings:
family historian David and Janet V. Turk;
North Country author Robert E. Pike;
Eatontown teachers Dotte Marshall, Ronald Danielson, and
William Bruce;
and especially, to Monmouth County historian George H. Moss Jr.

Contents

Acknowledgments

This endeavor to commemorate the whole of Eatontown and some of its forgotten pieces of history would not have been possible except for the efforts of Bill and Barbara Caffyn, Milt and Joyce Caffyn, Mike and Anne Nelson Caffyn, Millicent Bennett, Richard Bingham (Command Historian at Fort Monmouth), Margery Carroll, Alice DeBartolis, Joyce Dancisin, Kathy Dorn, Inez Dudick, Ted McGinness, Nancy Hall, Virginia Stofflet Hammond, Lou Herring, Colonel Quentin Keith, Charles H. Maps Jr., Mildred Magathan, Eddie Ostrander, Eileen Thompson (at the Monmouth County Historical Association Library), Monmouth University, George and Marie Foggia Quackenbush, Barbara Ross, Dr. Norman and Meda Thetford, Paul Wolcott, and Rosemary Kelly Zimmerman.

Introduction

Eatontown began as most towns do, with commerce.

In 1670 Englishman Thomas Eaton surveyed colonial Shrewsbury, looking for falling water to build a mill in order to ply his trade. Nearly all the land around the Shrewsbury River was flat, and another colonist had already built a mill at Tintern Falls, naming it after his estate in Monmouthshire, England.

So Eaton traveled south on what might have been part of a Lenni Lenape Indian trail. A few miles away from his Quaker village, Eaton found what he was looking for: swift-moving water tumbling over rocks. Eaton dammed the brook at its narrows and built a grist mill on the south side of the resulting pond.

He wasn't the only miller looking for falling water in colonial Shrewsbury—a land grant that once extended as far south as Point Pleasant. On what was to become the road to Long Branch, another Quaker miller, John Williams, dammed Turtle Creek, and built his grist mill on the north side of the pond.

By 1796, a village had developed across from Eaton's mill with a tannery and general store on the east side of the Red Bank Turnpike. A tavern for the New York-Philadelphia stage coach trade was built on what would become the intersection of Main and Broad Streets. A second stage coach stop was established in Mechanicsville on the ocean-bound road. This village would later be called West Long Branch.

By 1850, Eaton's village had grown to include four stores on Main Street and nearly forty homes. The Eatontown Steamboat Company built docks on Oceanport Creek to ship milled flour and other farm produce up the South Shrewsbury River to markets in New York City. Entrepreneur James P. Allaire built a four-story stone warehouse at the docks, from which he shipped his bog iron forged at the Howell Works 15 miles away.

In return for all this commerce, New York sent back revenue as well as residents for long summer sojourns. During the next fifty years, Eatontown Township would get a train station that served regional transportation needs, trolley lines for local traffic, a racetrack for leisure enjoyment, and several fancy hotels. Horse and vegetable farms would dot the outskirts of all three of the township's original villages.

Just after the United States entered World War I, the War Department began buying up briar-covered fields in Eatontown and Oceanport where Monmouth Park once stood, in order to enlarge its Signal Corps Camp already established in Little Silver. It would first name the camp after the New Jersey inventor who helped develop the Morse telegraph. Later, it would be renamed after a pivotal battle in the American Revolution fought just outside Monmouth Courthouse.

This book, compiled and written during Eatontown's 325th founding year, is an overview of its evolution from a small community with agricultural and equine roots to the modern-day industrial and suburban hub that it is today.

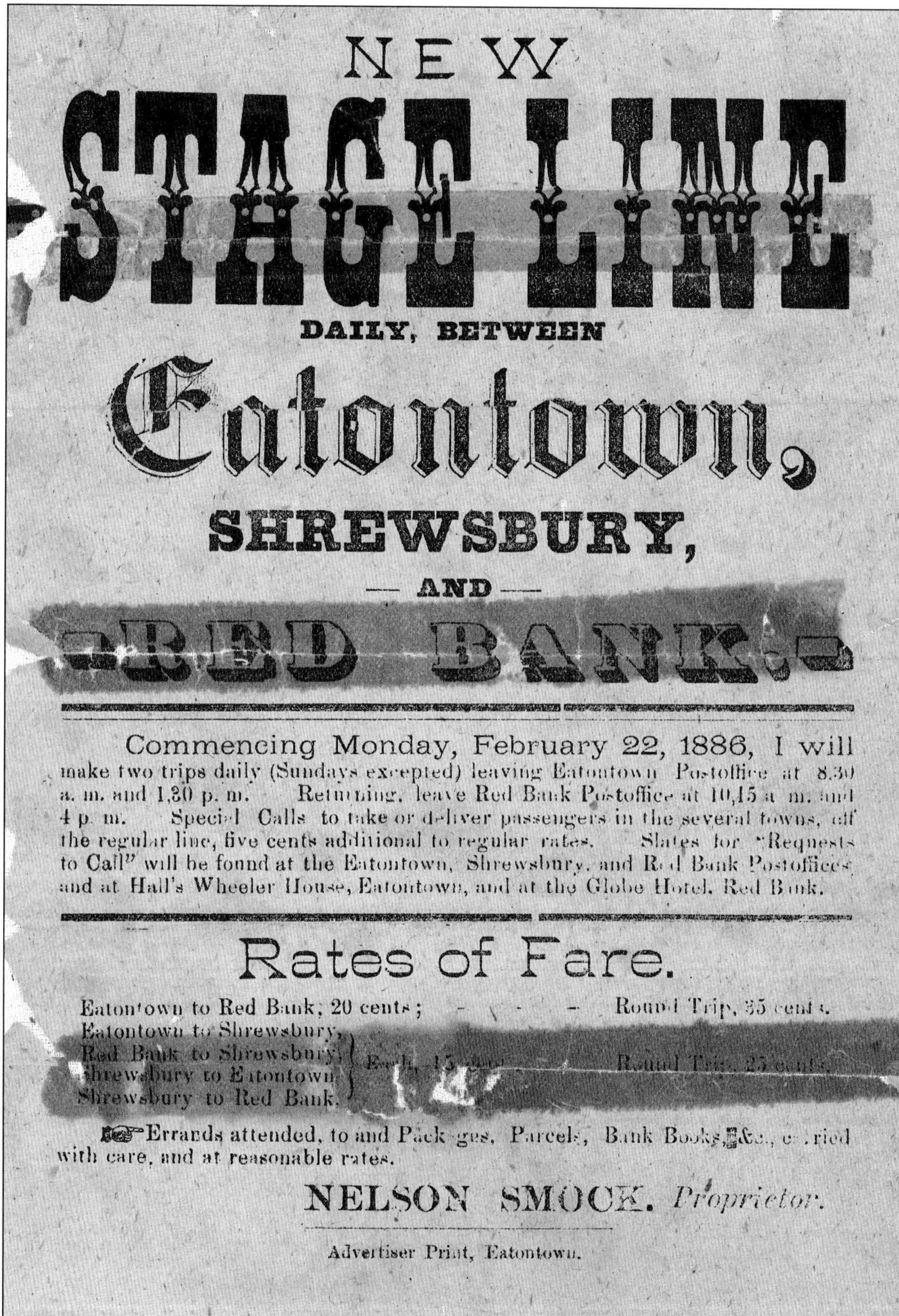

NEW
STAGE LINE
DAILY, BETWEEN
Eatontown,
SHREWSBURY,
— AND —
RED BANK.

Commencing Monday, February 22, 1886, I will make two trips daily (Sundays excepted) leaving Eatontown Postoffice at 8.30 a. m. and 1.30 p. m. Returning, leave Red Bank Postoffice at 10,15 a. m. and 4 p. m. Special Calls to take or deliver passengers in the several towns, off the regular line, five cents additional to regular rates. Slates for "Requests to Call" will be found at the Eatontown, Shrewsbury, and Red Bank Postoffices, and at Hall's Wheeler House, Eatontown, and at the Globe Hotel, Red Bank.

Rates of Fare.

Eatontown to Red Bank, 20 cents; - - - Round Trip, 35 cents.
Eatontown to Shrewsbury, Red Bank to Shrewsbury, Shrewsbury to Eatontown, Shrewsbury to Red Bank, } Each, 15 cents. Round Trip, 25 cents.

☞Errands attended, to and Packages, Parcels, Bank Books, &c., carried with care, and at reasonable rates.

NELSON SMOCK, *Proprietor.*

Advertiser Print, Eatontown.

Nelson Smock, a Civil War veteran, ran a stage line for eleven years. During Monmouth Park's Eatontown heyday he ran three lines through town. Smock also had the daily mail run between the Eatontown railroad station on Lewis Street and the post office when it was on Main Street.

One

Commerce

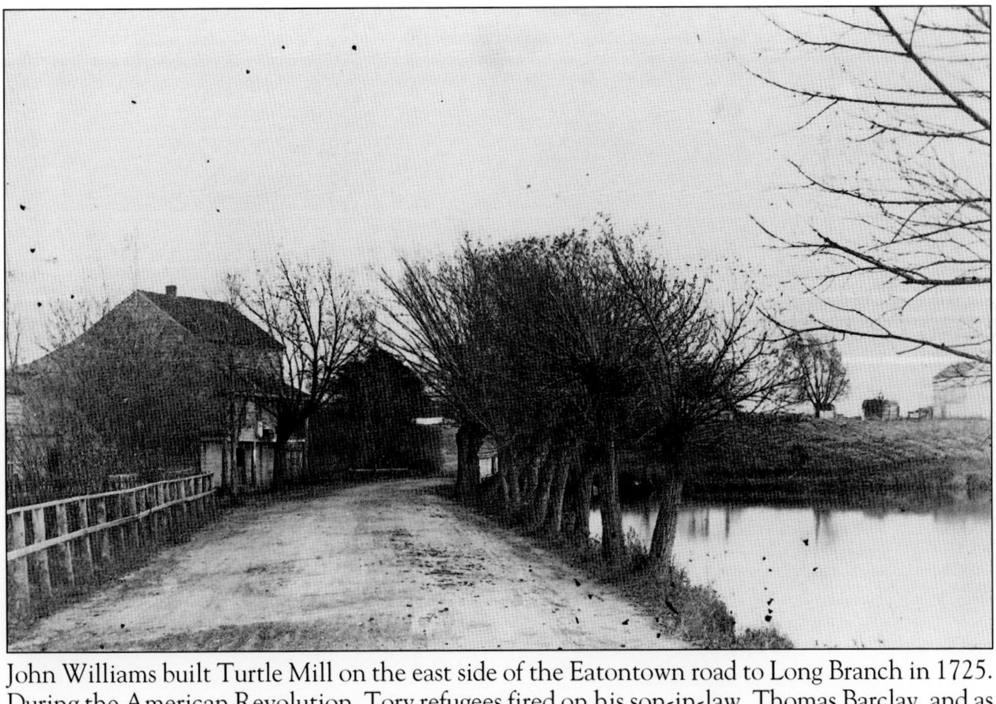

John Williams built Turtle Mill on the east side of the Eatontown road to Long Branch in 1725. During the American Revolution, Tory refugees fired on his son-in-law, Thomas Barclay, and as late as 1900 the bullet holes could still be seen in a post in the mill. The mill's location today is under a driveway south of Wolf Hill Farm on Eatontown Boulevard in Oceanport.

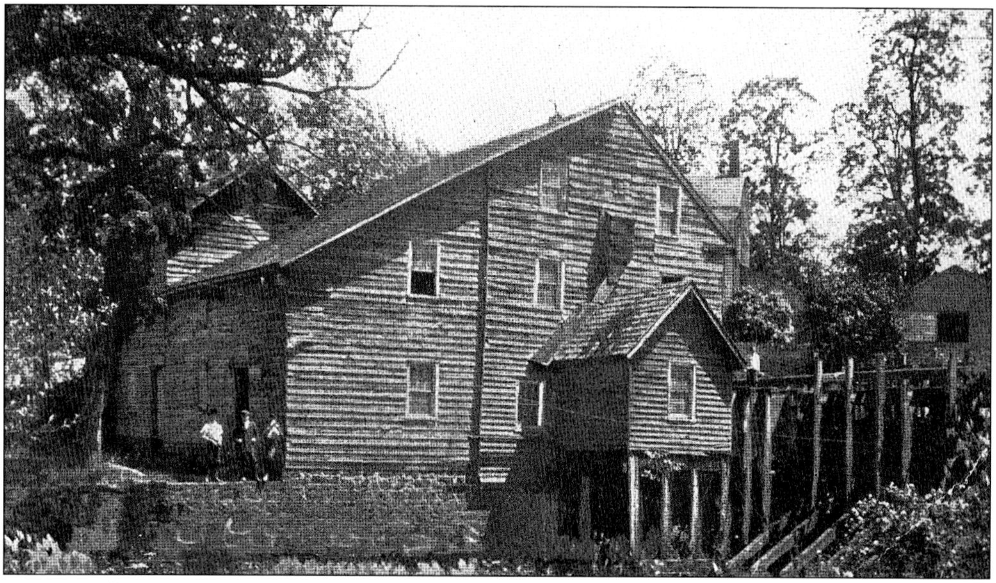

In 1670 Thomas Eaton built his mill. When he died, his wife, Jerusha Wing Eaton, operated the business until their son John reached maturity. The mill eventually wore out and in 1780 then-owner Peter Walcott, a carpenter, had it replaced. This is the mill most people recognize. As painted by James Wolcott Sr., it is the one used as the Eatontown seal. From 1845 to 1890, Charles and Joseph Richmond operated the mill.

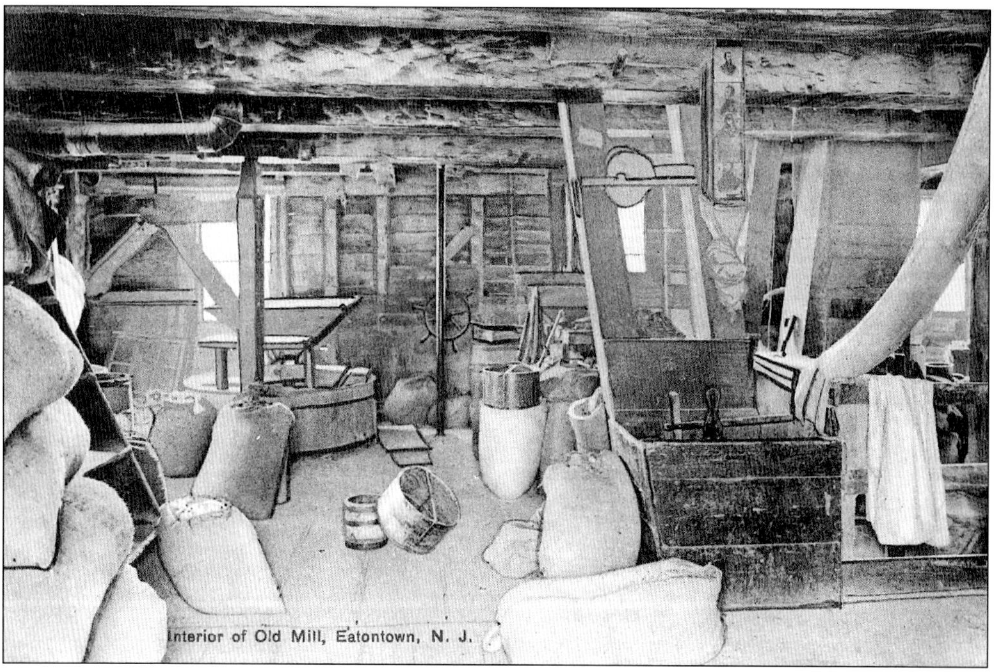

The interior of Richmond's mill showing milled rye and corn sold as cow feed. In 1927 Dr. Henry Reimar bought the empty mill for $3,500 with plans to turn it into a tea room.

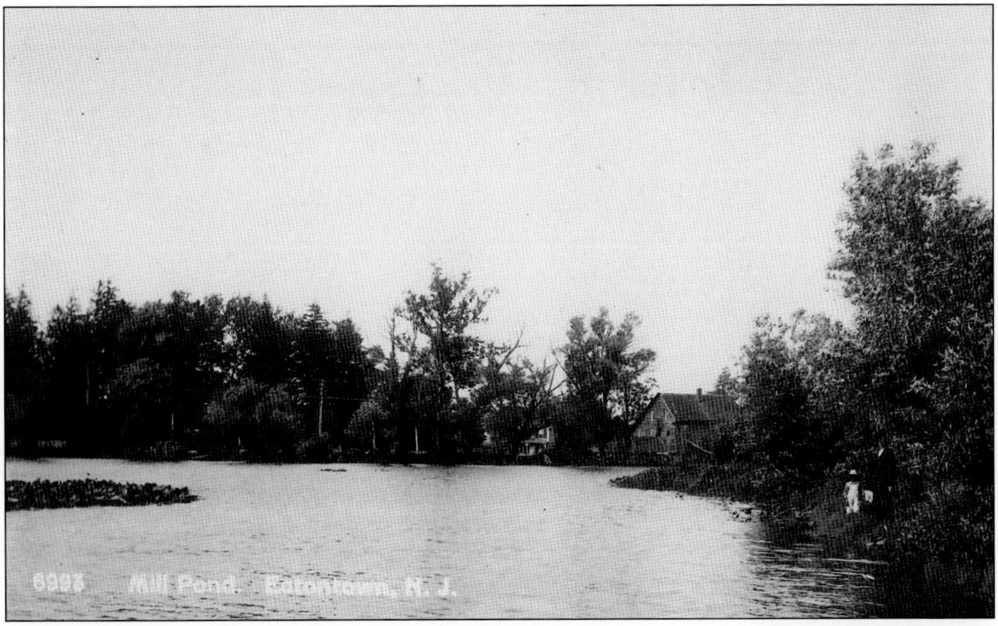

Mill Pond, looking east towards the Red Bank Turnpike, was used for fishing, boating, and skating. The mill is on the right.

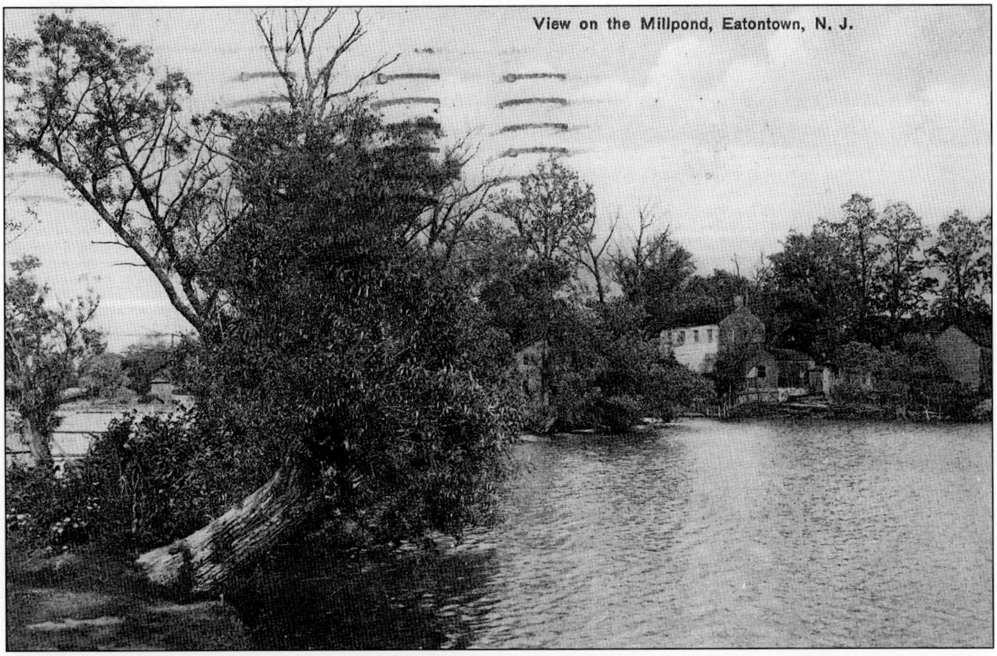

Mill Pond, surrounded by buttonwood trees, as seen from the north side of the pond, c. 1910. The ice house on West Street can be seen at the far right.

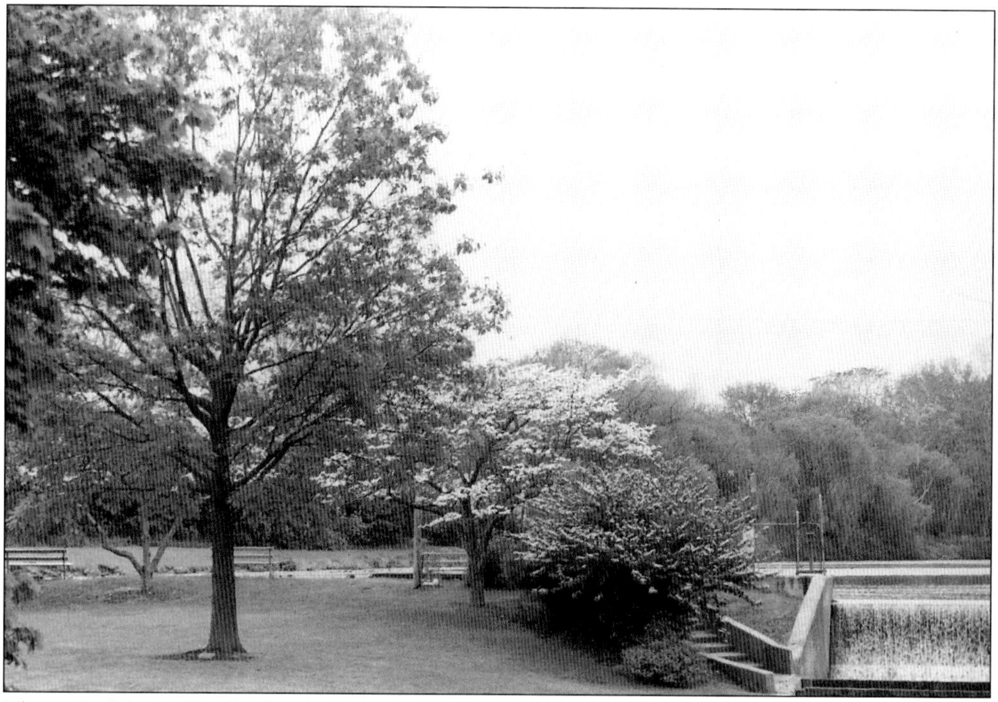

The site of Eaton's mill today, as seen from Route 35. The borough bought the property in 1931, and rebuilt the dam where it had collapsed.

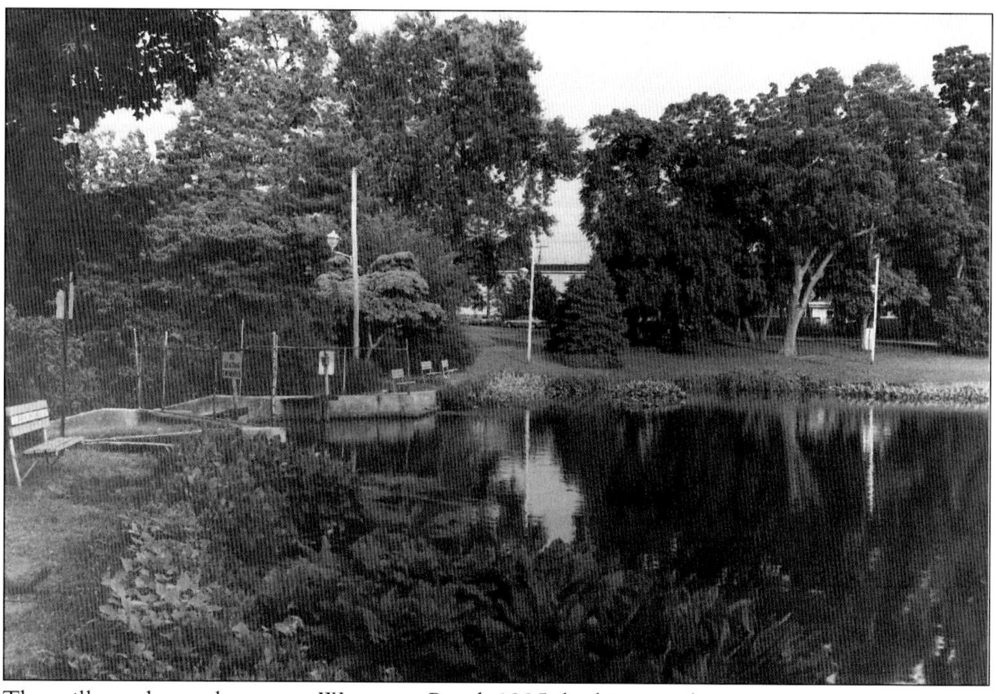

The mill pond, now known as Wampum Pond, 1995, looking south.

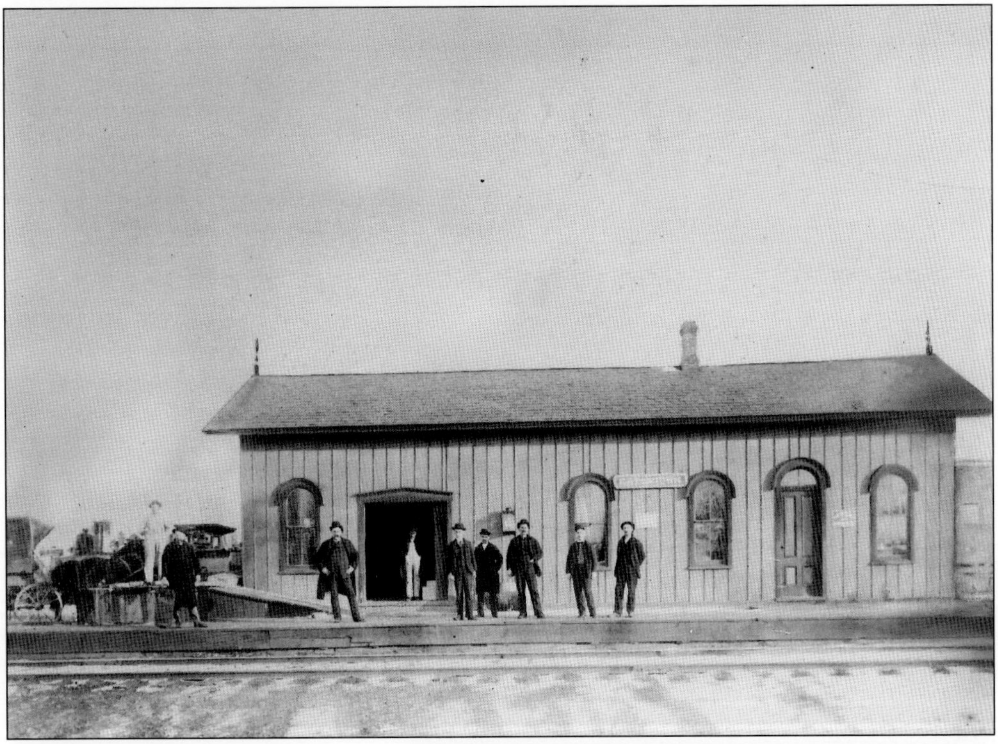

The train station for Eatontown Junction had three locations in Eatontown, going as far back as 1873. This photograph was taken about 1890 when the station was located at the curve of Lewis Street and Maxwell Avenue.

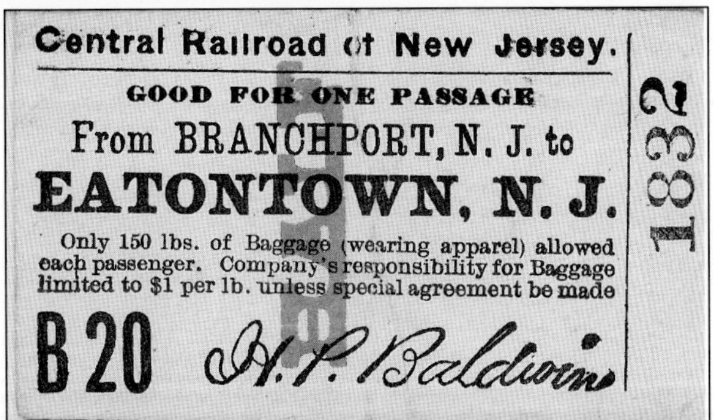

Central Railroad of New Jersey.
GOOD FOR ONE PASSAGE
From BRANCHPORT, N. J. to
EATONTOWN, N. J.
Only 150 lbs. of Baggage (wearing apparel) allowed each passenger. Company's responsibility for Baggage limited to $1 per lb. unless special agreement be made
B 20 H. P. Baldwin
1832

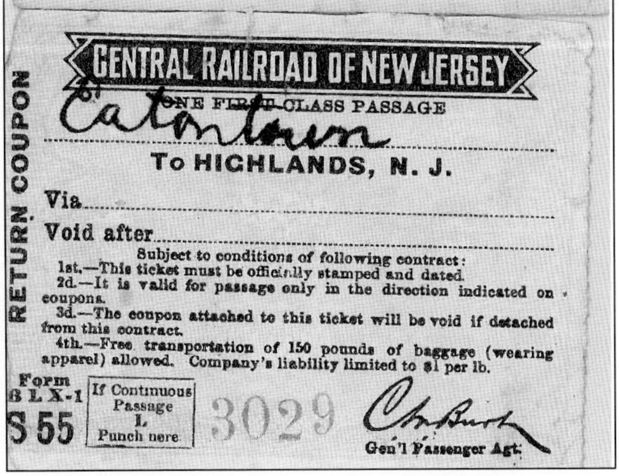

CENTRAL RAILROAD OF NEW JERSEY
ONE FIRST-CLASS PASSAGE
Eatontown
To HIGHLANDS, N. J.
Via
Void after
Subject to conditions of following contract:
1st.—This ticket must be officially stamped and dated.
2d.—It is valid for passage only in the direction indicated on coupons.
3d.—The coupon attached to this ticket will be void if detached from this contract.
4th.—Free transportation of 150 pounds of baggage (wearing apparel) allowed. Company's liability limited to $1 per lb.
RETURN COUPON
Form BLX-1
S 55
If Continuous Passage L Punch here
3029
[illegible]
Gen'l Passenger Agt.

The station was in existence until the mid-1960s. From World War I until then the tracks were used to ship freight to Fort Monmouth. The top ticket dates from 1895; the bottom one, from 1906.

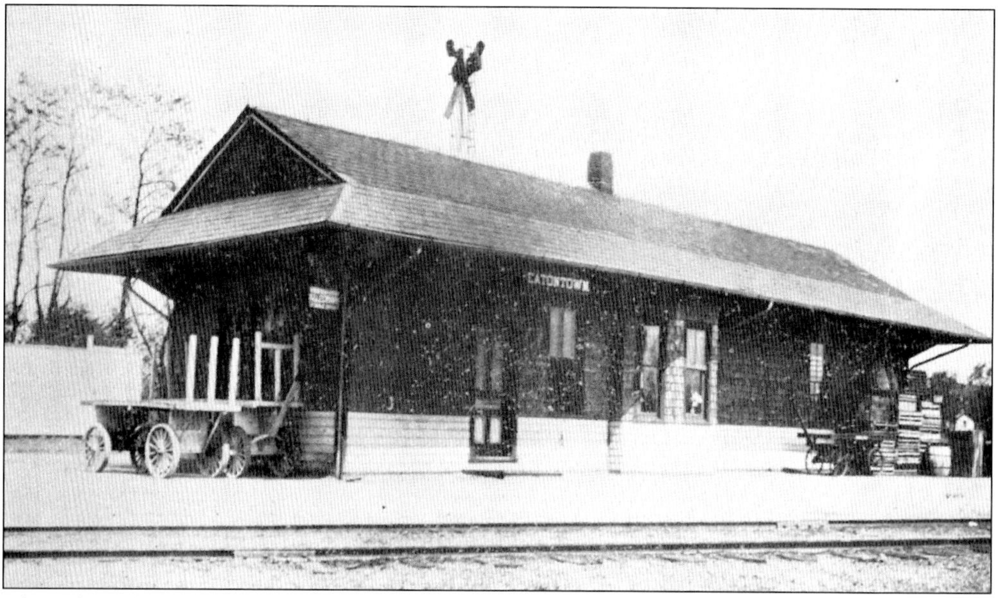

This is how the station looked in 1906. The tracks in front of the station sent passengers on the Seashore Line to Oceanport, Branchport (that station is where the Casa Comida restaurant is today), Monmouth Beach, Sea Bright, and Highlands. The tracks behind the station belonged to the Central Railroad of New Jersey that ran trains from Red Bank to Farmingdale and points south.

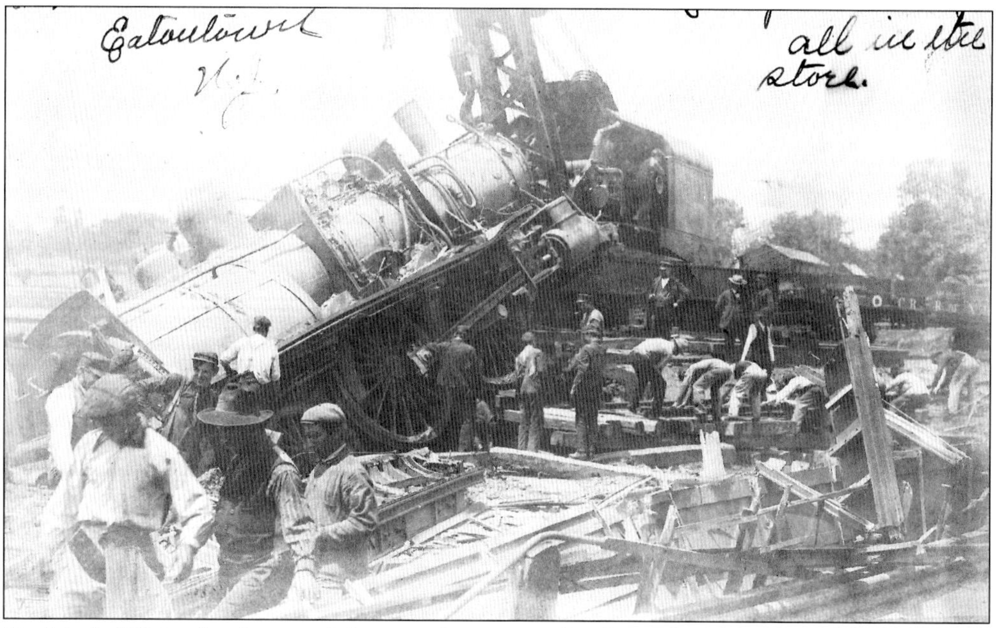

On July 2, 1906, a freight crew left a switch open on the Central Jersey tracks. At 11 a.m. that Monday, the Atlantic City Flyer was heading north in Eatontown Junction when it ran the open switch. The locomotive, tender, baggage, and smoking cars passed over the switch safely. But when the pullman car passed through, the switch opened and the rear half traveled up the siding, stretching the entire train line-up and causing the locomotive, tender, and smoking car to topple over.

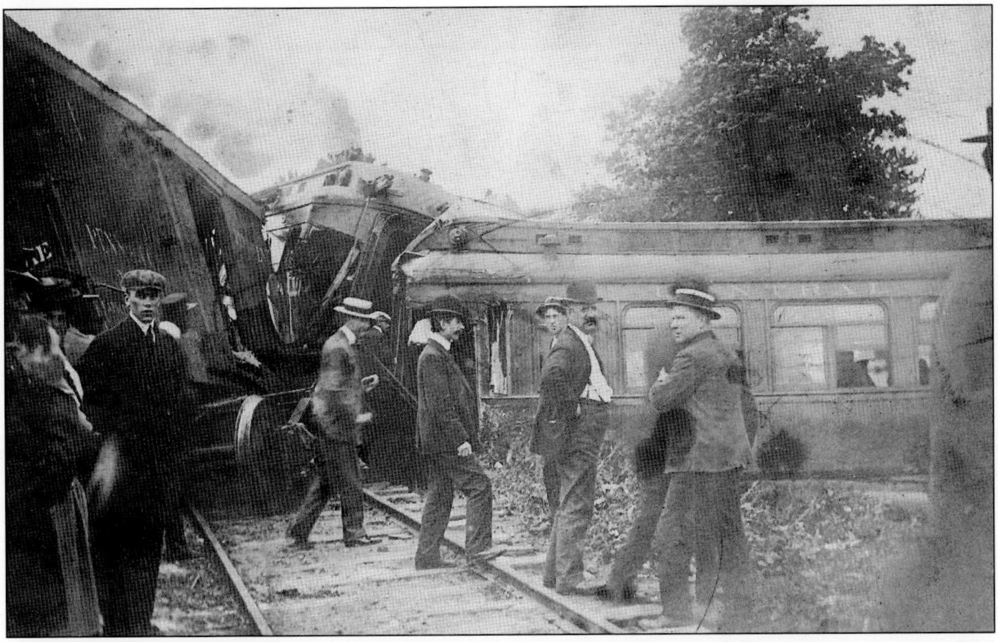

The curious, the thrill-seekers, and the helpful came out to the wreck site where one man died and more than a score were injured. Later, people would send postcards of the wreck taken by enterprising photographers.

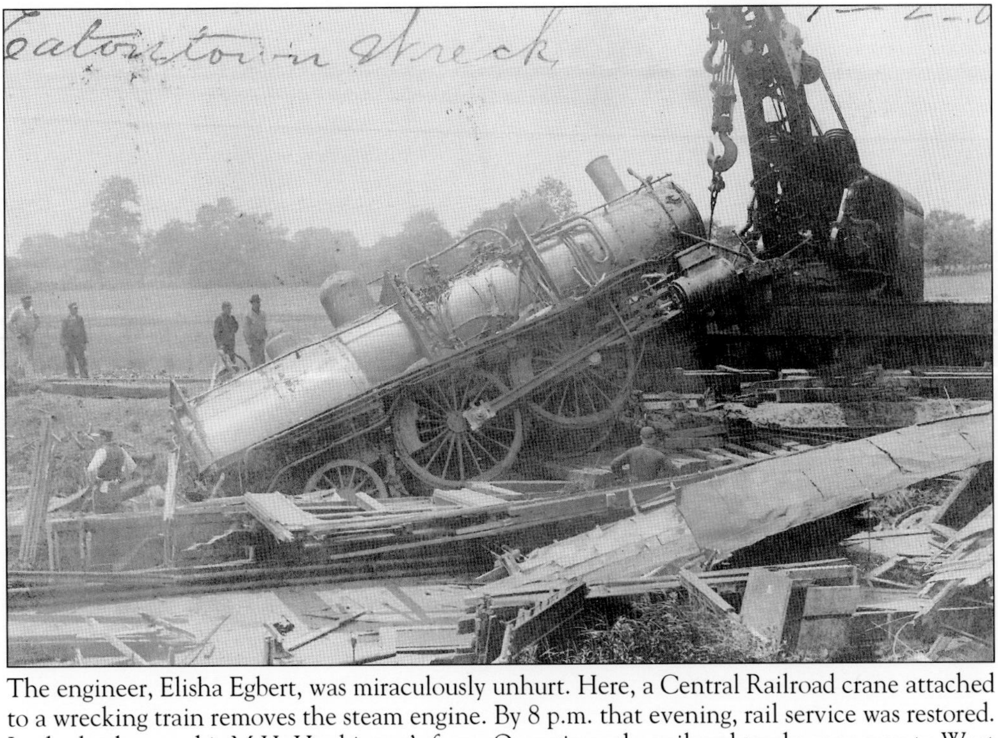

The engineer, Elisha Egbert, was miraculously unhurt. Here, a Central Railroad crane attached to a wrecking train removes the steam engine. By 8 p.m. that evening, rail service was restored. In the background is M.H. Hankinson's farm. Over time, the railroad tracks gave way to West Street on the west side of Main Street and Throckmorton Avenue on the east side.

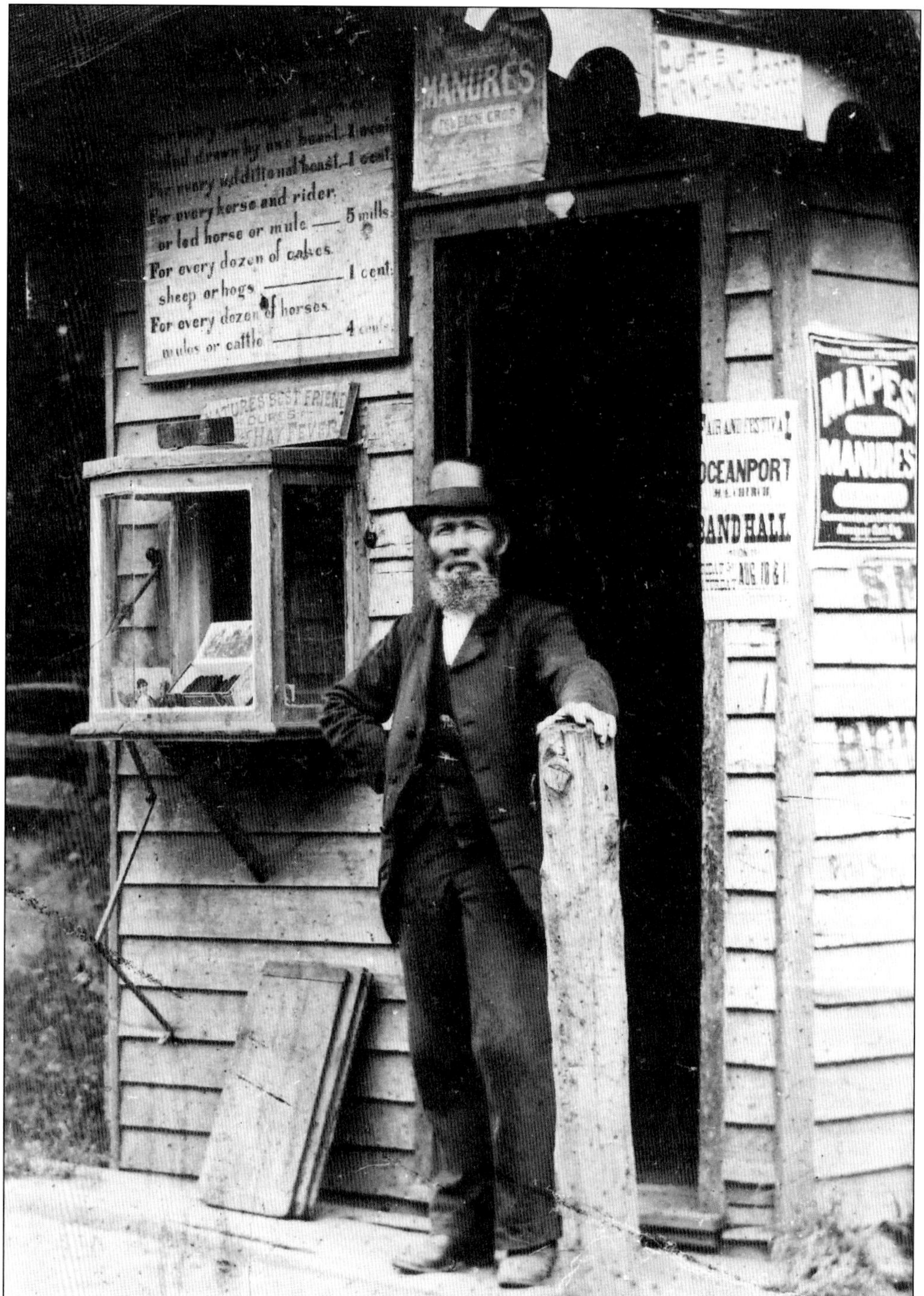

Turnpikes that criss-crossed Eatontown often went through private land. John Smock operated a toll house at the edge of his farm on Eatontown Boulevard in Oceanport village in 1870. Another toll house was located on the Eatontown-Colts Neck Turnpike that is today the intersection of Tinton Avenue and Wayside Road.

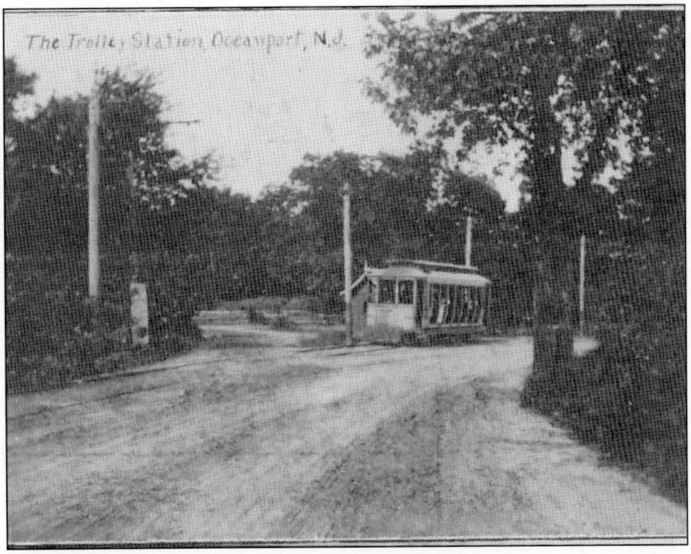

Smock's toll house eventually became the Oceanport trolley stop at Eatontown Boulevard and Wolf Hill Avenue, c. 1912.

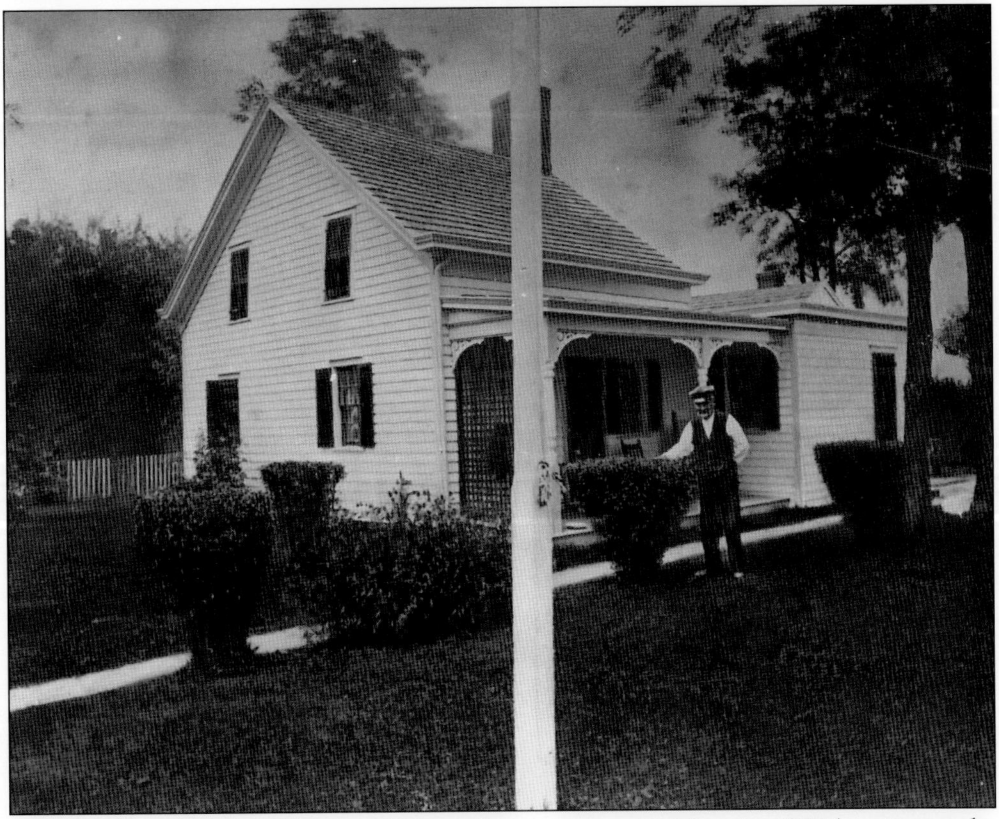

The Monmouth Road toll house at Palmer Avenue was moved from its 1779 location on the Old Plank Road near the shores of Corlies Pond (today, Deal Lake) by Egbert Hopper just before the Civil War. Near the front door was the niche where the toll taker collected his fee. Hopper was an early farmer in the village of what would become known as West Long Branch.

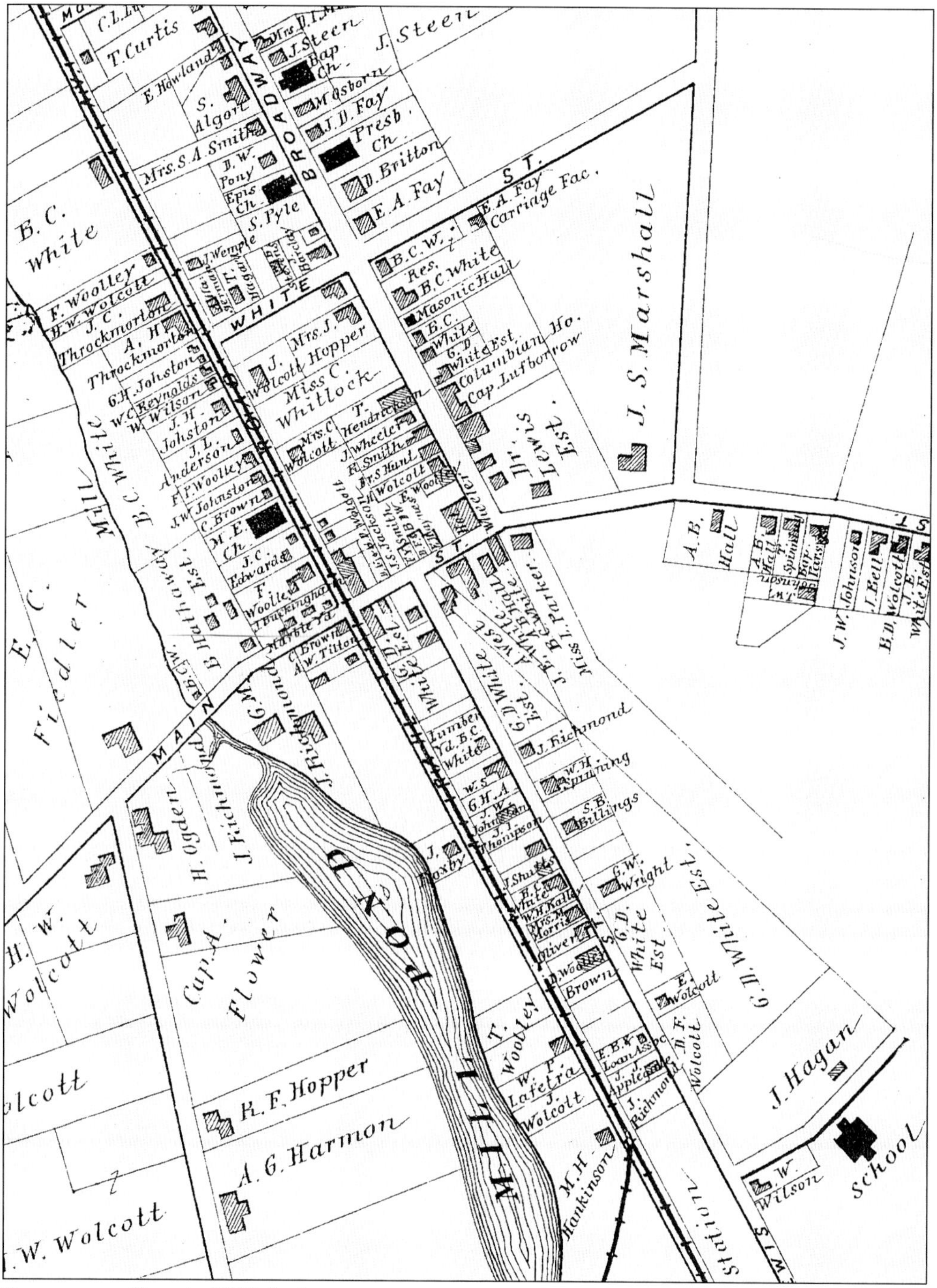

Eatontown village in 1878, looking east.

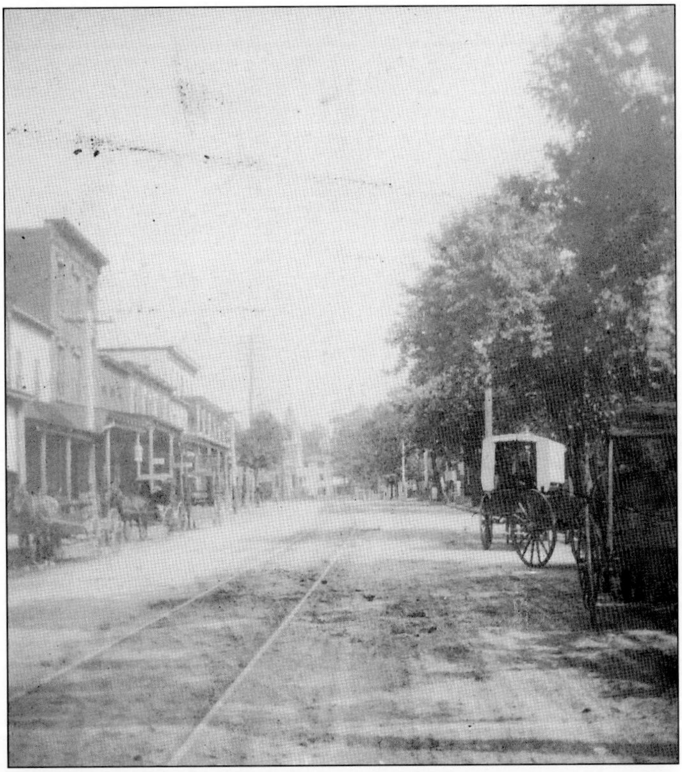

Main Street looking south, c. 1905. The Second Advent Church can be seen in the distance where Main Street curved right into South Street, then also known as Locust Street. The tall, three-story brick building was the Eatontown Pharmacy, which would house other businesses over the years, including the ice cream and cigar store operated by Ed Smock.

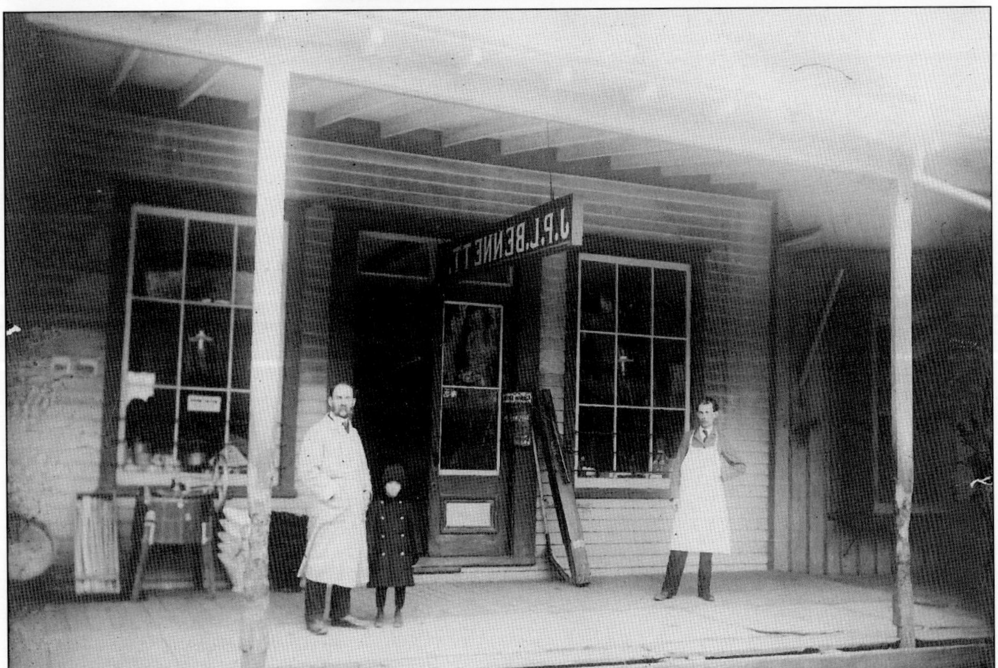

J.P.L. Bennett's general store sold groceries, provisions, canned goods, flour, feed, and grain. By 1911 it was known as Bennett & Wright. An advertisement for the store told customers: "Orders called for and goods delivered."

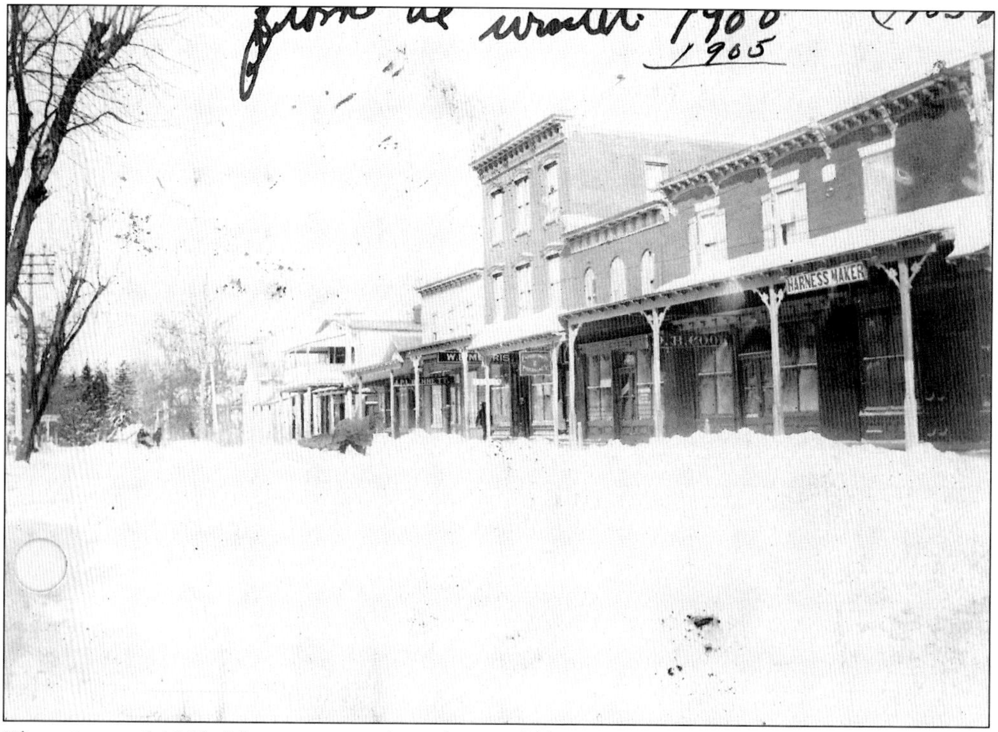

The winter of 1905–06 saw quite a bit of snow fall. Here is a view of the east side of Main Street looking north past storefronts for a harness maker, P.B. Cook, Eatontown Pharmacy, W.E. Morris Clothier, and J.P.L. Bennett.

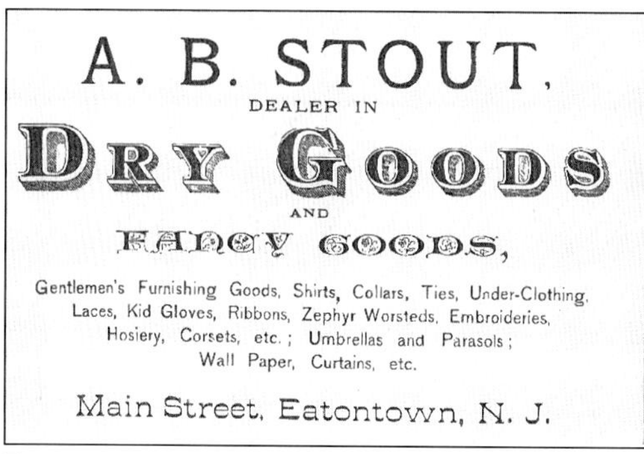

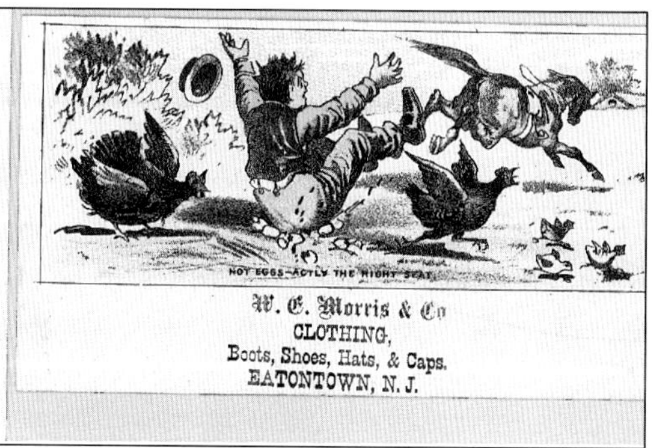

Eatontown merchants gave out advertising cards to their customers. Children would collect the trade cards into albums.

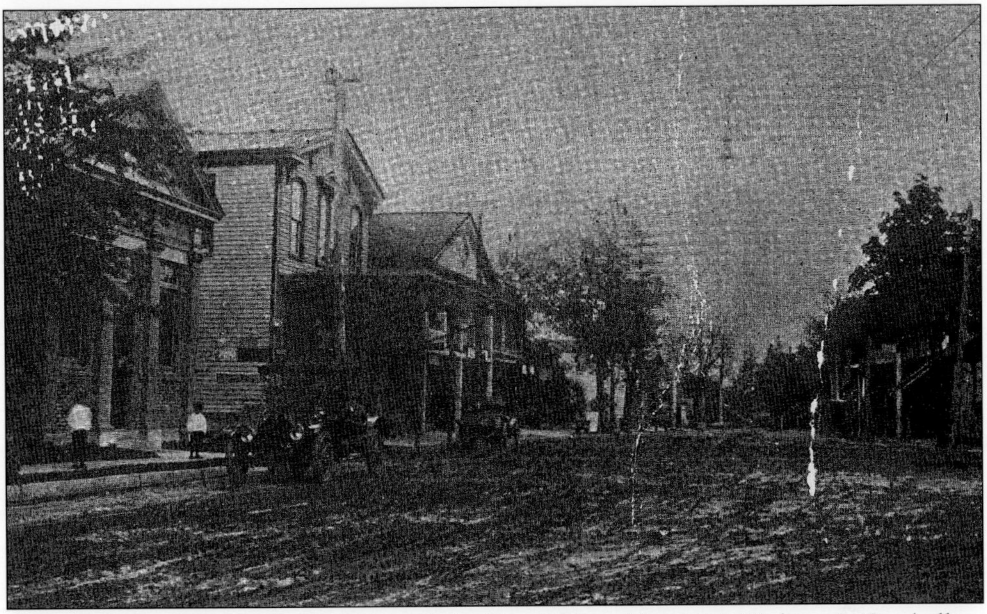

Main Street, looking north, *c.* 1912, with the First National Bank, H. Wolcott & Co. (selling dry goods, groceries, hardware, paints, and oils), and Taylor's Cigar, Confectionery, and Ice Cream Store on the west side of the street.

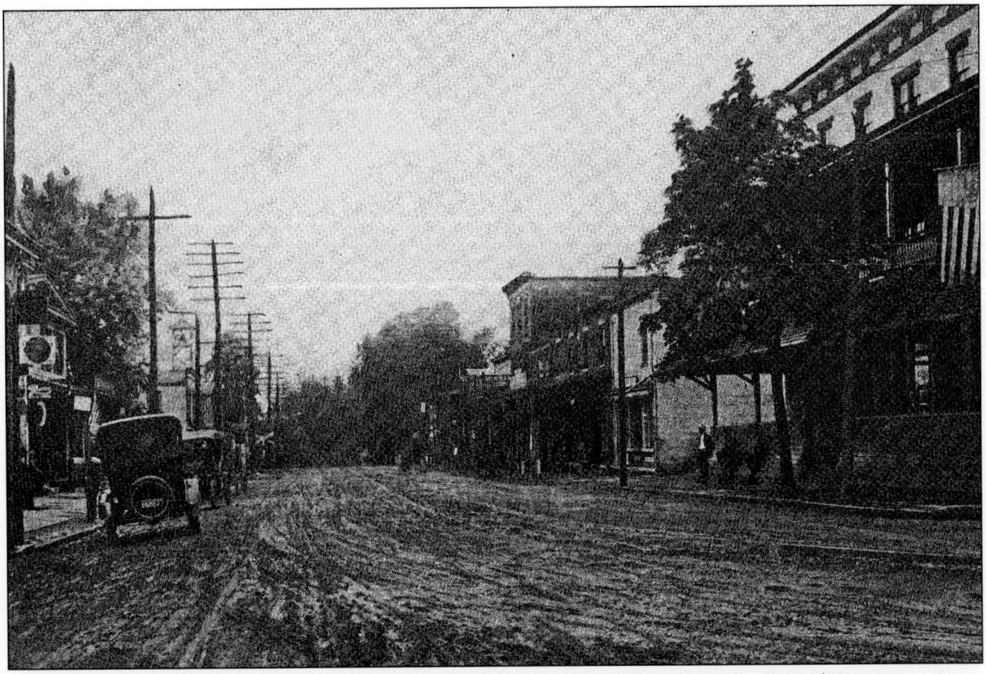

Main Street, looking north, *c.* 1915, with the Metropolitan Hotel on the Broad Street corner.

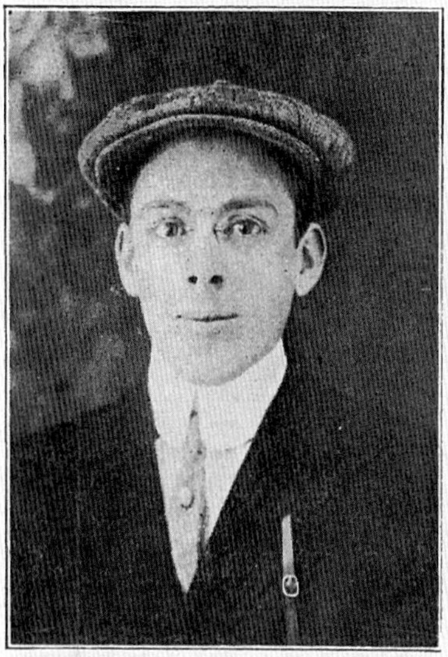

TAYLOR BROS.

FRUITS
CONFECTIONERY
CIGARS, ETC.

Among the best known and most active of Eatontown's younger business men that have come to the front within the last few years should be included the names of Arthur and William Taylor, who, in 1907, succeeded J. S. Clark to the Cigar, Confectionery and Ice Cream place almost opposite the Metropolitan Hotel. These enterprising young men have since made considerable improvements and increased the patronage, and this stand is today headquarters for the young men of the village. Here may be found a complete line of all the standard brands of Cigars, Cigarettes, Smoking and Chewing Tobacco and Pipes, as well as Choice Box Confectionery, while in summer a Soda Fountain and Horton's Ice Cream help to make the place popular, not only among Eatontown people, but by those stopping temporarily in the village. They are members of the Eatontown Lodge, Junior Mechanics, and the Hook and Ladder Company, Arthur Taylor being a member of the Elks, and are classed among the progressive element that is today gaining a foothold in Eatontown.

And don't forget they are the only ones in town that keep

HORTON'S
ICE
CREAM

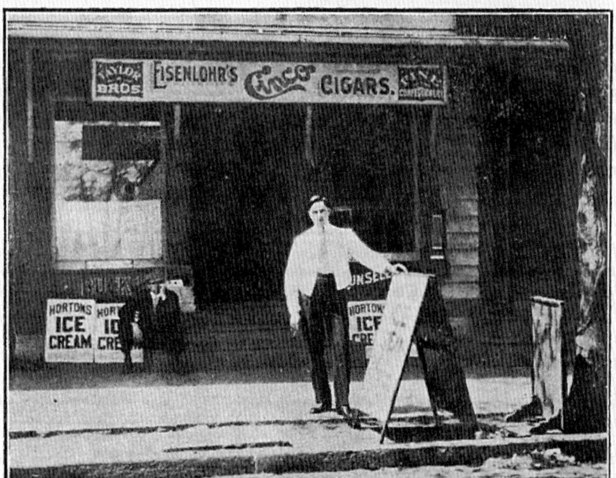

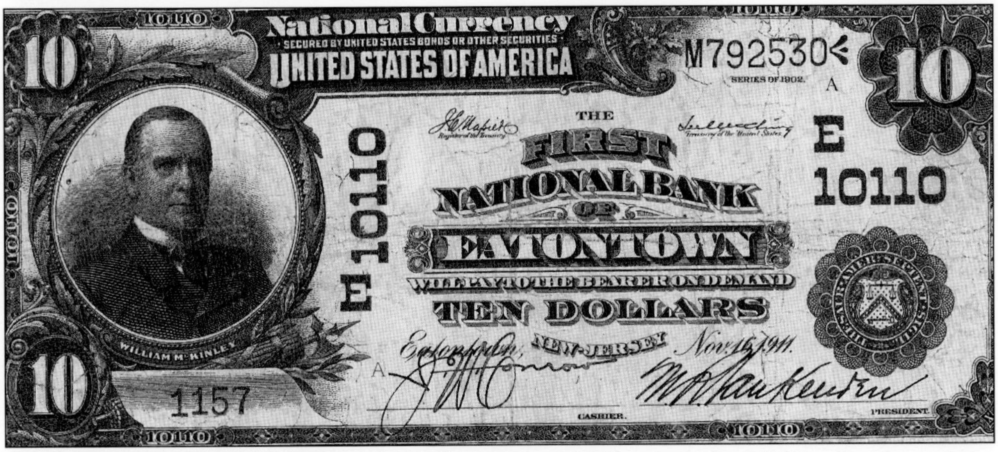

The First National Bank of Eatontown, chartered in 1911, was one of 323 in the state whose assets contributed to more than $500 million in resources in New Jersey at the time. This $10 bank note was signed by the bank's first president, Melvin R. Van Keuren, who owned a coal and lumber store on the corner of Main and West Streets.

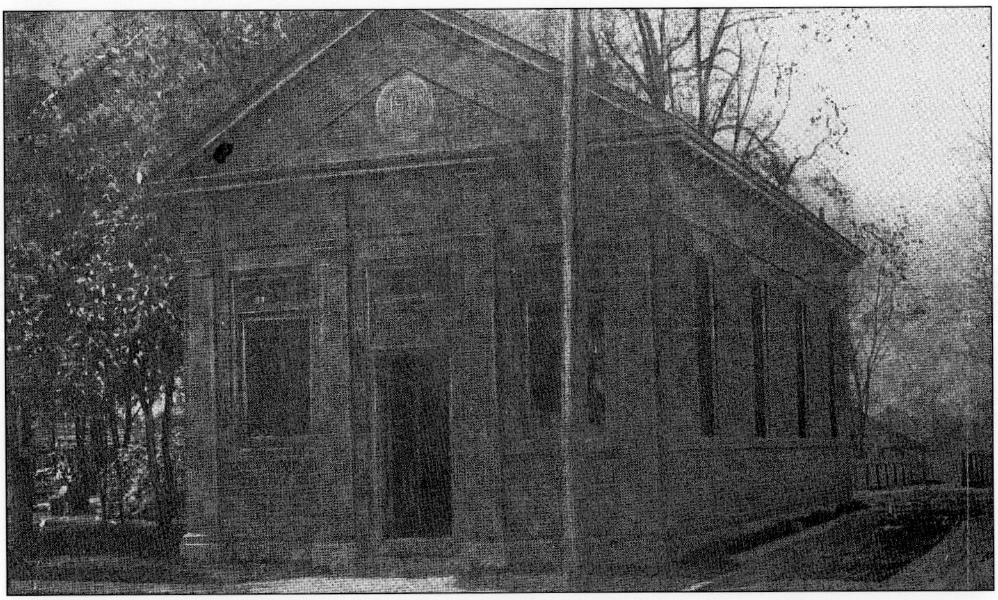

In 1926 the bank became known as the Allenhurst National Bank and Trust Company. In 1954, the bank moved down Broad Street and eventually became the Central Jersey Bank and Trust. Today it is known as the National Westminster Bank. The original bank building was used as a post office annex until it was torn down in 1961 to make way for the Route 71 South jughandle.

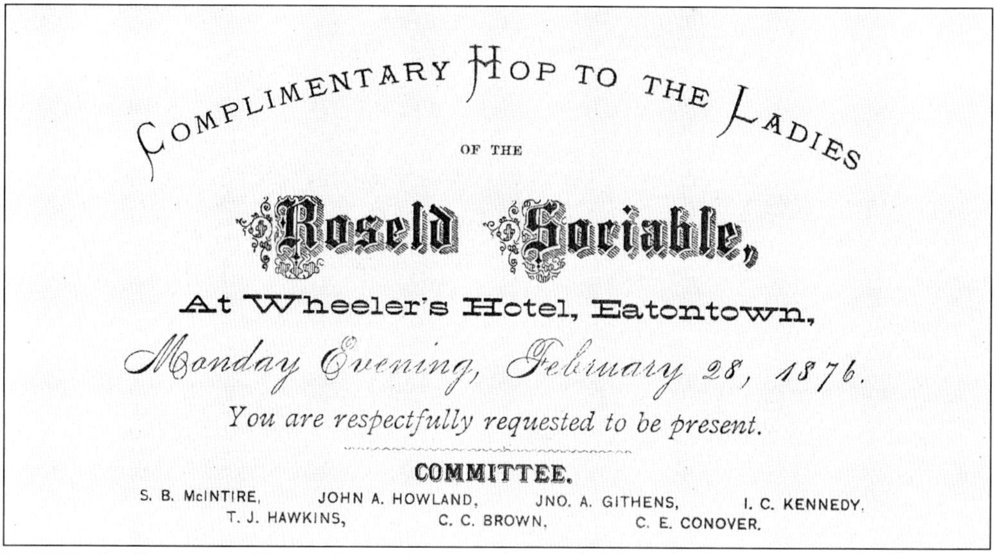

Complimentary Hop to the Ladies

OF THE

Roseld Sociable,

At Wheeler's Hotel, Eatontown,

Monday Evening, February 28, 1876.

You are respectfully requested to be present.

COMMITTEE.

S. B. McINTIRE, JOHN A. HOWLAND, JNO. A. GITHENS, I. C. KENNEDY, T. J. HAWKINS, C. C. BROWN, C. E. CONOVER.

In 1873 the Eatontown Tavern burned. In its place, John S. Wheeler built a three-story brick hotel and tavern with livery stables and garden. Various town functions were held here, including this Roseld Sociable. In 1878 Peter R. Hall bought the hotel and operated it as Hall's Hotel, catering to racing enthusiasts at nearby Monmouth Park. Hall also operated a beer-bottling establishment in one of the barns behind the hotel.

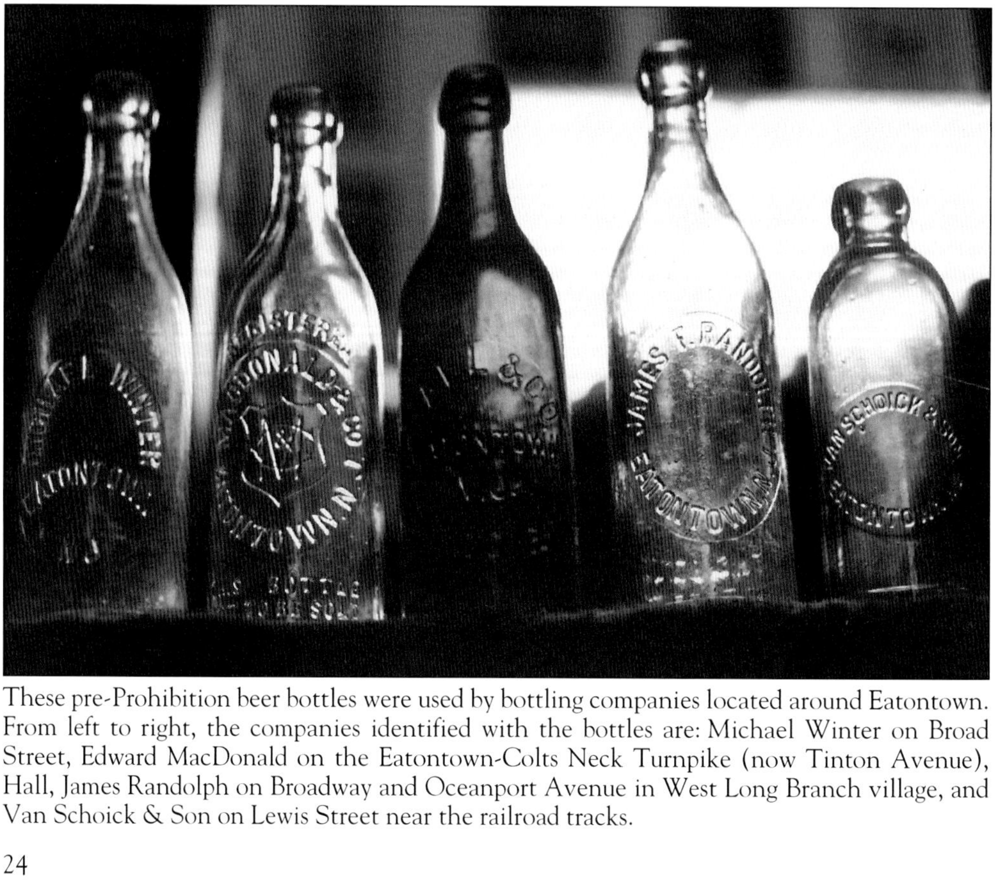

These pre-Prohibition beer bottles were used by bottling companies located around Eatontown. From left to right, the companies identified with the bottles are: Michael Winter on Broad Street, Edward MacDonald on the Eatontown-Colts Neck Turnpike (now Tinton Avenue), Hall, James Randolph on Broadway and Oceanport Avenue in West Long Branch village, and Van Schoick & Son on Lewis Street near the railroad tracks.

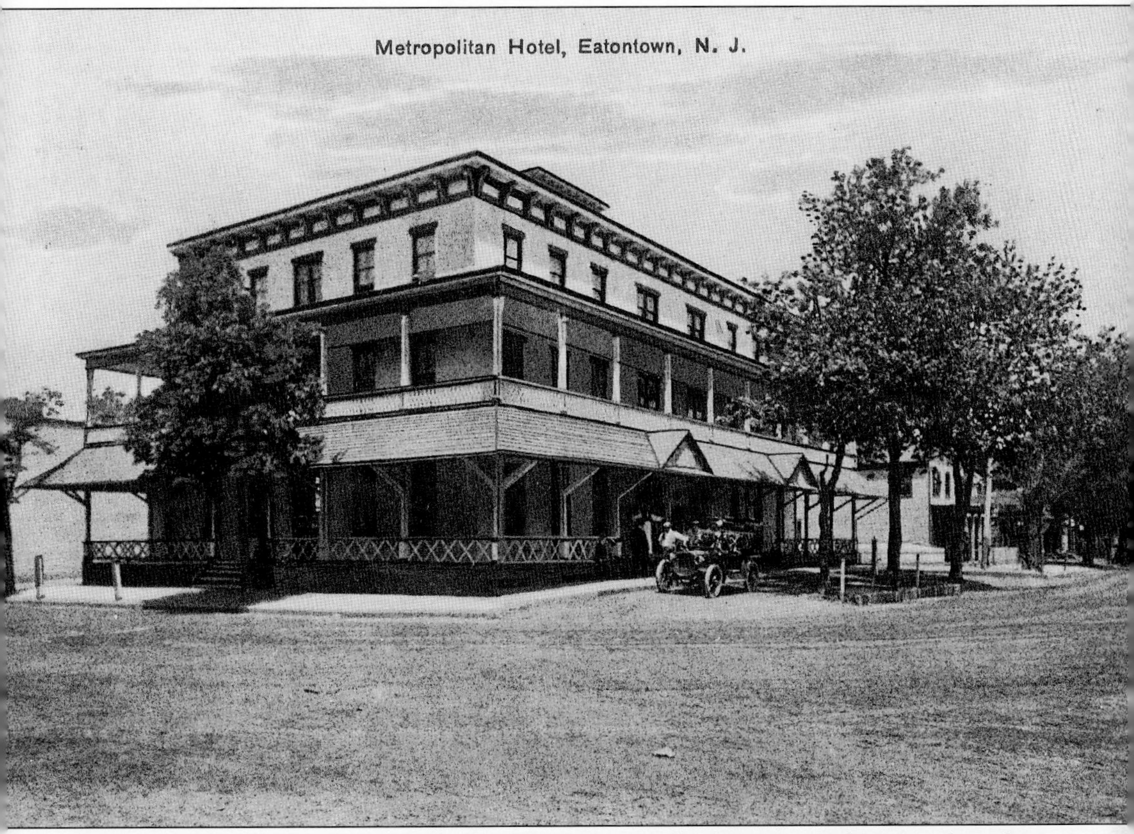

In January 1895 Thomas Elwood Snyder Jr. took over the business and renamed it the Metropolitan Hotel. He spent thousands of dollars in modern plumbing and heating. In 1907 he bought his competitor's hotel, the Columbian Hotel down Broad Street, and closed it. Snyder's father owned and operated the Colts Neck Inn which is still standing today on Route 537 in Colts Neck Township.

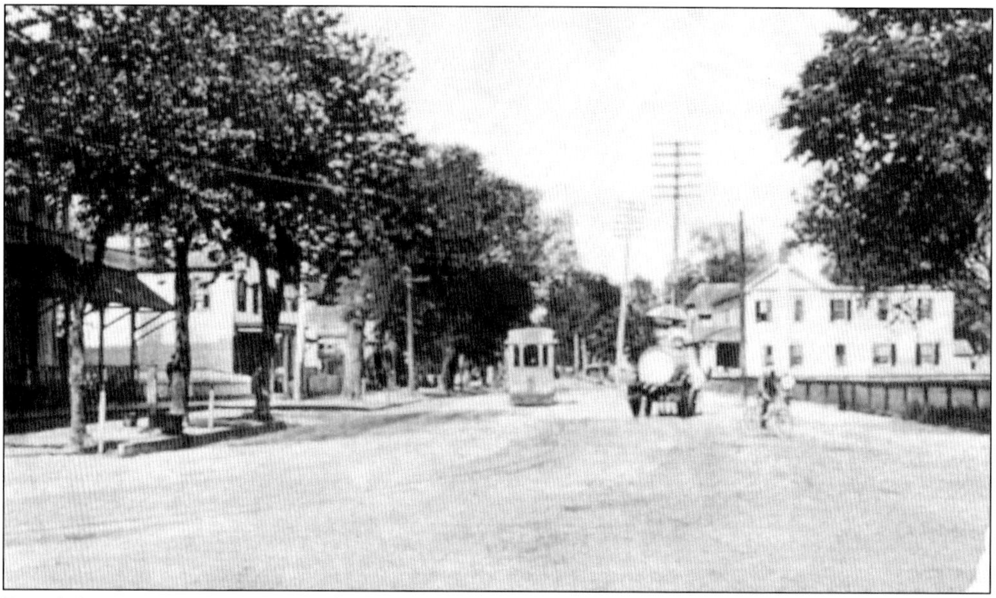

Broad Street at Main Street. The Metropolitan is on the left, followed by Michael Winter's Saloon and Bennett's Bakery. On the right is the fenced-in property of Dr. John Lewis, who practiced medicine from 1811 to 1861. In 1833 he let Joseph Barclay operate a general store in a building on the property. It was destroyed in a fire in 1839. Barclay, a judge, was the son of Quaker patriot Thomas Barclay. The next building is the Columbian Hotel.

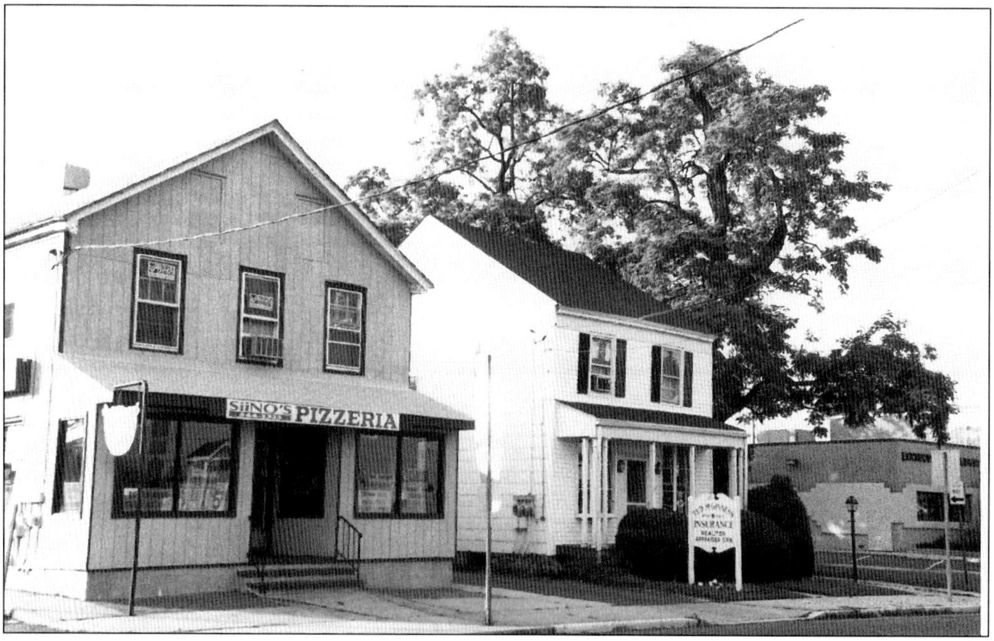

In 1889 these premises were used as a drugstore by Dr. S.H. Hunt (left) and a newspaper and bakery in the building owned by R. Smith (right).

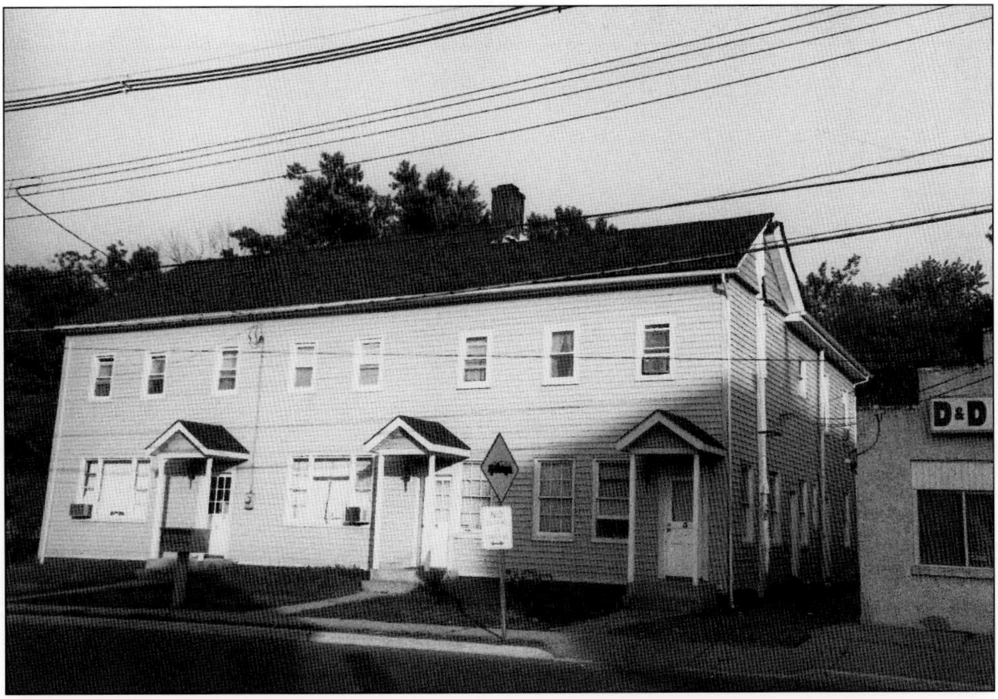

The Columbian Hotel was built in 1831, and had various uses and owners, including a colorful ship captain by the family name of Lufborrow. The building is now an apartment house.

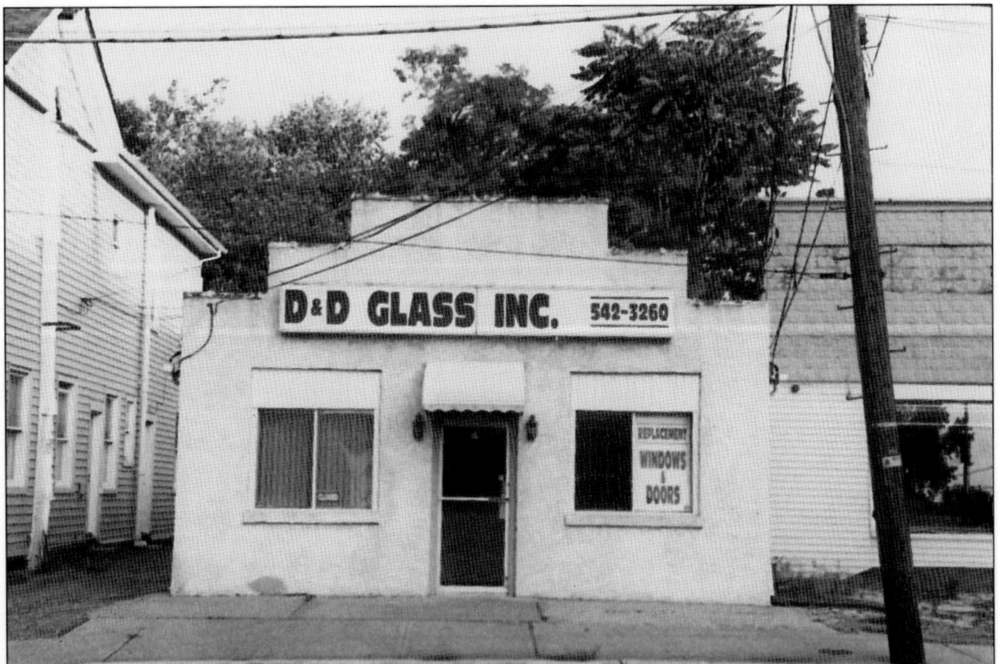

Ed Taylor owned and operated Taylor's Bowling Alley, the village's first public lanes on Broad Street.

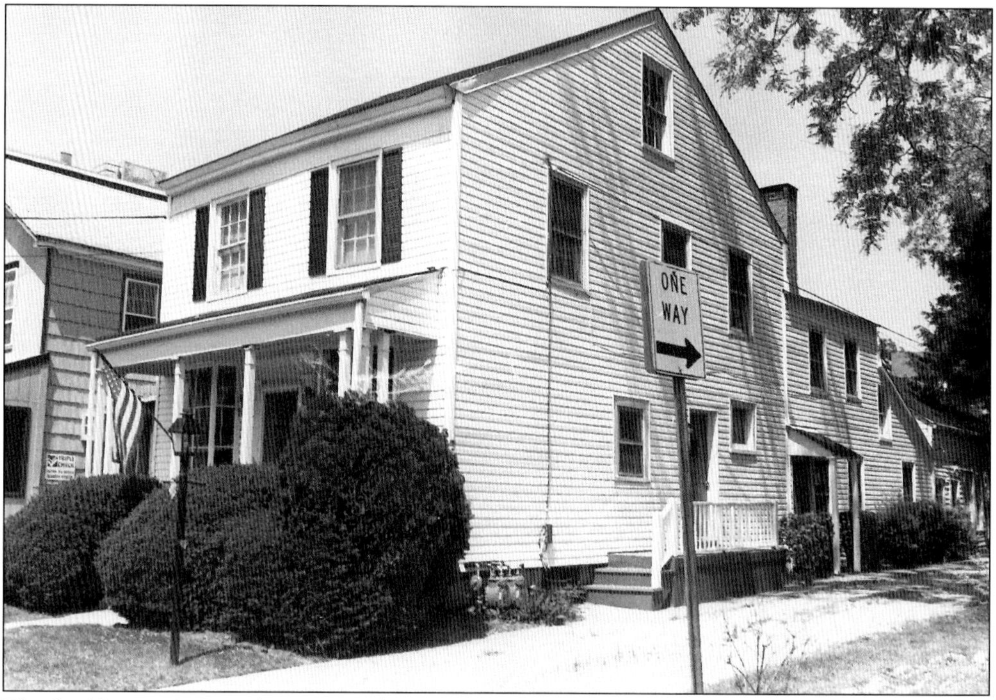

This building at 21 Broad Street was built in 1801. Throughout Eatontown's history, it has been used by a variety of businesses. Its present owner is real estate appraiser Ted McGinness.

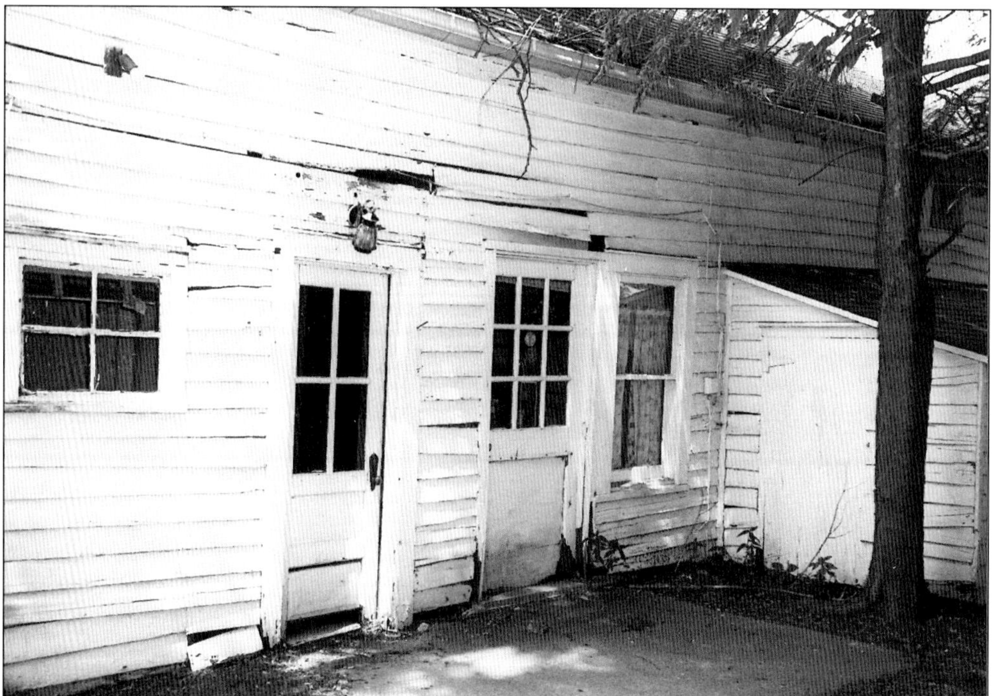

The side doors to what had been at one time Bennett's Bakery and then a toymaker's workshop. The ovens date from the 1820s, predating those at the Allaire Village.

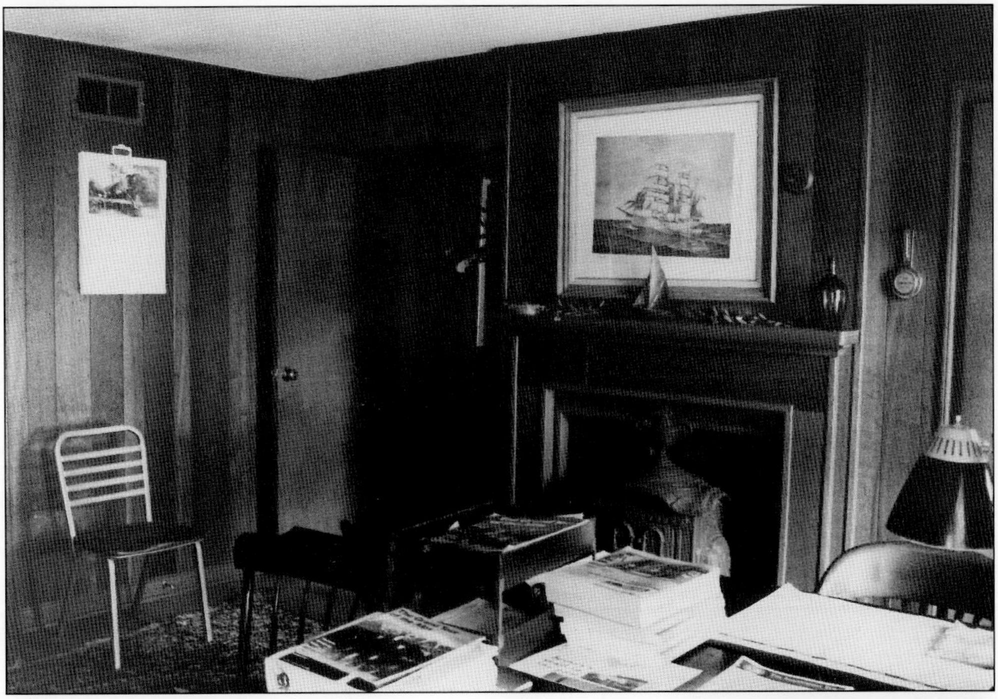

Eatontown has had many different hometown newspapers in its history. In 1877 James Steen established the township's first newspaper, *The Eatontown Advertiser*, at 21 Broad Street. In 1946 the building was once again a newspaper office, this time for *The Eatontown Sentinel*.

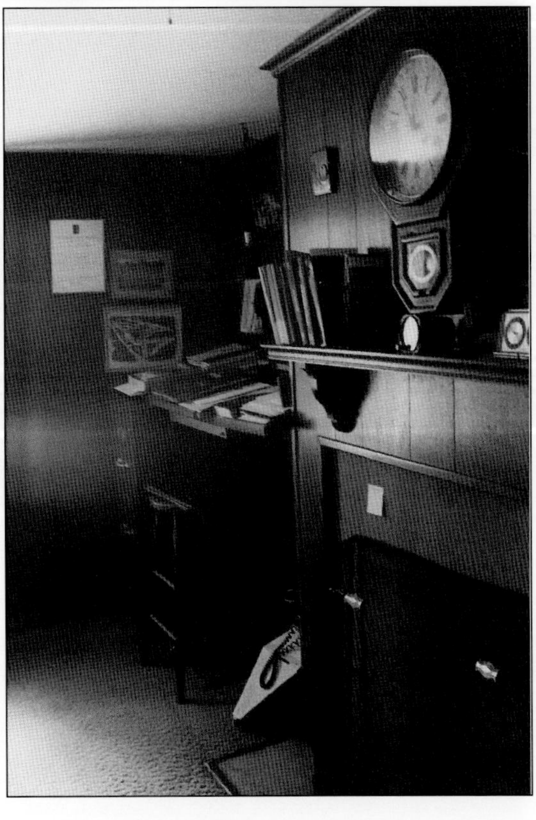

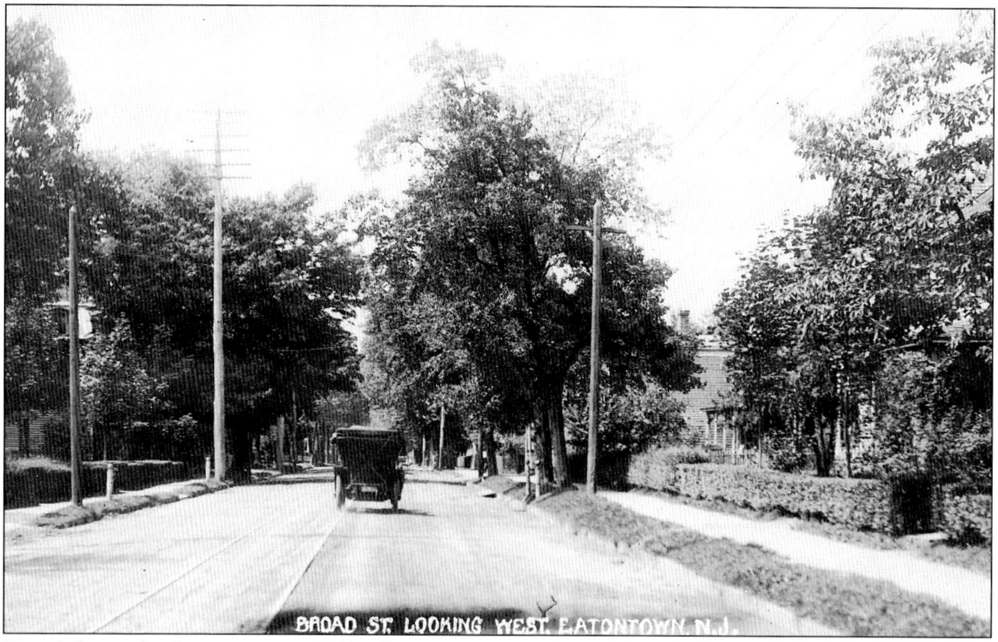

Broad Street looking west, *c.* 1908, showing a vintage automobile and trolley tracks laid down by the Monmouth County Electric Company.

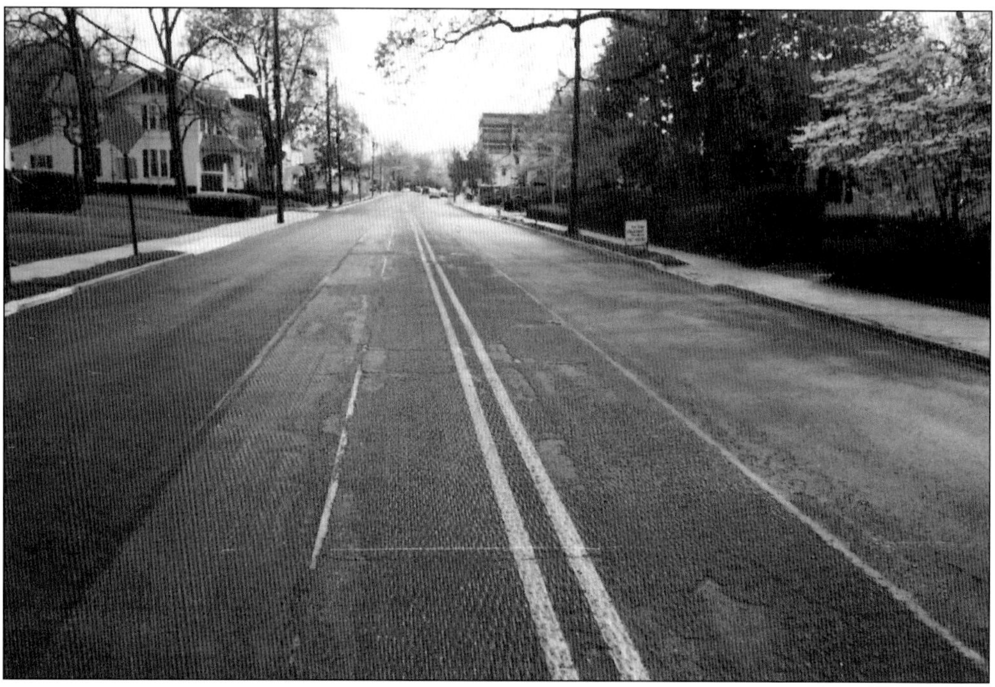

Broad Street looking west, 1993, when the Monmouth County Road Department milled the roadway in order to repave it. This process exposed the trolley tracks.

William Allgor operated a blacksmith shop on Broad Street known locally as "the forge." In 1944 he moved his business to Lewis Street where the empty florist shop stands today, and shoed horses for Monmouth Park. These pictures were taken in the mid-1950s, just before the forge was torn down to make way for a new driveway into the Allenhurst National Bank and Trust.

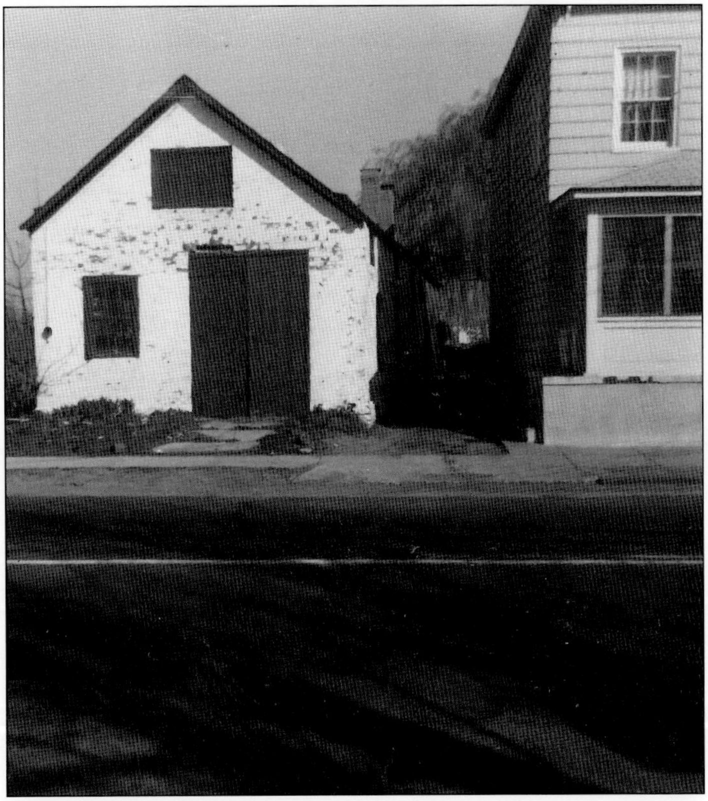

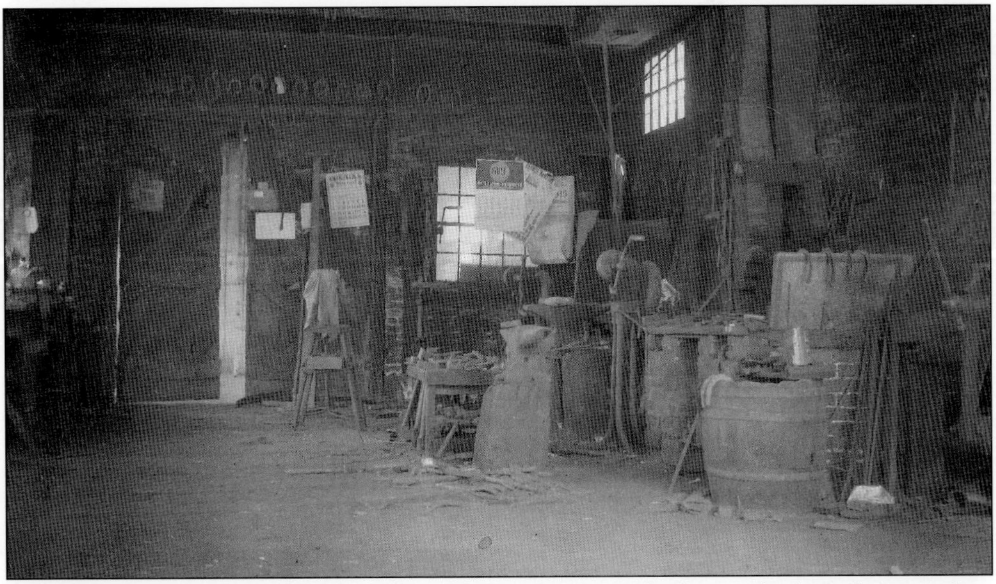

The interior view of Allgor's shop, where two anvils, a water bucket, and a large floor-standing vise can be seen. One of his anvils is on display in front of the Eatontown Historical Museum on Broad Street. National Westminster Bank is on the site of the blacksmith's shop today.

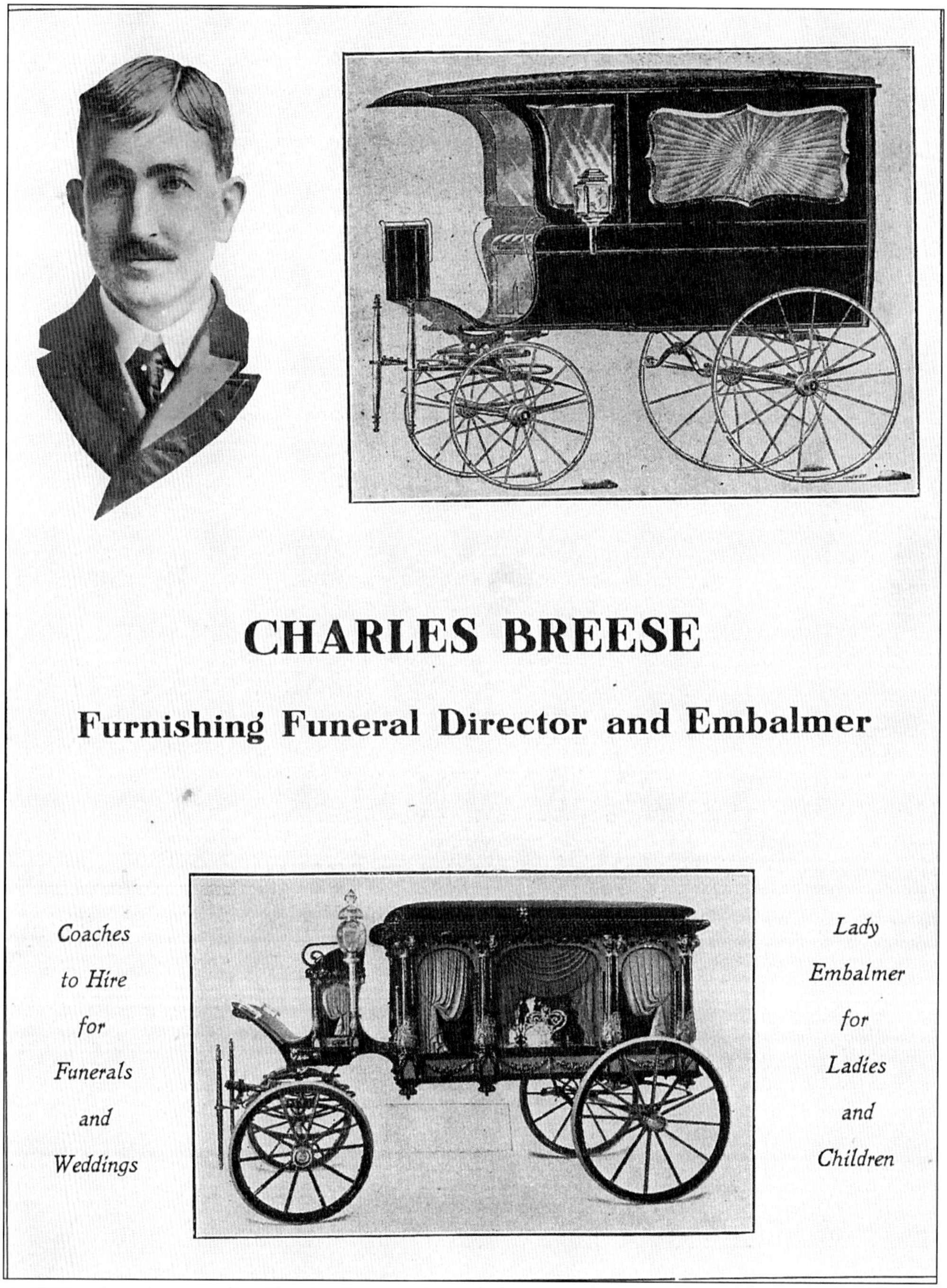

A 1911 advertisement for Charles Breese, funeral director.

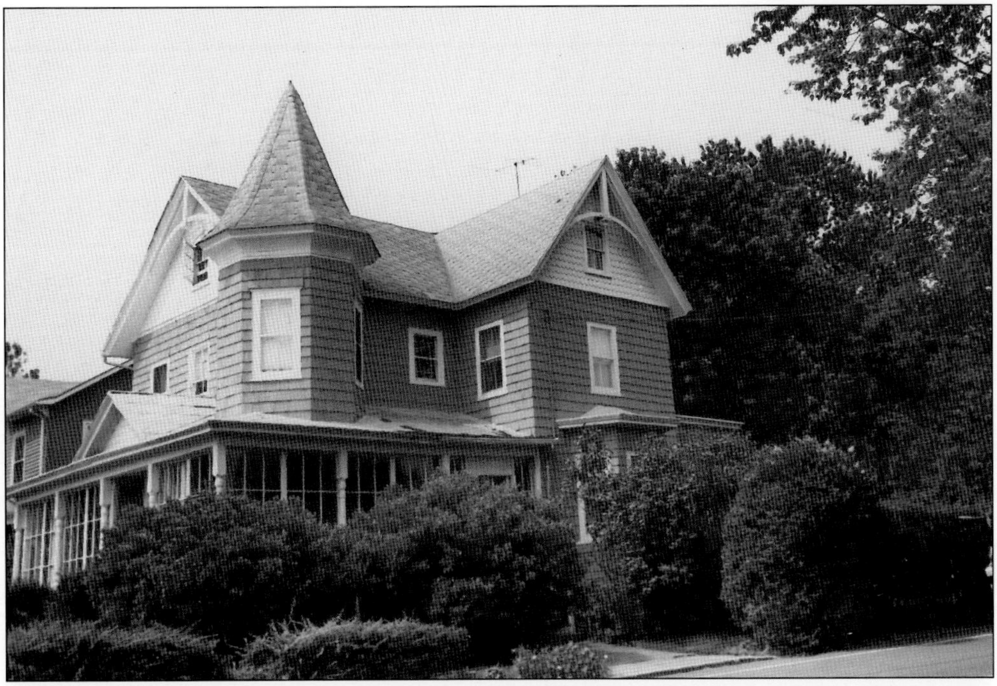

Breese operated his business from his home on South and Willow Streets. From 1946 to 1976 Dr. Norman Thetford and his wife Meda, a nurse, used it as a doctor's office. Dr. Norman Thetford is a collateral relative of Gabriel West, a founding member of St. James Episcopal Church.

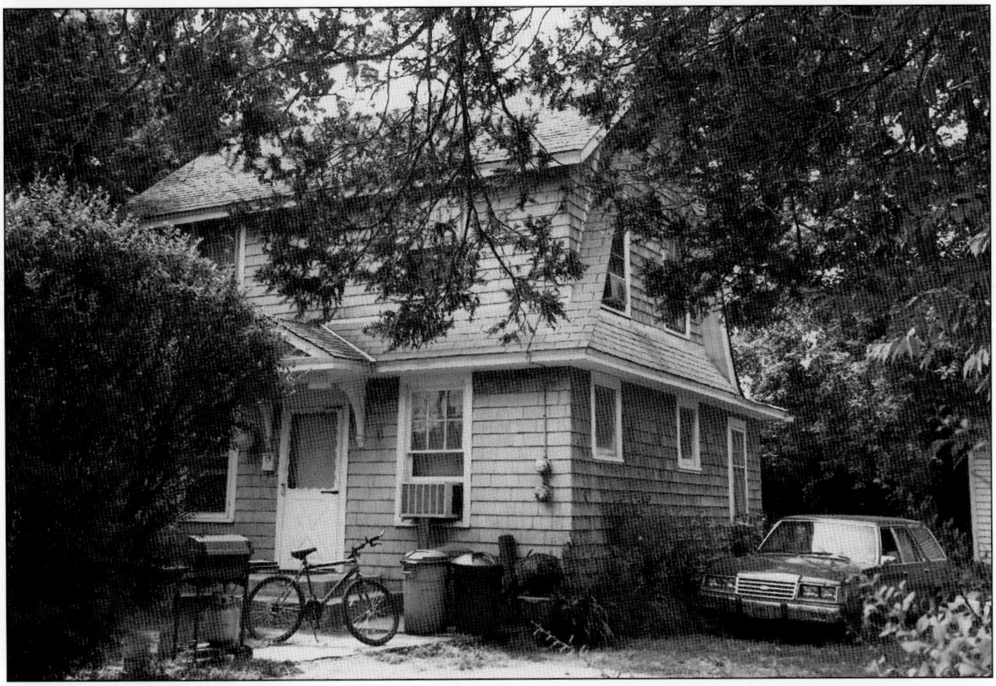

Breese's funeral operations included a chapel at the rear of his property. Today it is a private residence.

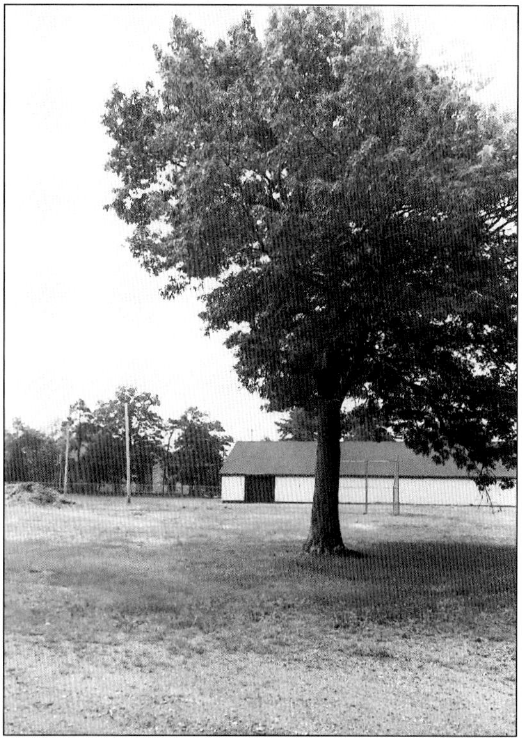

The site of the Crescent Brick Works on the corner of Pinebrook and Hope Roads. The company made fire bricks that were sold throughout Monmouth County, and employed as many as twelve people at its height. It was started in 1913 and was operated into the early 1920s. The property is now part of Fort Monmouth.

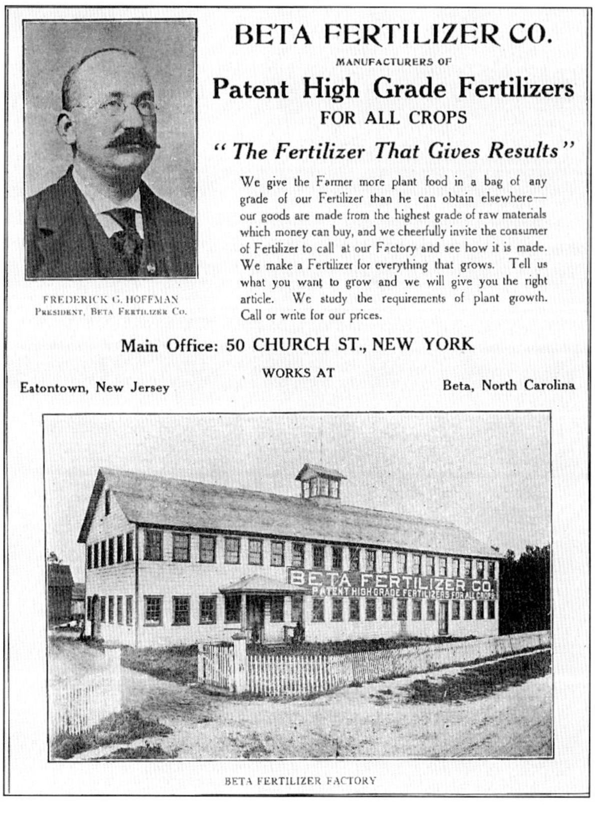

The Beta Fertilizer Factory was located on Lewis Street, near Maxwell Avenue in Eatontown's first recognizable industrial neighborhood. New businesses located here because of the easy access to markets via the Central Railroad of New Jersey. Over time the area included sawmills, a bottling works, and factories for canning tomatoes and making hats, underwear, and horse carriages.

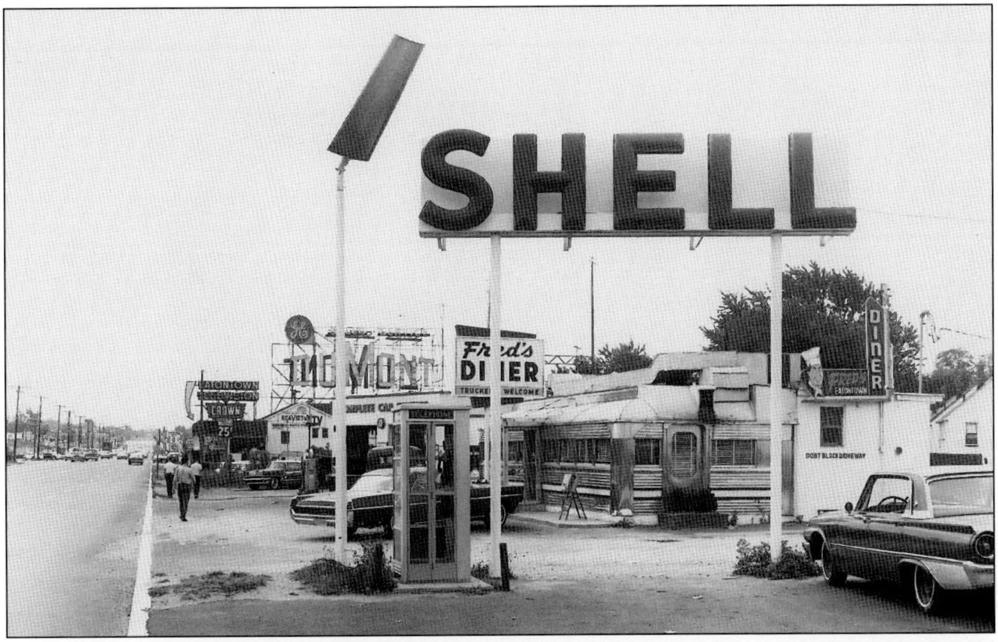

In 1929 the state claimed part of Eatontown's central farmland in order to straighten out the old turnpike. Neptune Highway was the local name given to Route 35. This view is looking south. The Shell station is bordered by South Street on its west side. Fred Klaproth owned the diner pictured here in 1950 that has since been moved back on an angle to the highway and is now a Japanese restaurant called Tokyo. The James Frangella family continues to operate Eatontown TV today.

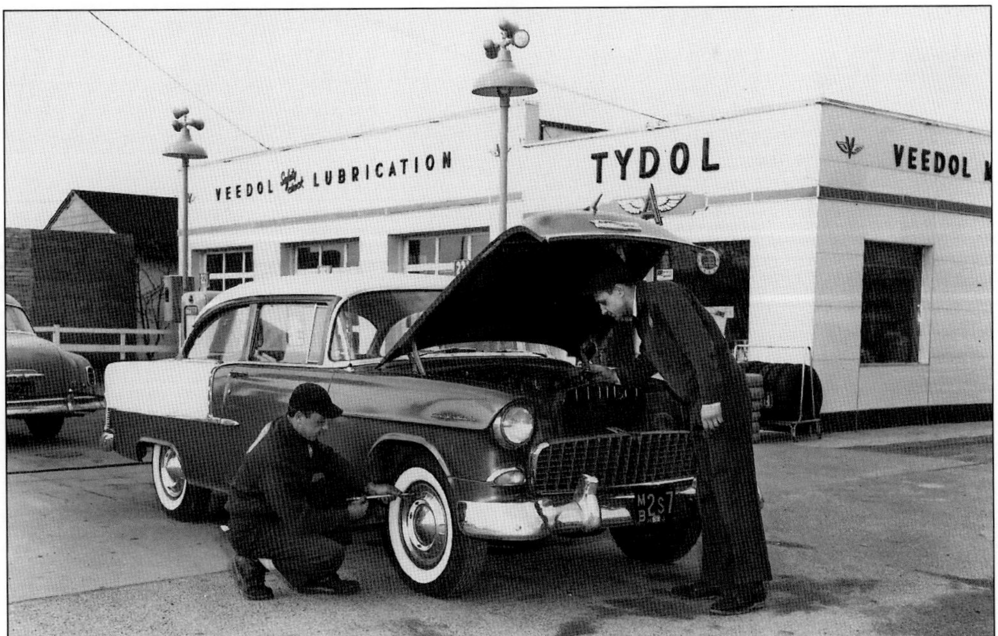

Dr. Lewis's corner estate gave way in the 1950s to the Tydol service station. Today it is Meineke Discount Muffler at 14 Broad Street.

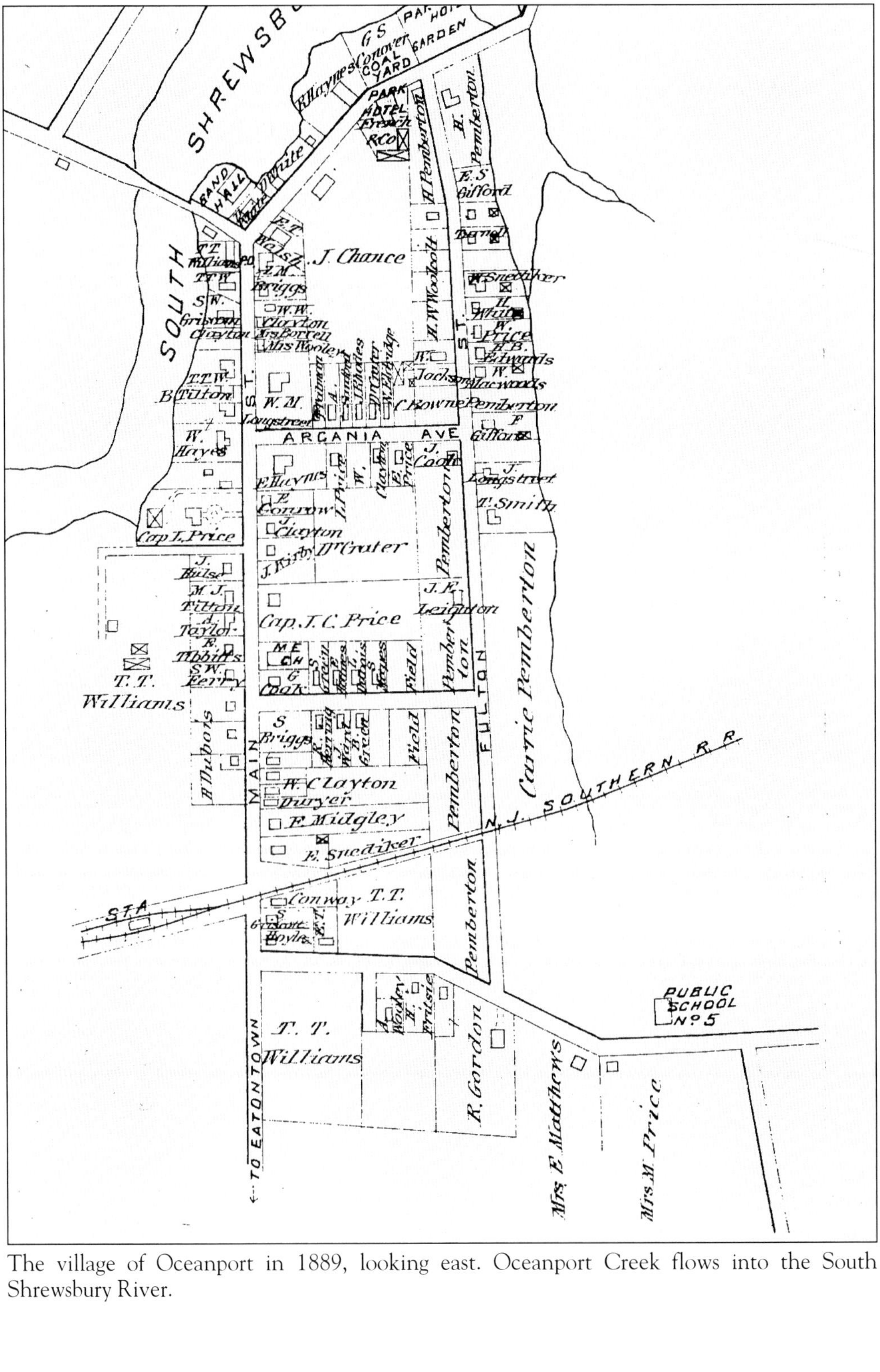

The village of Oceanport in 1889, looking east. Oceanport Creek flows into the South Shrewsbury River.

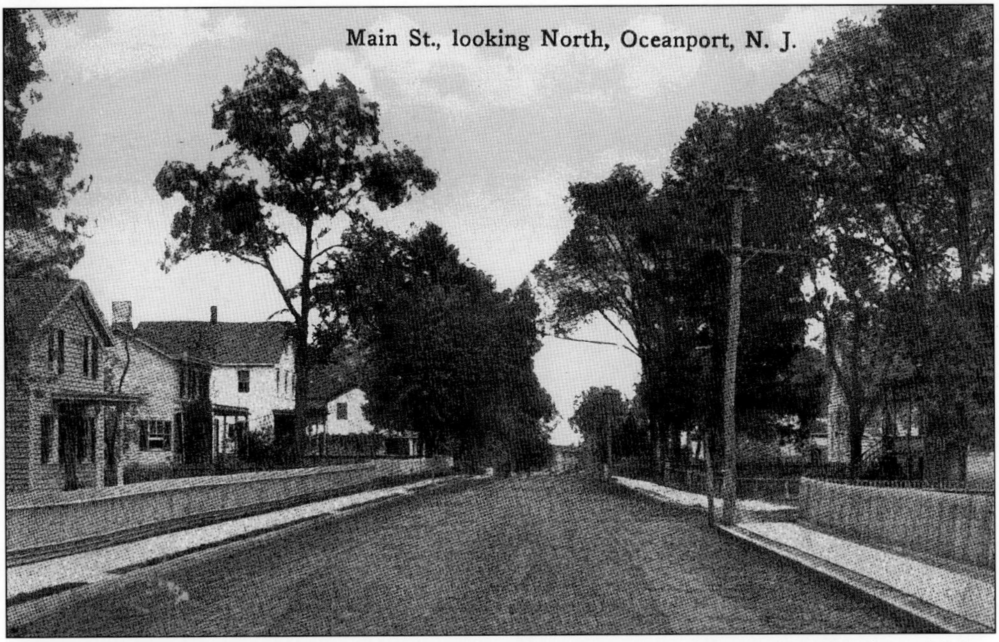

Main Street heading east from the intersection of Broad Street and Eatontown Boulevard. Most of these buildings, constructed during the colonial era, are still standing today. The picture was taken about 1908.

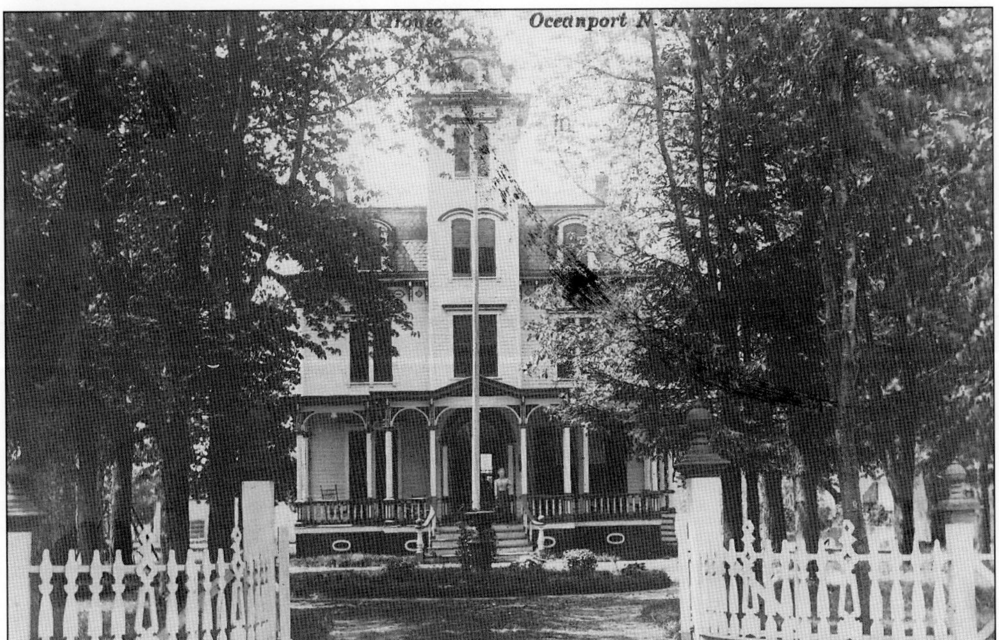

In 1873 Captain Lawrence Price built Riverside Cottage on Main Street. The summer hotel, which overlooked Oceanport Creek, could sleep thirty-five guests. From 1903 to 1920 it was known as the Amelia House when Thomas Woodwards operated it as a rooming house. By the 1960s it had been turned into an apartment house.

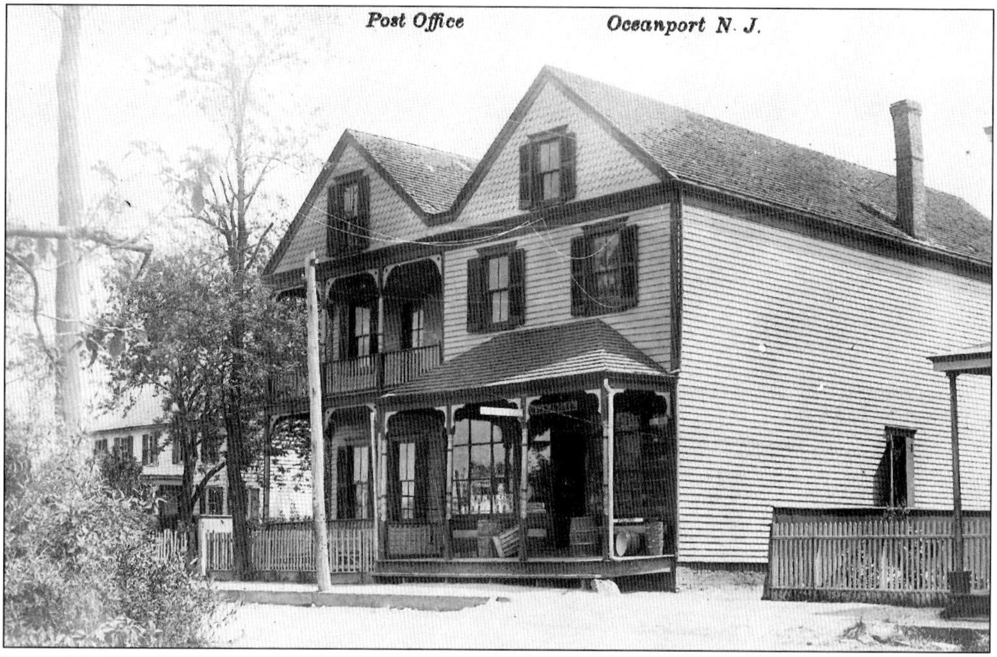

Lewis M. Van Anglen operated a grocery store and the Oceanport village post office out of this building from 1905 to 1910.

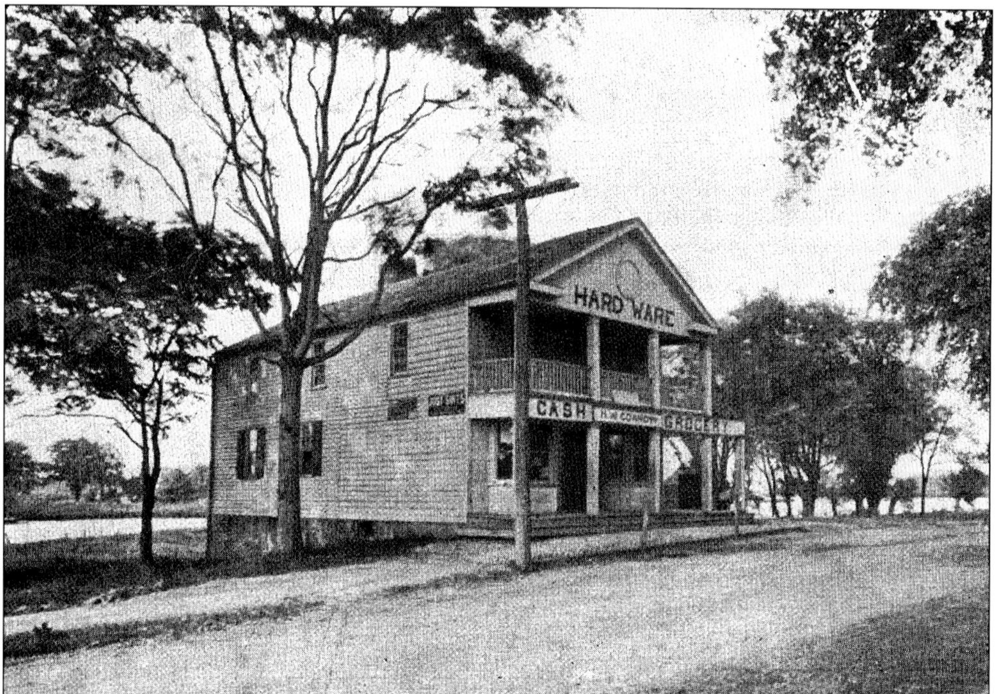

Harry W. Conrow owned a grocery and hardware store, and operated the post office out of this building from 1912 to 1918. His wife Loretta then took over as postmistress, and served until 1934.

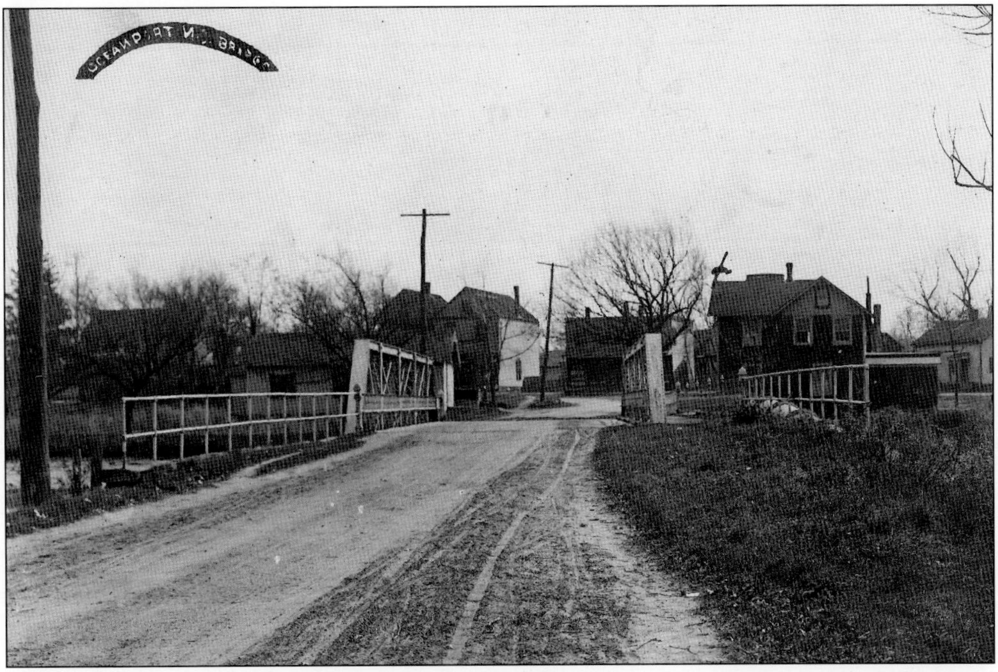

Oceanport Avenue heading south from Little Silver into Oceanport's commercial center, c. 1909. The band hall, seen through the left guard rail, was the setting for concerts and civic functions. The property in the foreground would eventually become part of Fort Monmouth.

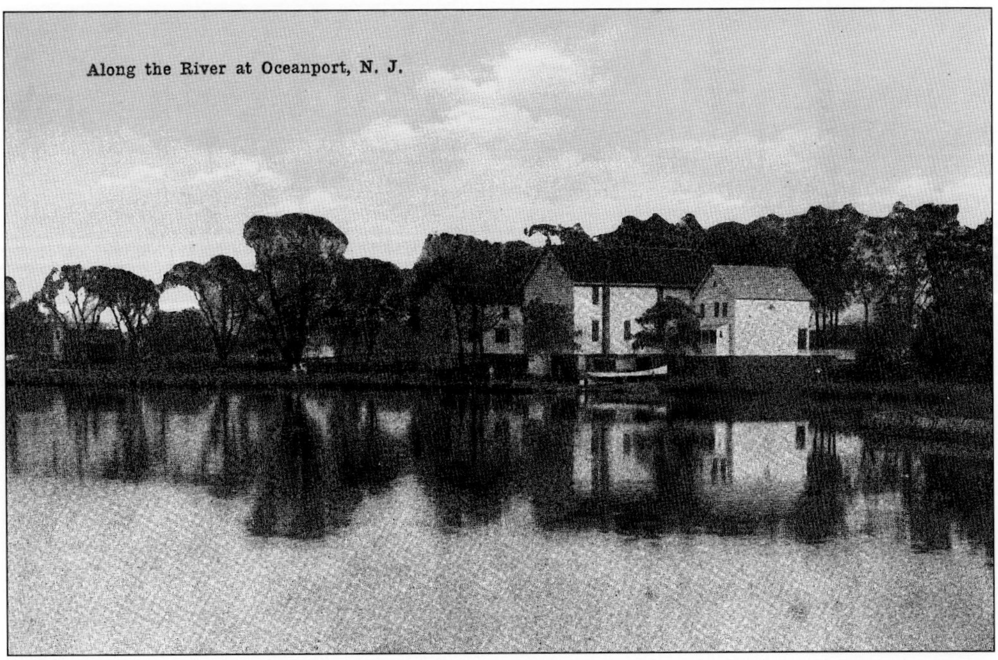

The developing business block of Oceanport village on the South Shrewsbury River, east of the bridge.

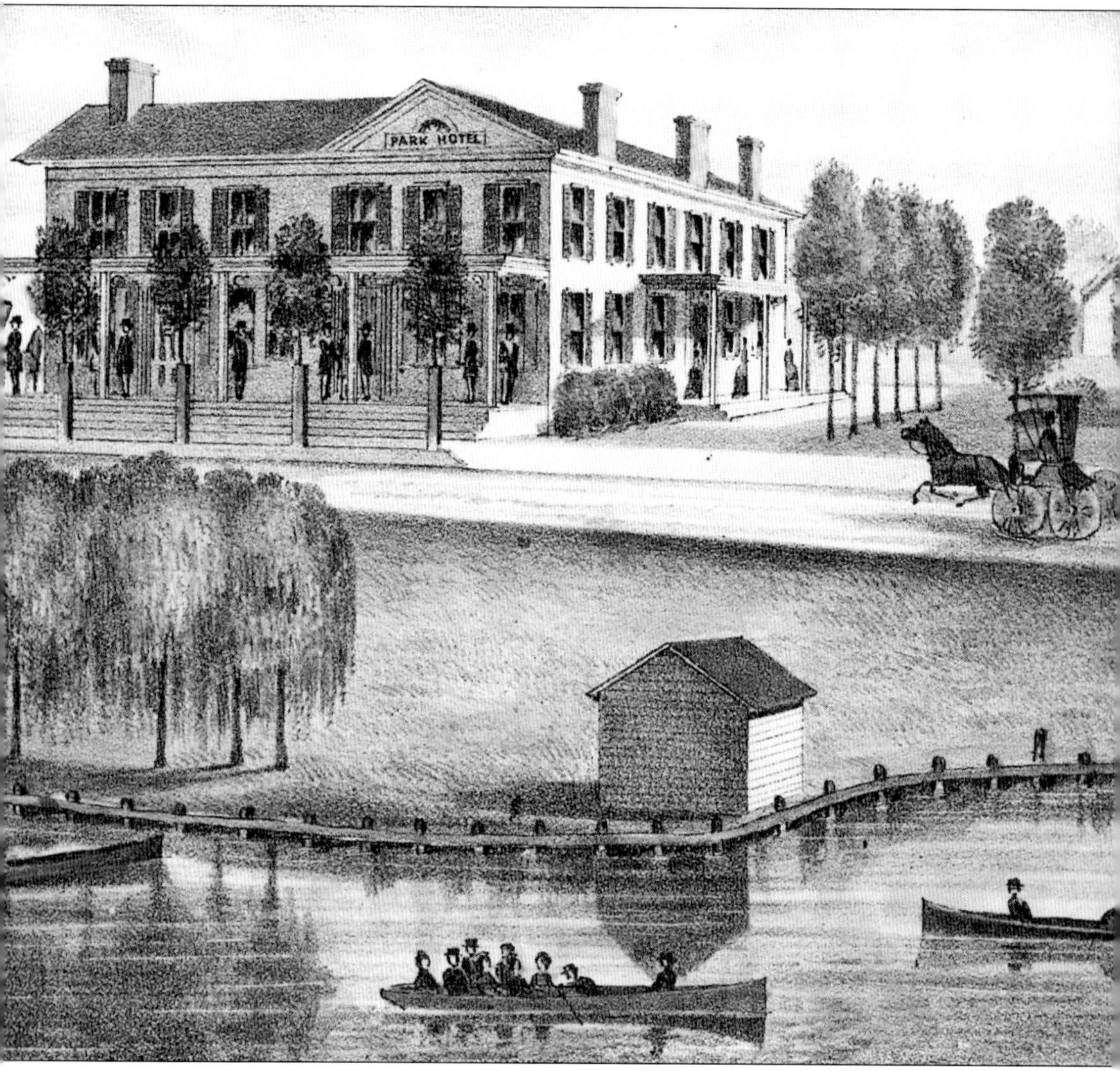

The Parker family, one of the original Shrewsbury colonists, built a hotel in 1846 at the corner of East Main Street and Pemberton Avenue to cater to the early seashore trade. New York summer guests would come by steamboat to the Eatontown docks only a few blocks away.

Known as the Park Hotel in 1878, it was owned by Henry Bart Edwards. W.A. French & Co., wholesale liquor dealers and bottlers from Red Bank, bought the hotel in 1888, and operated it until 1890.

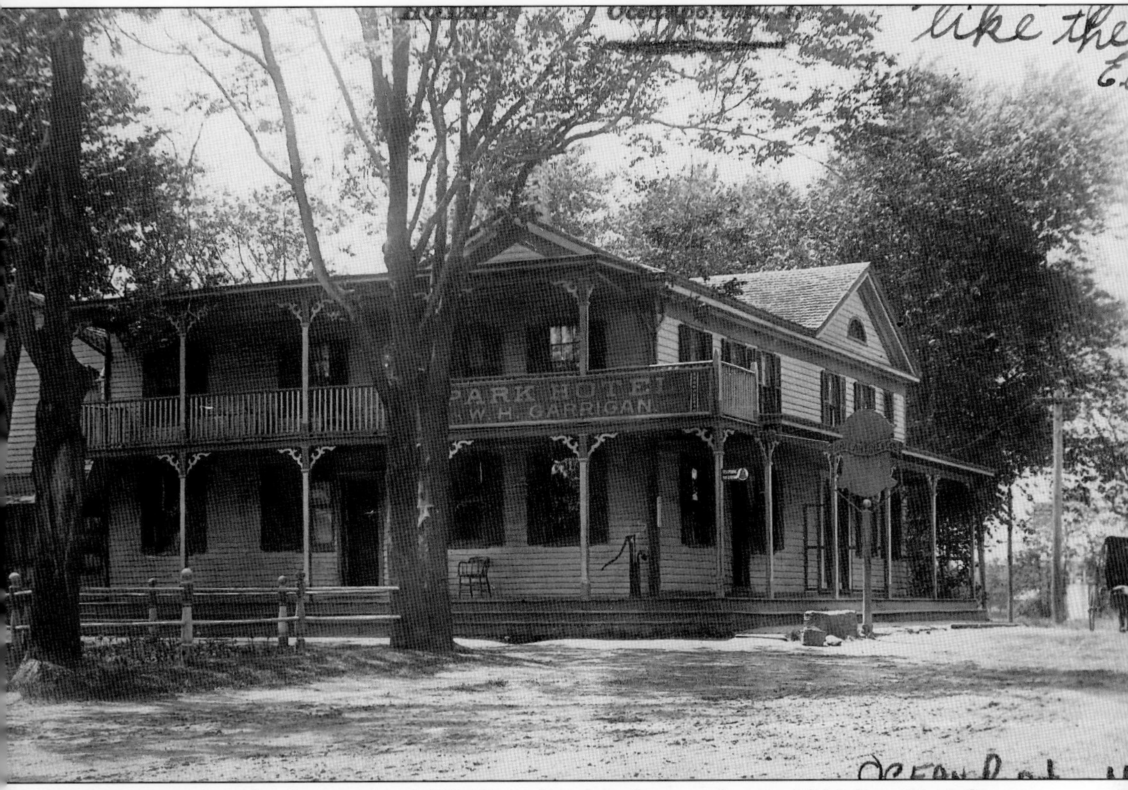

W.H. Garrigan bought the hotel in 1890. This photograph was taken in 1906. East Main Street is to the right. Note the Ballentine & Co. beer sign next to the carriage stepping stone. It advertised what brand of beer the hotel served. The hotel also boasted a public telephone. The Park Hotel was in operation through World War I. In the 1920s it was converted to an apartment house.

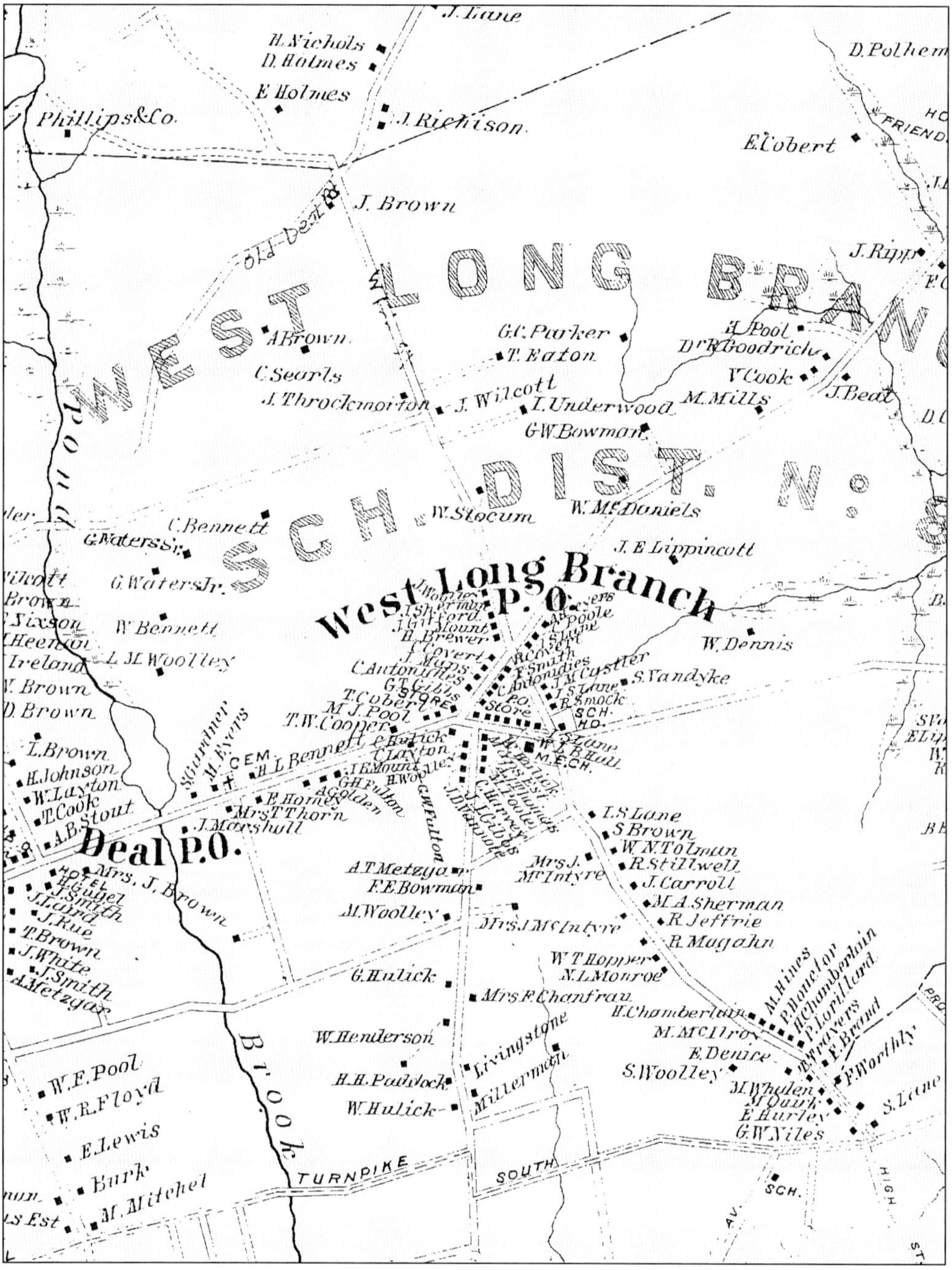

Eatontown's southern village was Mechanicsville, a stage coach stop on the way to the Jersey Shore, which could be reached either by the Red Bank-Long Branch Turnpike (today South and Wall Streets) or by one of the roads to Long Branch (today Monmouth Road or Route 71). By 1889 Mechanicsville was referred to as the West Long Branch P.O., its postal customers owning many large farming homesteads.

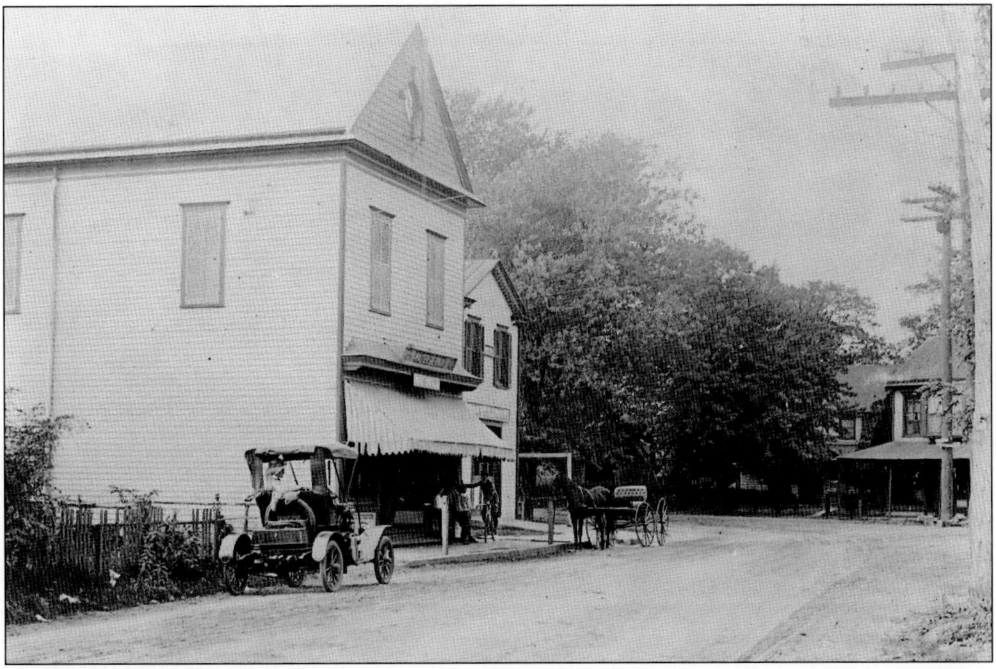

Monmouth Road looking north into the heart of West Long Branch. Note the three modes of transportation represented in front of Walter Sherman's store and post office. The automobile belongs to Atlick Merriman, a noted local postcard photographer. His daughter is sitting in the car.

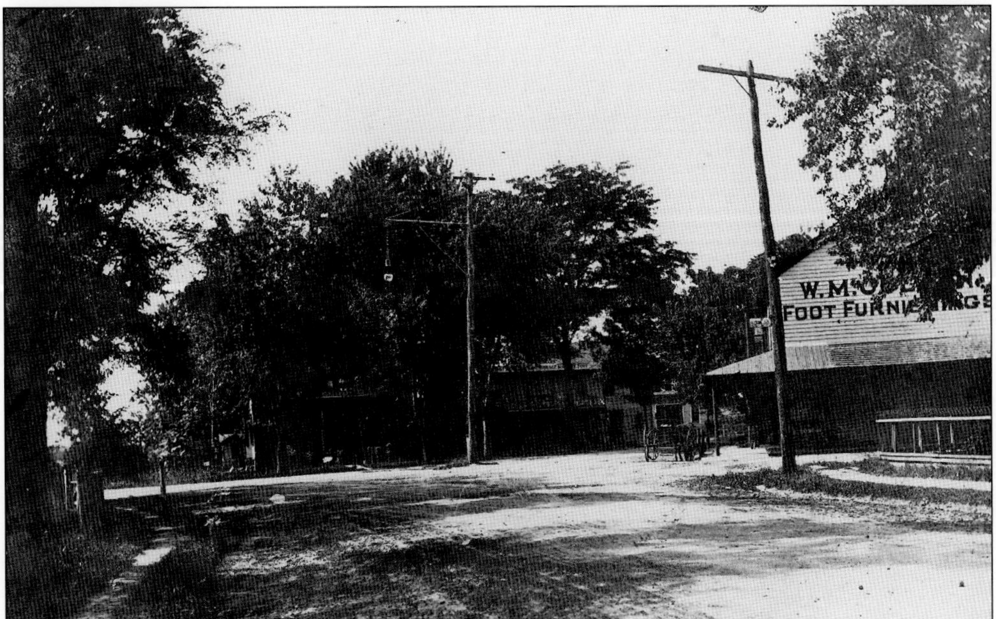

The same intersection seen from Cedar Avenue. The W.M. Golden Foot Furnishings store is on the Locust Avenue corner. Today a separate pizza and beauty shop occupy the building.

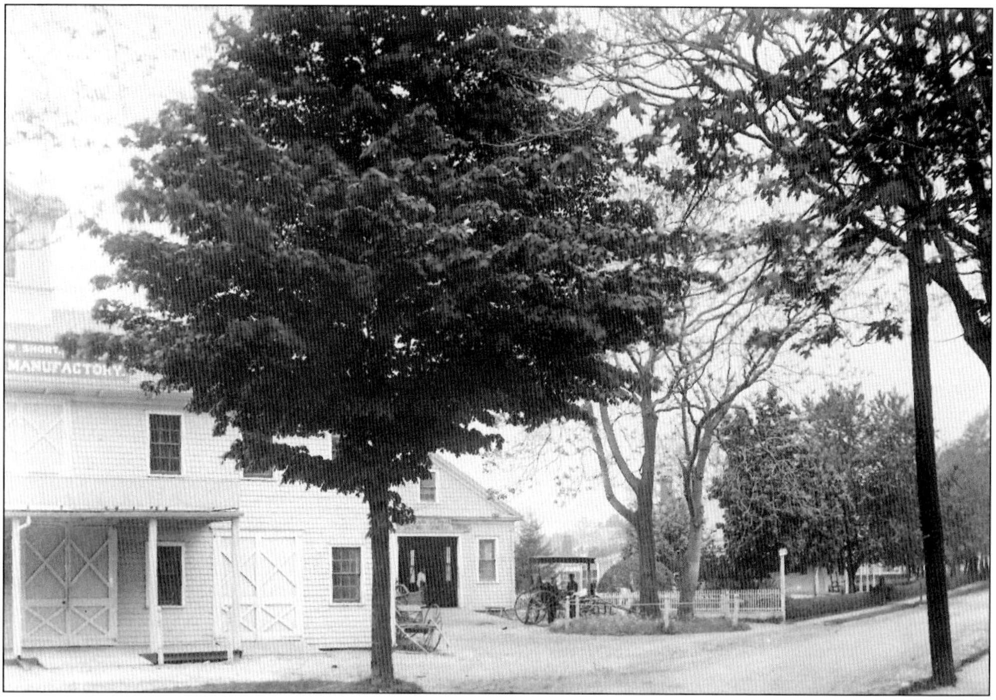

The John Short Carriage Manufactory and the Hank Sherman Shoeing and General Jobbing garage were located on the west side of Monmouth Road, where an Amocco gas station stands today.

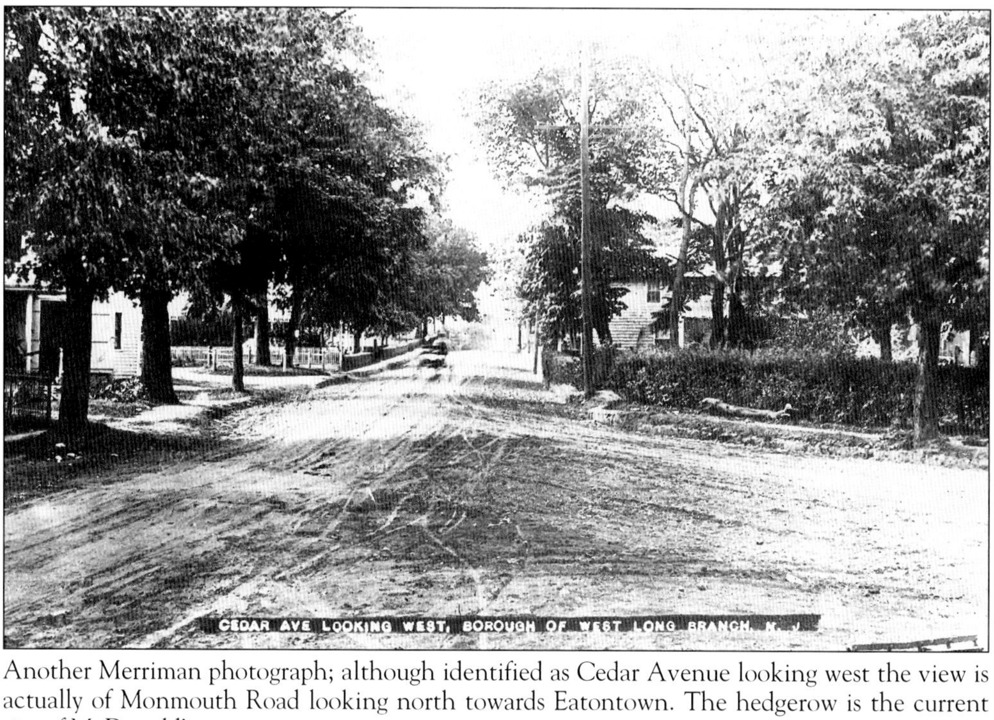

Another Merriman photograph; although identified as Cedar Avenue looking west the view is actually of Monmouth Road looking north towards Eatontown. The hedgerow is the current site of McDonald's.

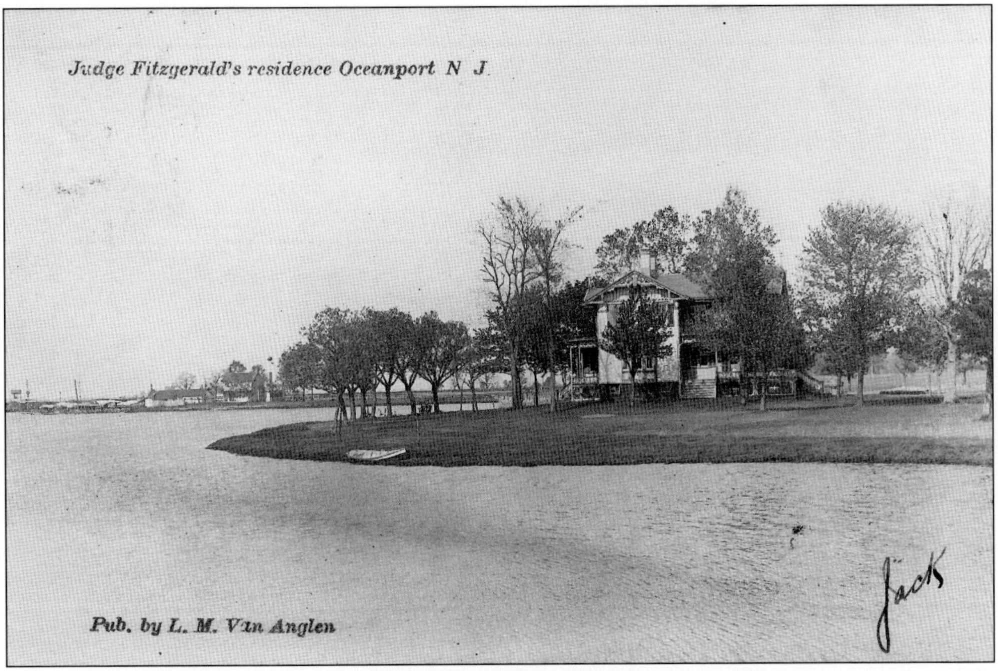

This is a view of what was at one time the Allaire Warehouse, stable, railway, and pier. It was adjacent to the Eatontown docks. Later the site became the private residence of Judge Fitzgerald. Today it is part of Old Wharf Park.

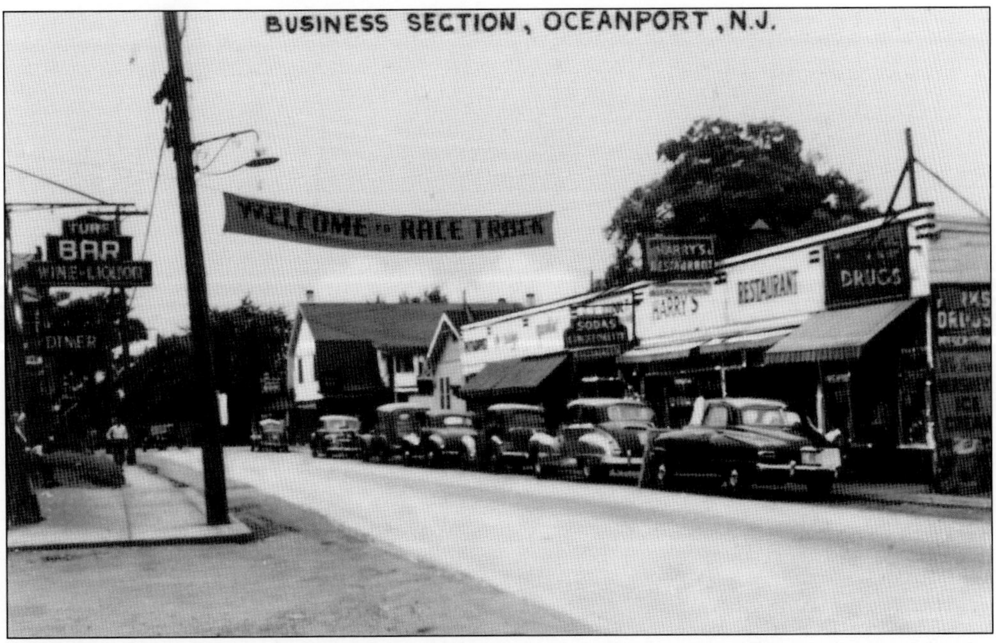

Oceanport declared its independence from Eatontown in 1919. In the 1940s, its business district was still concentrated on Main Street, and catered largely to the Monmouth Park racetrack clientele. By the 1990s this same intersection had become a municipal park on Oceanport Creek known as Old Wharf Park.

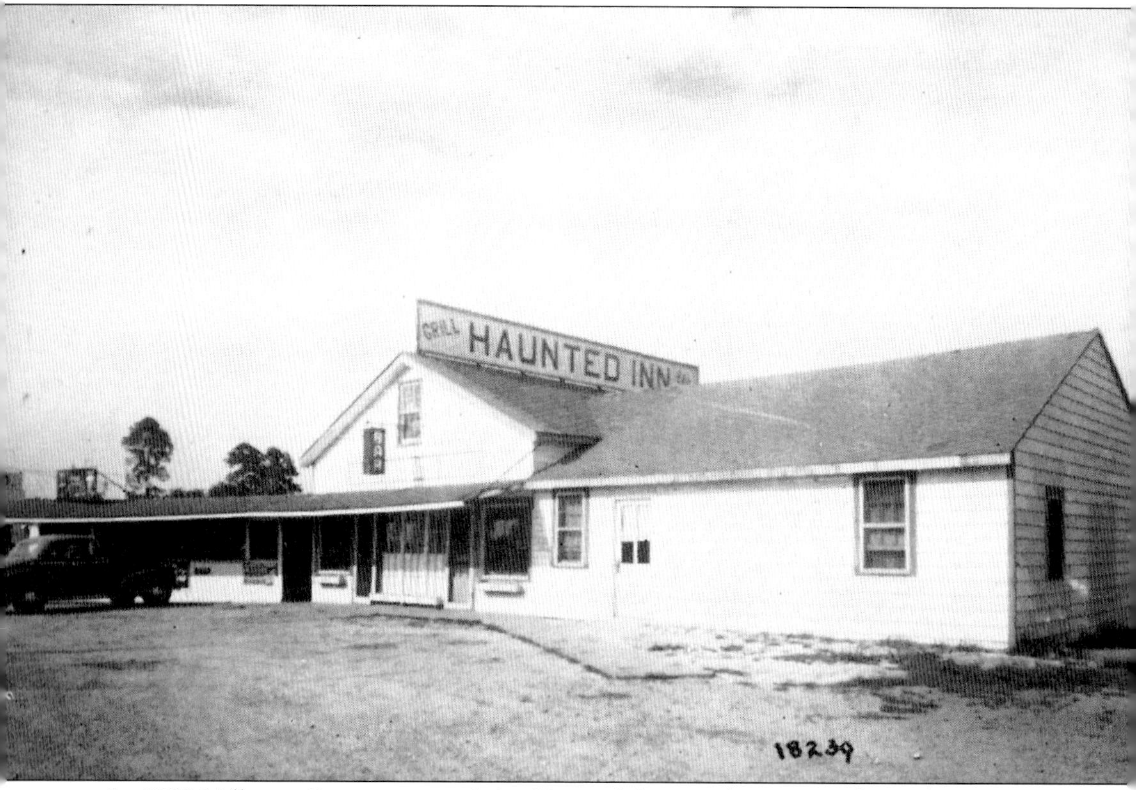

In 1938 Millicent Bennett opened the Haunted Inn on the corner of Broad Street and the Main Street to Oceanport, basing the name on a rumor that the building was haunted by the ghost of a woman who had committed suicide (her father owned the building). From 1940 to 1954 Mrs. Bennett and her husband operated the Haunted Inn on Route 35. Circle Cabins and Trailers were located behind the bar which is today Circle Court Trailer Park. The center of the park had communal outdoor showers where sycamores now thrive and shade the trailer park. Stillwell Van Pelt owned the Texaco station in the far left of the photograph (only the end of the sign can be seen).

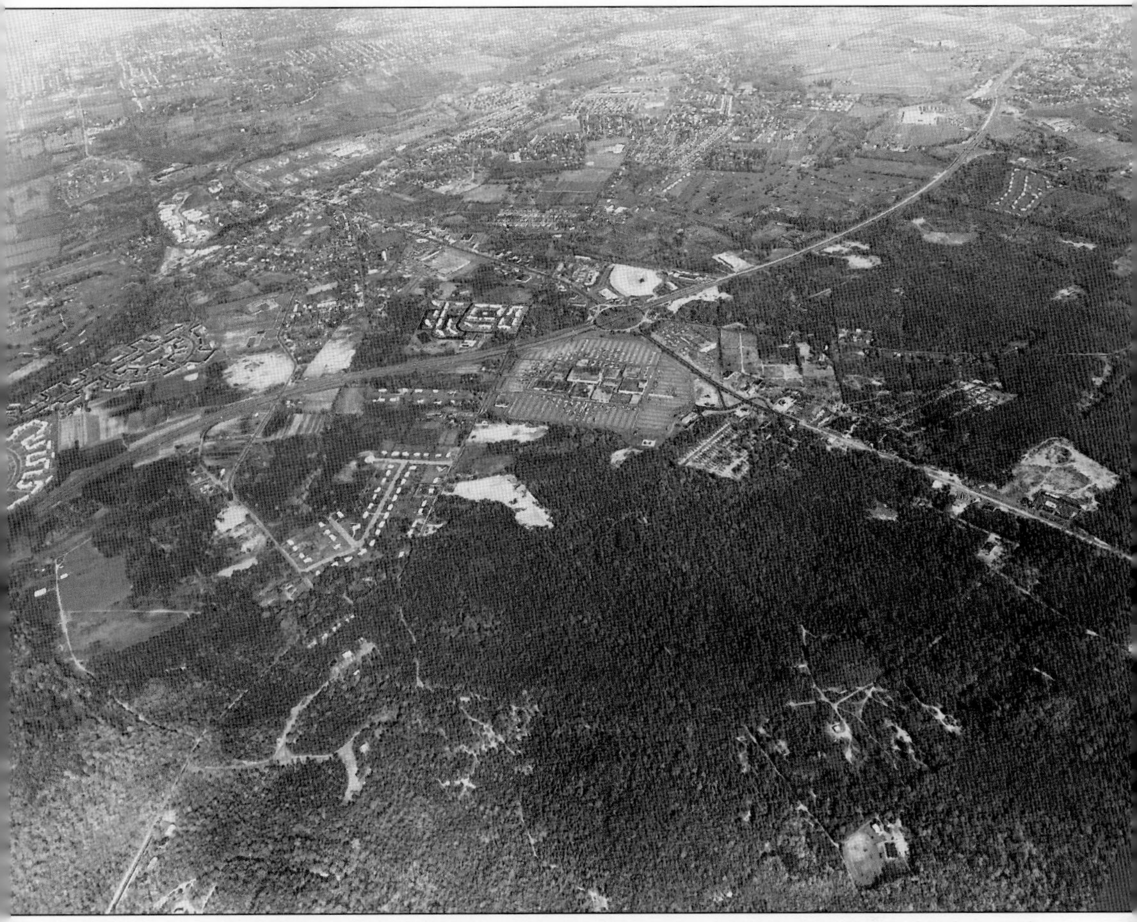

A 1964 aerial view of Eatontown, looking northeast. Newark realtor Irving Feist, the first real estate manager of new Monmouth Shopping Center (located in the middle of the photograph), said in May 1960: "One day I took a helicopter ride over the country. Over Eatontown I could see the outline of the Parkway and its approach to the Eatontown Circle. I could see a double axis developing between Red Bank and Asbury Park, Long Branch and Freehold. I saw that the area was served by highways and a tremendous number of feeder roads. It if wasn't the geographical center of the county, it was the highway center."

The shopping center was ten years in the planning; ground for the 600,000-square-foot outdoor retail mall was broken on May 12, 1958. At the time it was one of only three of its kind in New Jersey. Its builder and owner was the Massachusetts Mutual Insurance Co.

Most of the forested area in the foreground is the Woodmere neighborhood where many old-time village residents had wood lots and picked holly boughs at Christmas.

FLAG RAISING

AT THE

EATONTOWN PUBLIC SCHOOL

Wednesday, Dec. 23, 1908

PROGRAM.

PARADE—Line of march forms at 1.30 p. m. on Lewis Street, south to Wayside Avenue, north on Maple Avenue to Lewis Street, east on Lewis Street to Main Street to Broad, and thence to School Grounds.

EXERCISES AT SCHOOL GROUNDS.

MUSIC—"America," - By Band and Audience
INVOCATION, - - By Rev. A. D. Betts
MUSIC—"Star Spangled Banner," Band and Audience
RAISING OF FLAG—By Members of G. A. R., Salute of Flag by Children and Singing of second verse of "The Star Spangled Banner."
MARCH TO HALL.

EXERCISES AT CRESCENT HALL.

ADDRESS, - - By Rev. Martin L. Ferris
MUSIC.
ADDRESS, - - - By Rev. L. B. Giles
MUSIC.
ADDRESS, - - - By Prof. Sensor
MUSIC.
ADDRESS, - - By Rev. Joseph B. Kulp
BENEDICTION, - - By Rev. D. L. Parsons

If the Day should be Stormy, all Exercises wiil be held in Crescent Hall.

THE TIMES PRINT, Eatontown, N. J.

Two

Church and School

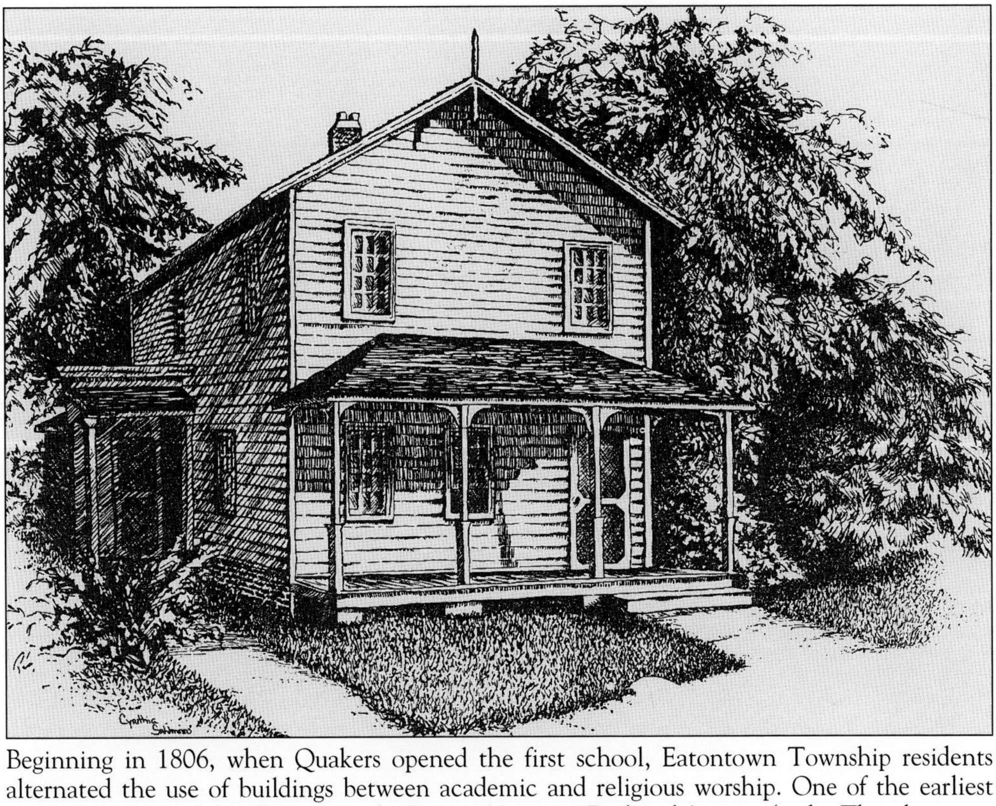

Beginning in 1806, when Quakers opened the first school, Eatontown Township residents alternated the use of buildings between academic and religious worship. One of the earliest buildings used as a schoolhouse was the Brower House on Railroad Avenue (today Throckmorton Avenue). The house also served as a Methodist meetinghouse in 1846.

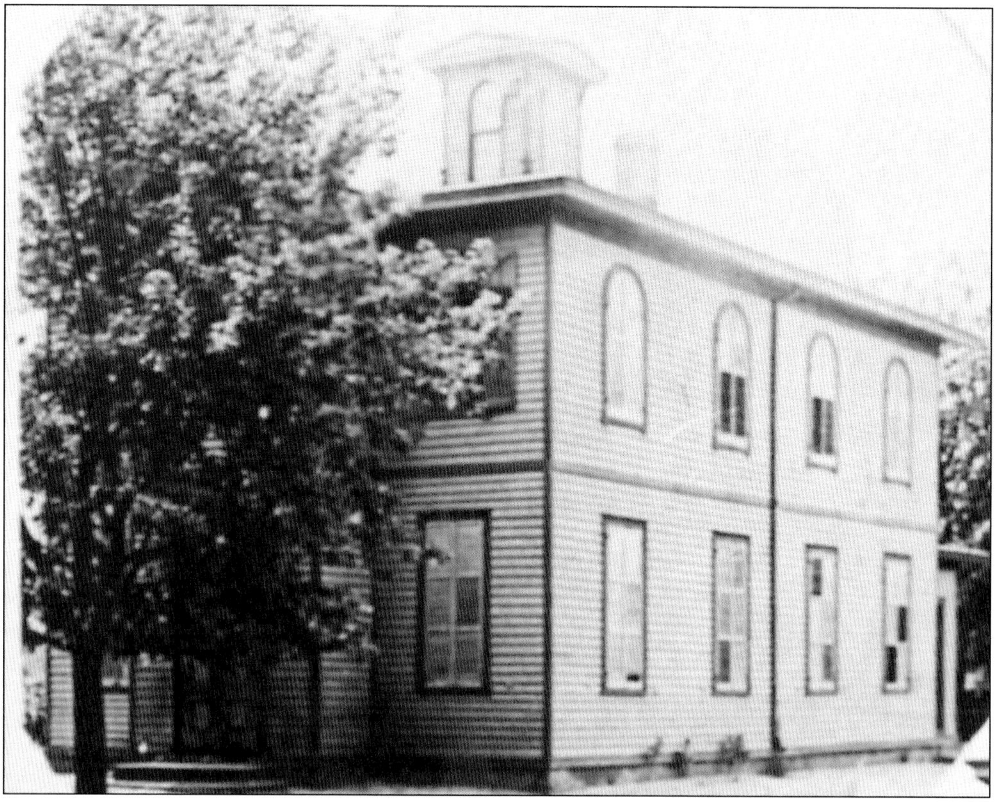

Free public education came to New Jersey in 1868. By 1870 the new two-story, four-room public school on High Street was opened. In 1909 this school was sold, and the building divided and rebuilt into two houses that are still standing side by side on High Street.

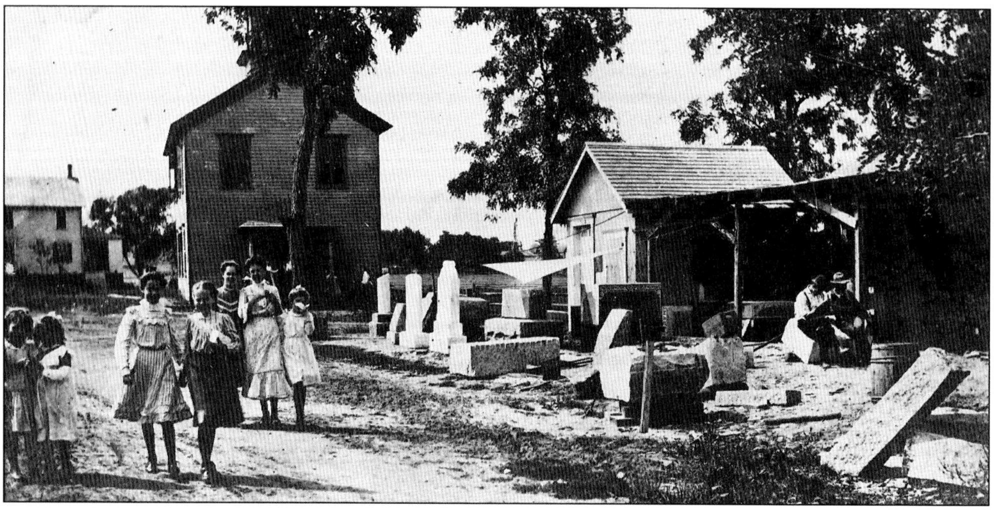

In 1870, on the northwest corner of Wall Street and Locust Avenue, this two-story frame structure was constructed for school purposes. This school was closed in 1904, and pupils went to the new two-story brick school on the corner of Wall Street and Monmouth Road. A monument company stands on the site of the frame schoolhouse today while Deal Yeshiva, a private academy, occupies the former brick public school building.

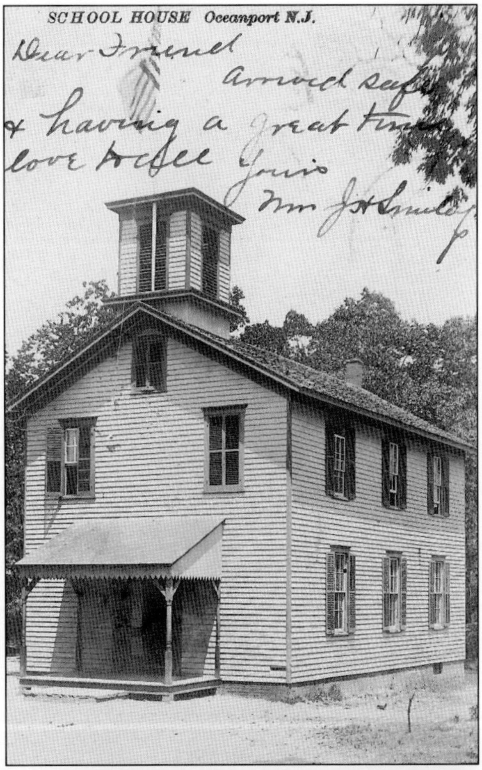

In 1869 a two-story, wood-frame schoolhouse was built on Wolf Hill Avenue in the village of Oceanport. This photograph was taken about 1905.

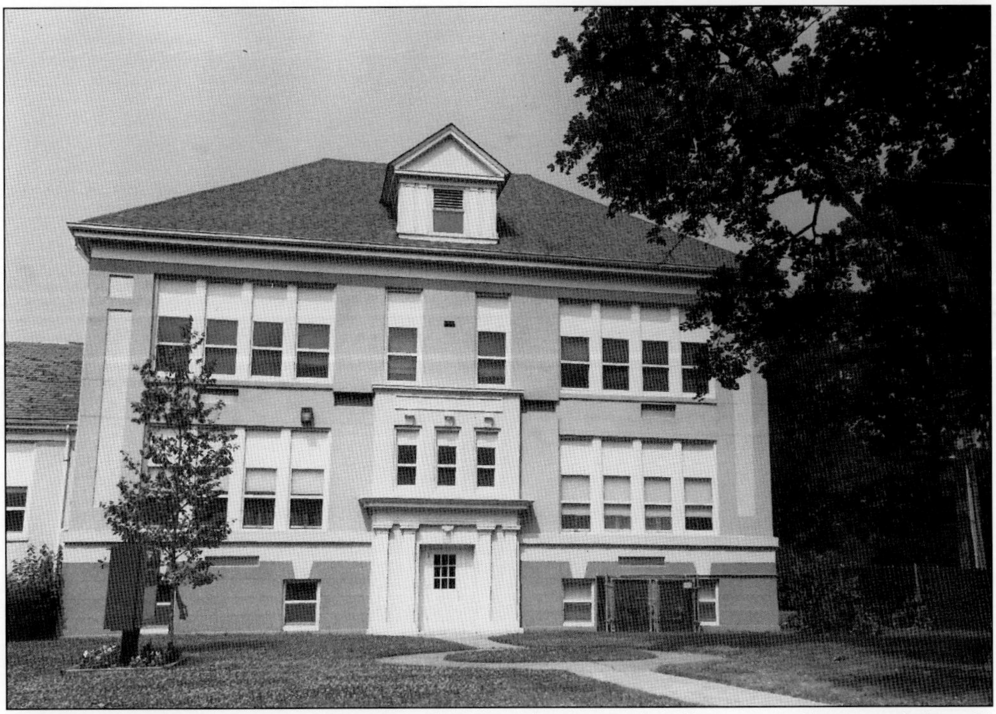

In 1911 this three-story brick building became the new schoolhouse on the site of the old wooden school. It has since been expanded.

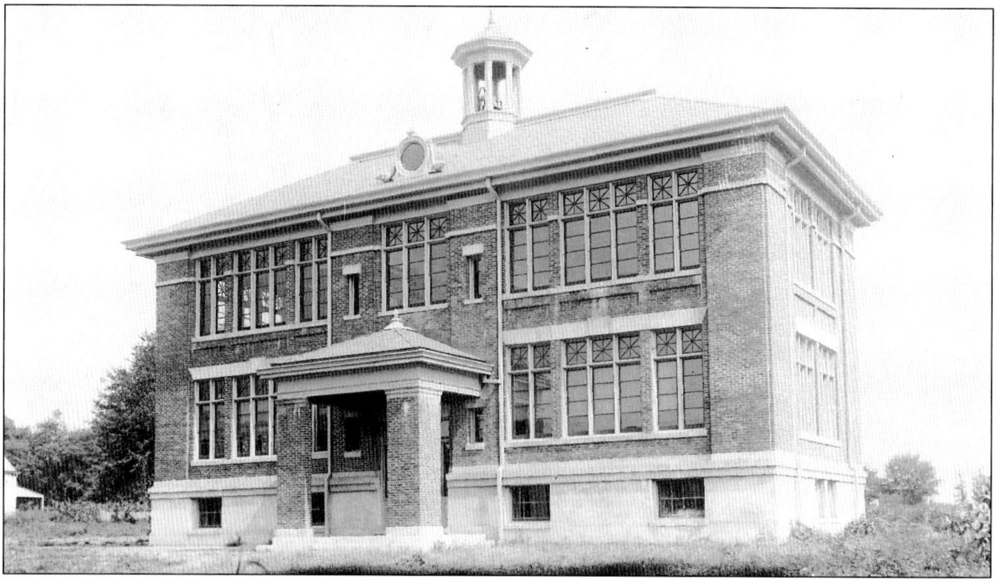

Eatontown Public School No. 1 was built on Broad Street in 1907 at a cost of $21,500, and integrated the children at the school on High Street with those attending the one-room schoolhouse in Locust Grove on the southeast corner of Wyckoff Road and South Street.

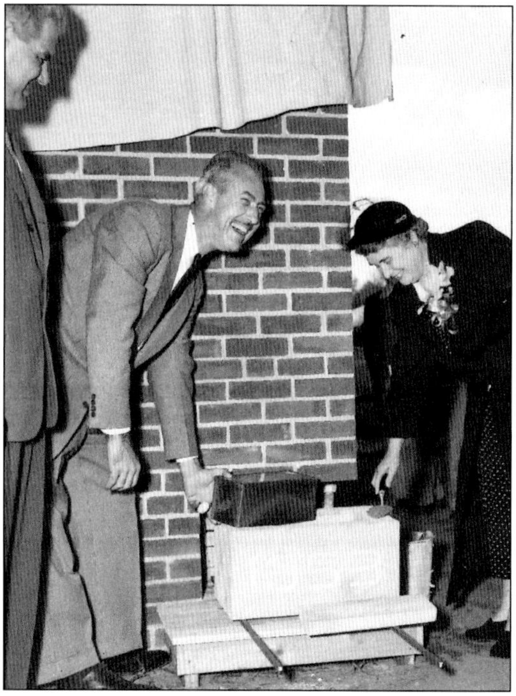

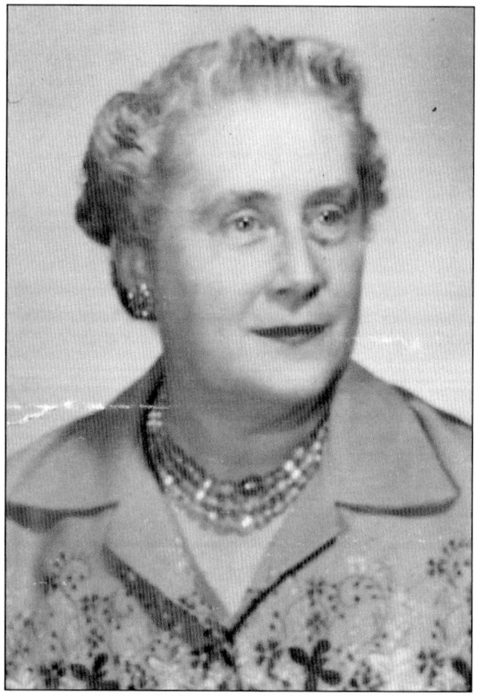

Left: In 1953 Margaret L. Vetter, Eatontown schools' second overall and first woman principal, helped lay the cornerstone of the new elementary school on Grant Avenue, named in her honor. With her is Leo J. Carling, president of the Eatontown Board of Education and co-sponsor of the town's first planning board. Both Vetter and the adjoining Memorial Junior High School were built on farms owned by the Wolcott family.
Right: Another view of Margaret L. Vetter.

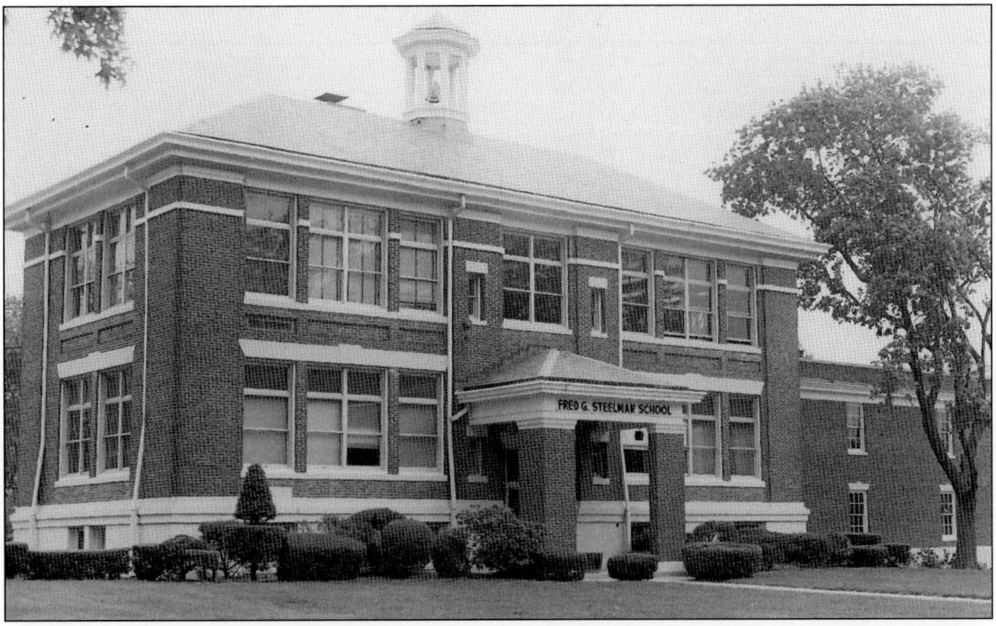

In 1894 the Eatontown Board of Education was organized. Fred G. Steelman came to teach in 1916. He took a short leave of absence to serve in World War I, but then returned to teach, and was principal until 1940. Public School No. 1 was renamed in his honor in 1955. Today it is used as the offices of the Eatontown Board of Education.

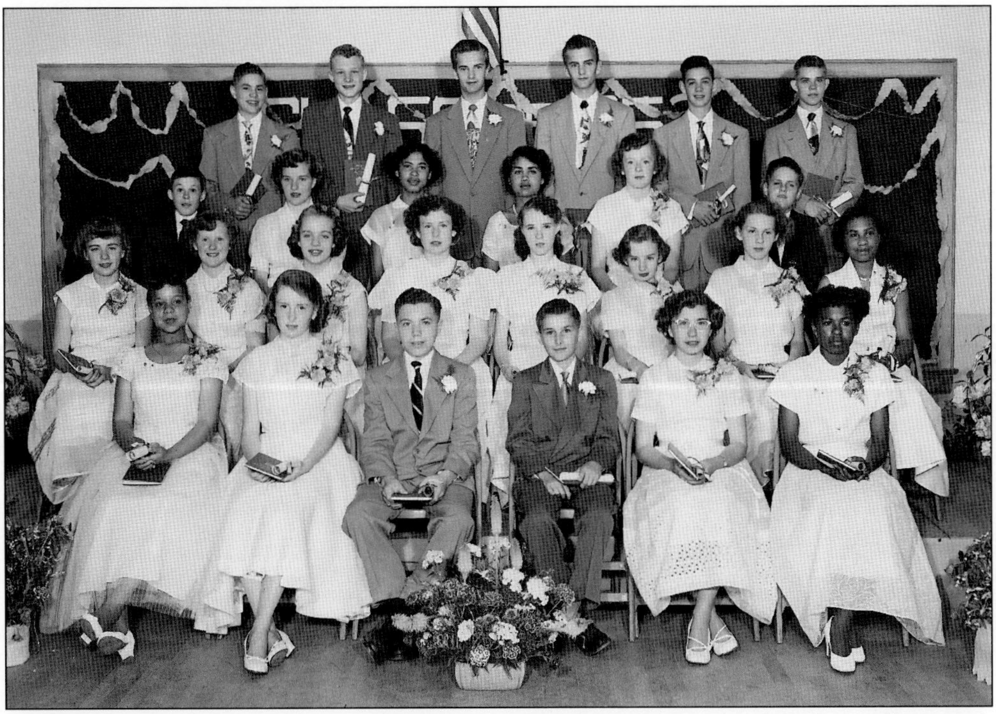

In 1952, a two-story, four-room extension was added to the Steelman School. That year's graduating class had its portrait taken in one of the new classrooms. These eight graders went on to be freshmen in Long Branch High School.

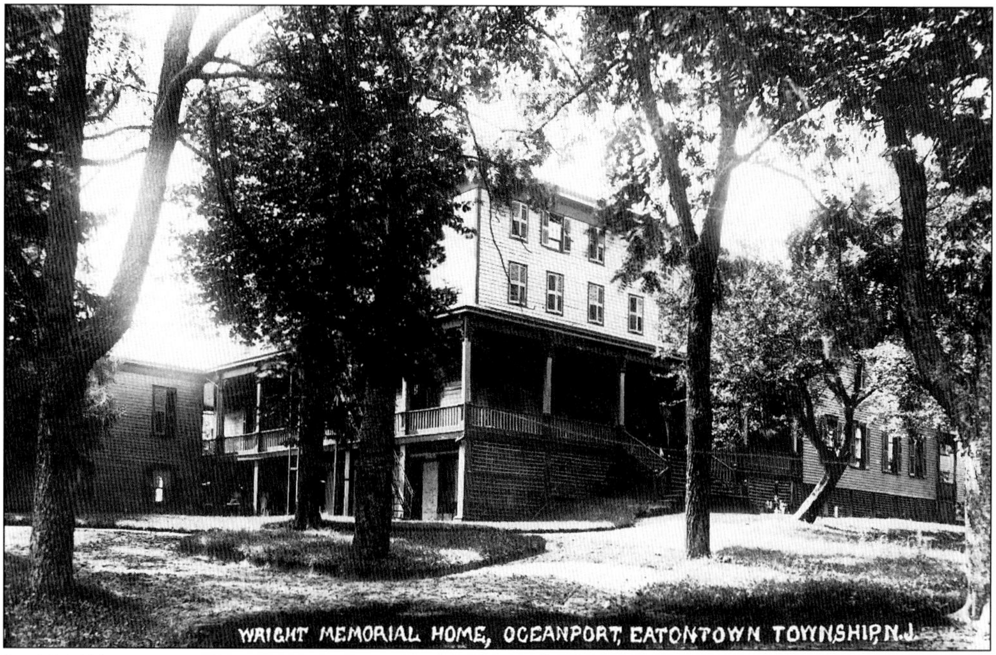

In 1844 Eatontown Seminary, a private school, was built on land bordered by Monmouth Road and Eatontown Boulevard. In 1850 it was sold to H.F. Spaulding, who changed the name to the Ocean Institute and operated it as a day school.

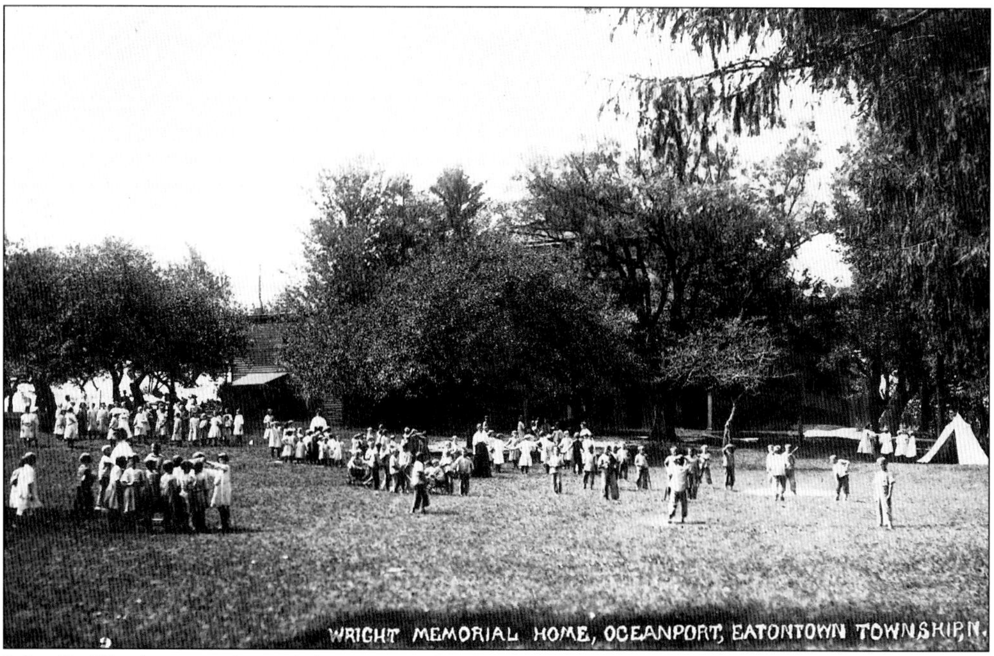

John D. Wright, president of the Society for the Prevention of Cruelty to Children, bought the property in 1875. He gave it to the American Female Guardian Society of New York for use as a summer home for the Society for Friendless and Cruelly Treated Children.

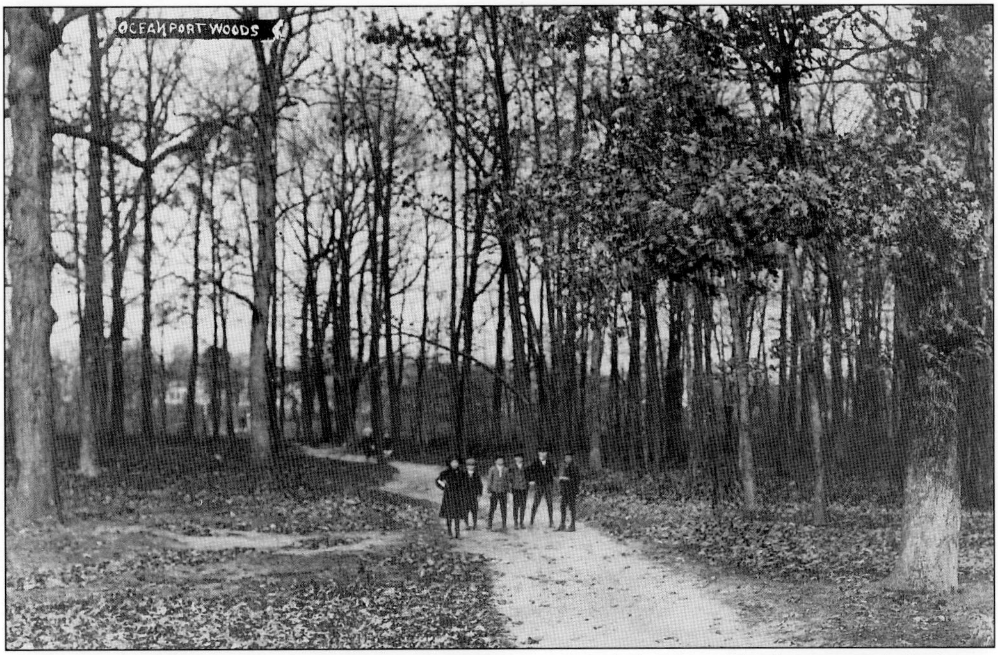

Known as the Wright Memorial Home, the property included a chapel built in 1882 (which was also used as a schoolroom), dormitories, a caretaker's cottage, and a dispensary. A young Mary Pickford played at this summer retreat.

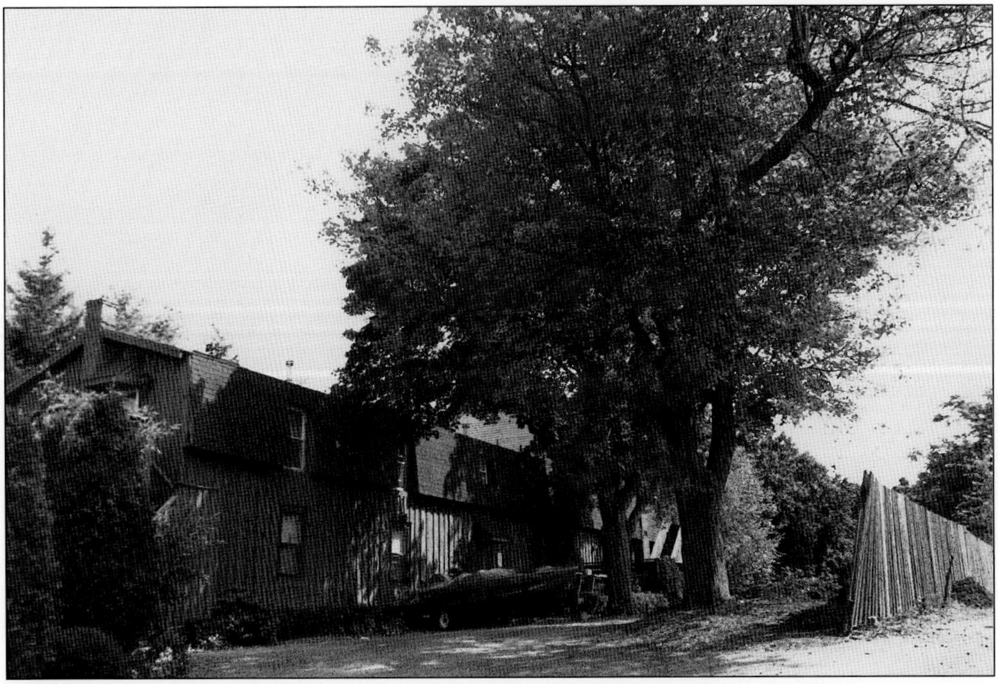

The home closed in 1946 and the main buildings burned down several years later. In more recent times, the remaining buildings were turned into dwellings on the Oceanport side of Monmouth Road.

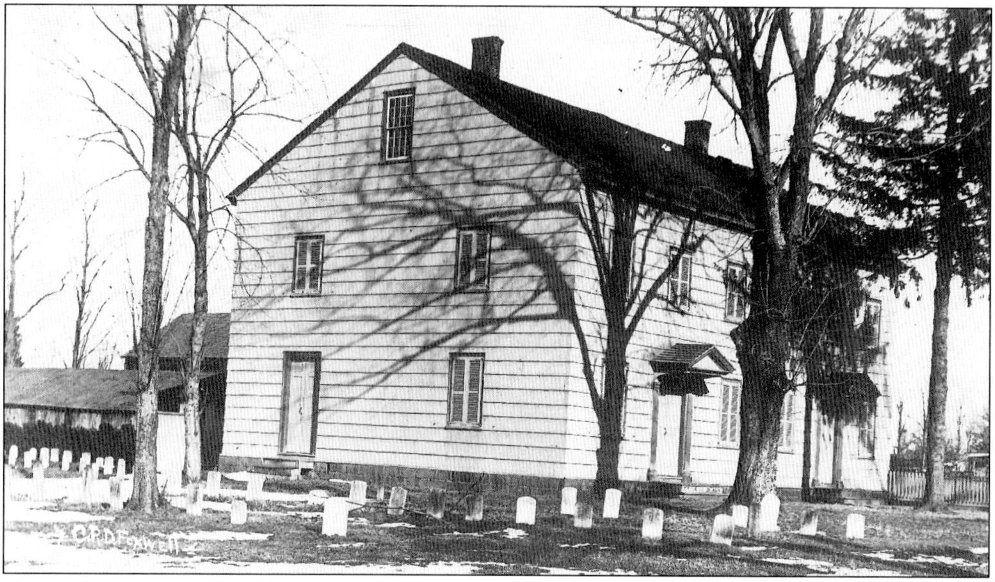

Many of Eatontown's earliest residents, including Thomas Eaton, were Quakers who worshiped in the Friends Meetinghouse on Sycamore Avenue and Broad Street in Shrewsbury. This picture was taken about 1905.

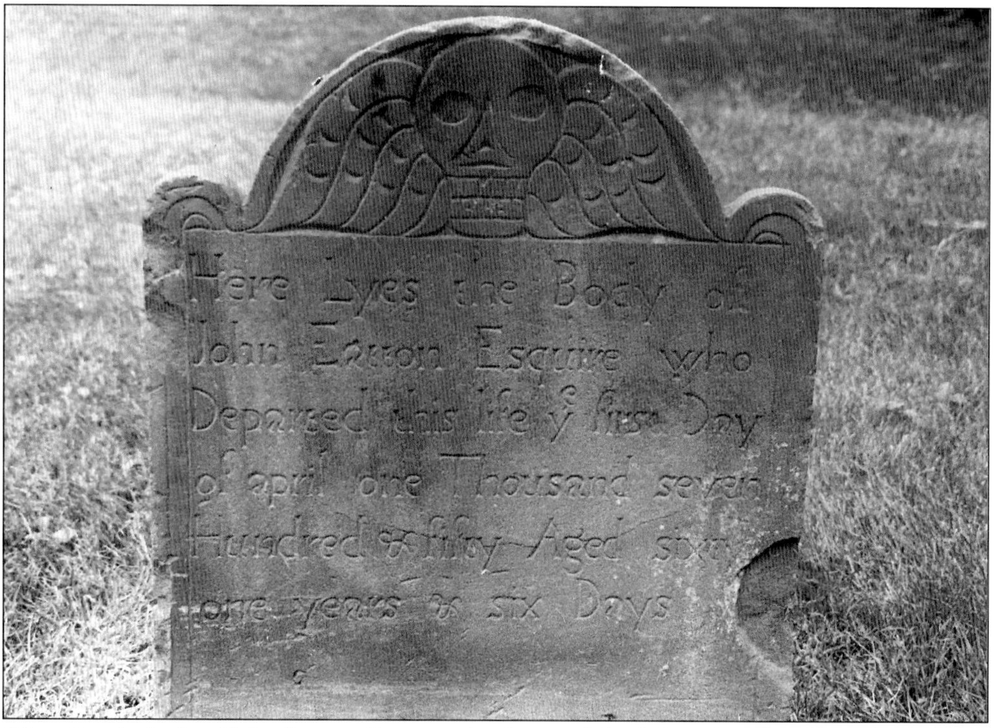

"Here lies the body of John Eatton, Esquire who departed this life ye first day of April 1750 aged 61 years and 6 days." This is the slate headstone of Thomas Eaton's son which can be found in the Quaker burial grounds. The carved skull and angel wings are typical of colonial headstones. Note the early spelling for Eaton, who was a member of the Provincial Assembly from 1723 to 1750. He was also a justice in the "10-pound court.".

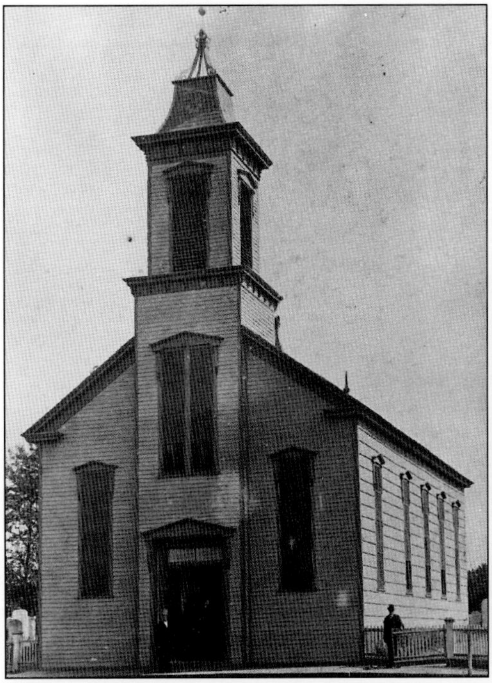

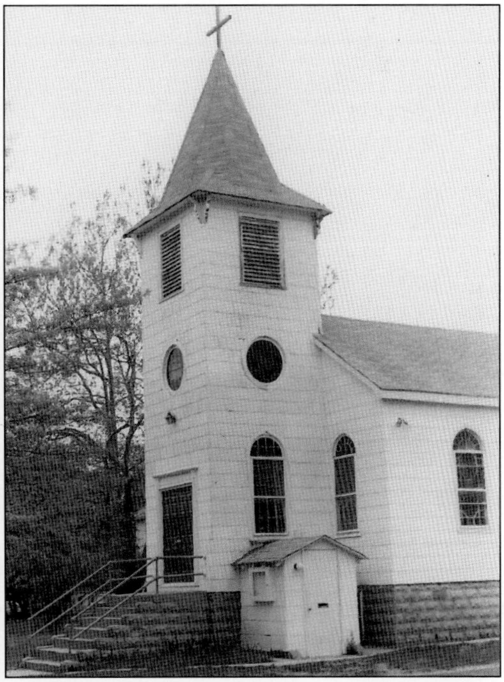

Left: In 1809 the Methodist church on Locust Avenue in Mechanicsville was erected; it is affectionately referred to as "Old Faithful." After 264 German immigrants perished when the *New Era* ran aground north of Asbury Park in 1854, they were buried in a mass grave in this church's cemetery. A monument to them went up in 1892.
Right: The African Methodist Episcopal Zion Church was built in 1845 on South Street in Locust Grove, the village's African-American community. Today it is Eatontown's oldest church, celebrating its 150th anniversary.

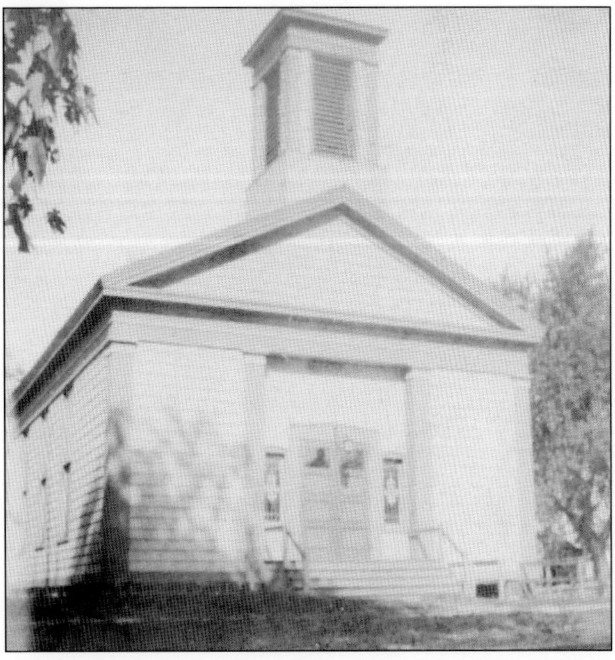

The Methodist church in the village of Eatontown first went up in 1852 on Railroad Avenue.

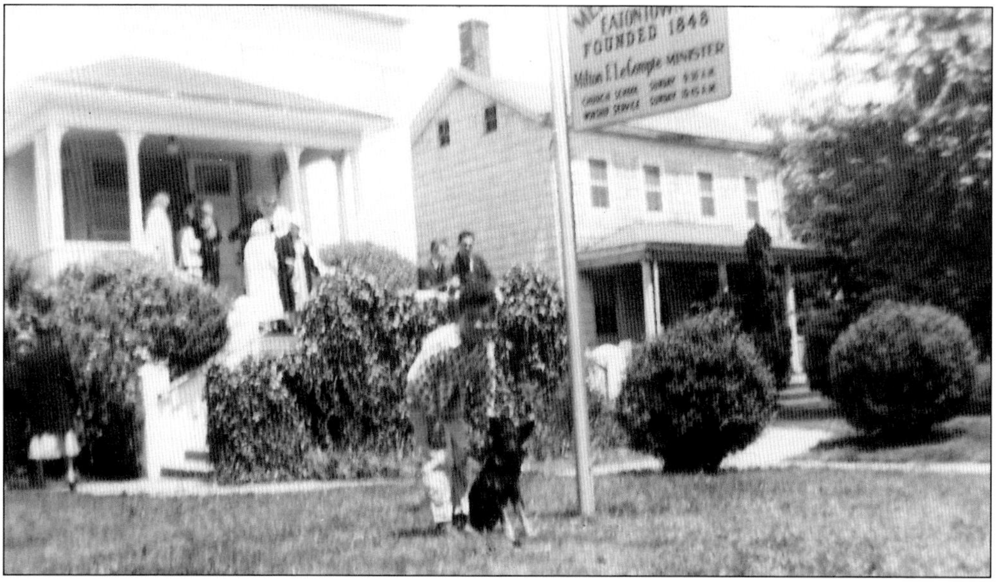

In 1913 the Methodist church was moved to Broad Street and became known as the Methodist Episcopal Church until 1959, when the congregation moved to Wyckoff Road. The public library is located on this site today. This picture was taken in 1959. The rectory is to the right.

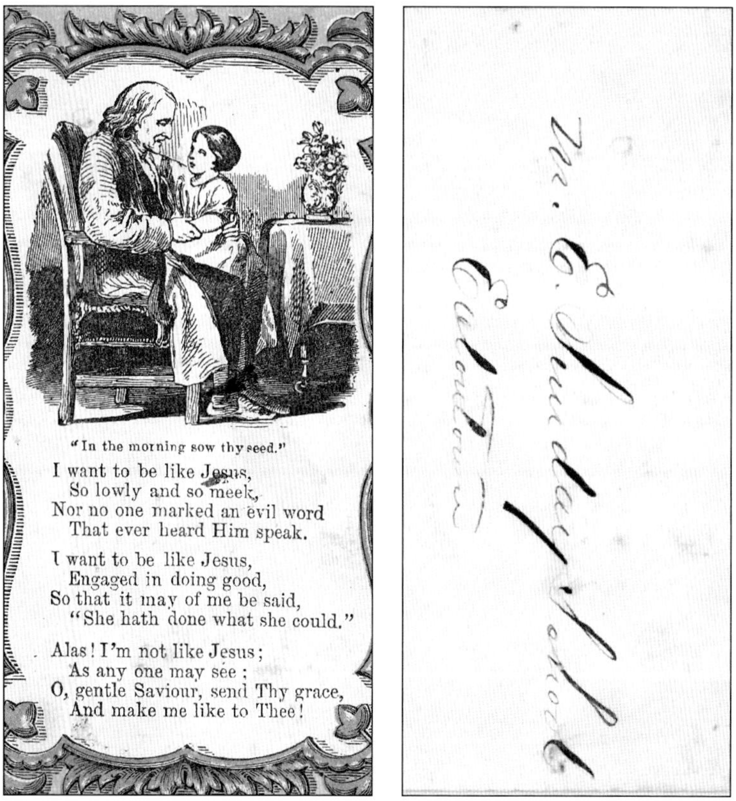

Methodist Episcopal Church prayer cards given out by Sunday school teachers to their pupils.

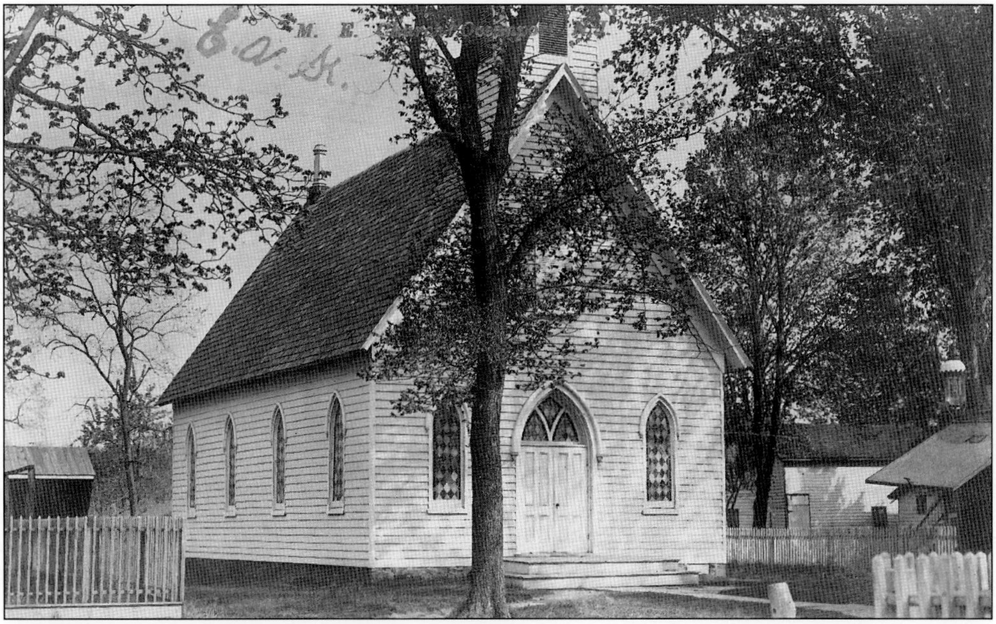

The Methodist church built in 1868 on Main Street in the village of Oceanport. This picture was taken about 1906.

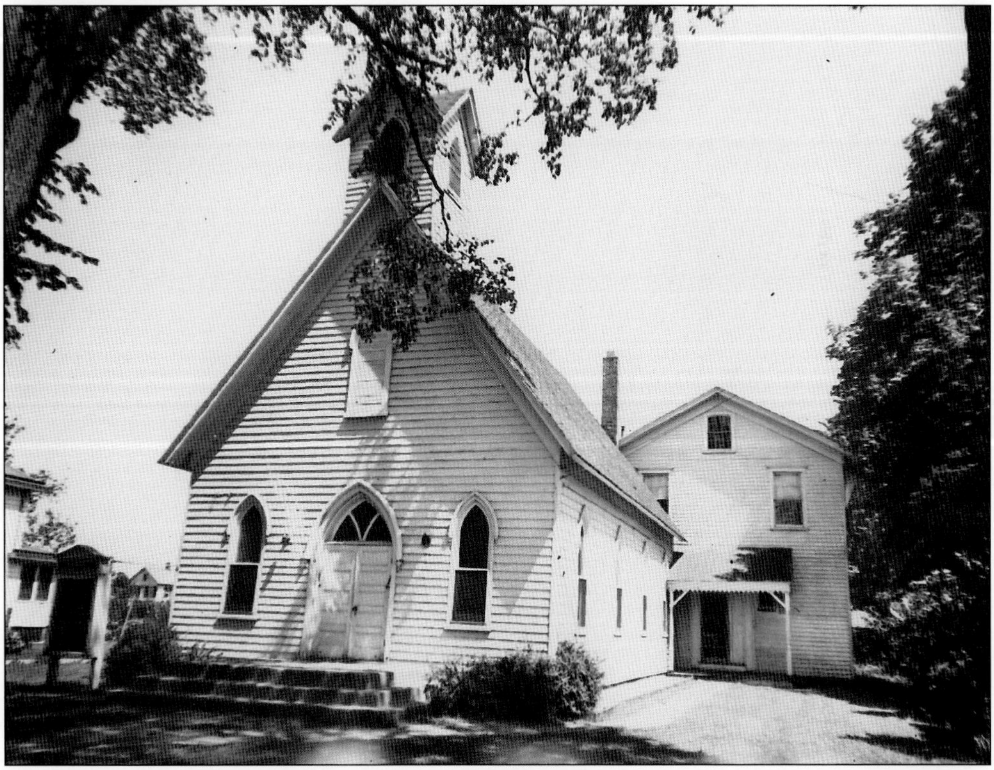

In 1911 the 1870 schoolhouse on Wolf Hill Avenue was moved to the Methodist church property. It was attached in 1930. This picture was taken before a modern foyer was added to the front of the church's doors.

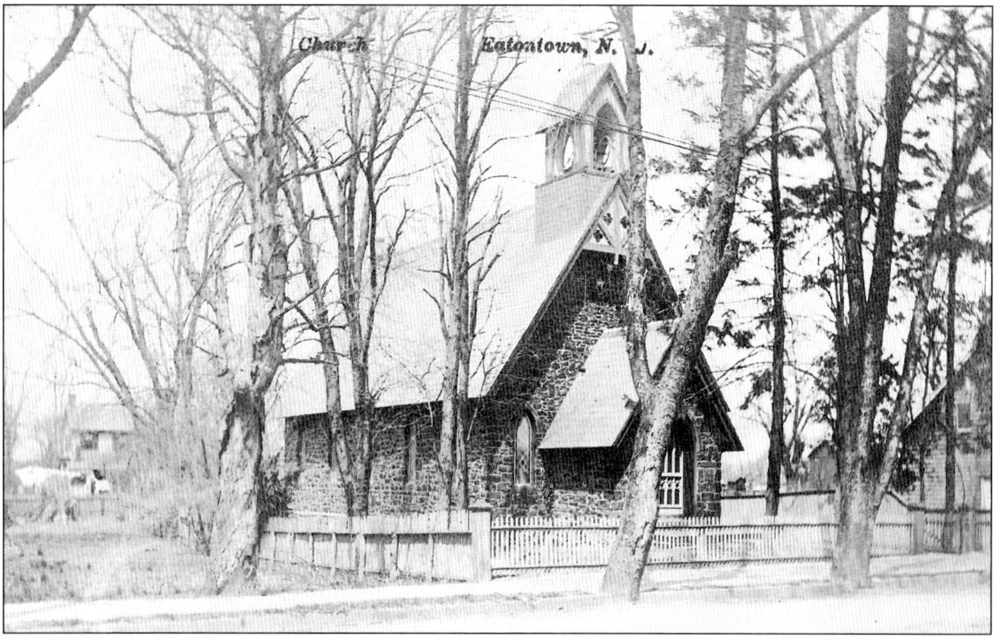

The St. James Memorial Episcopal Church was organized in 1866, and construction of the stone church on Broad Street was begun in the same year.

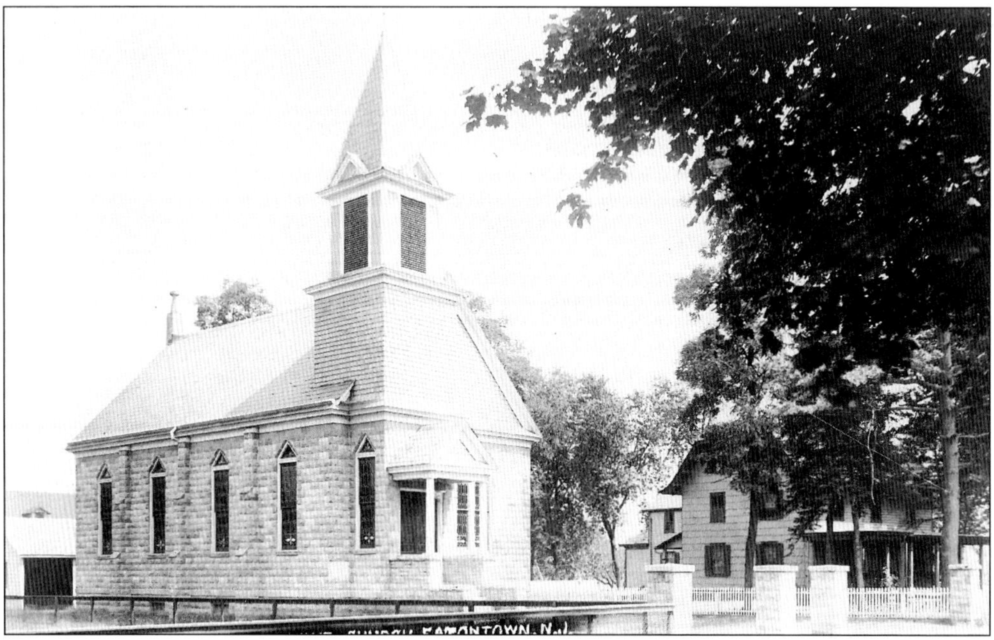

The Advent Church, organized about 1840 and with at least two other locations in the village, moved into this stone edifice built in 1905. It was located at the southern end of Main Street just before the road curved onto South Street. In more recent times, it was known as the Monmouth Baptist Church. The Route 35 Wendy's is now located on this site.

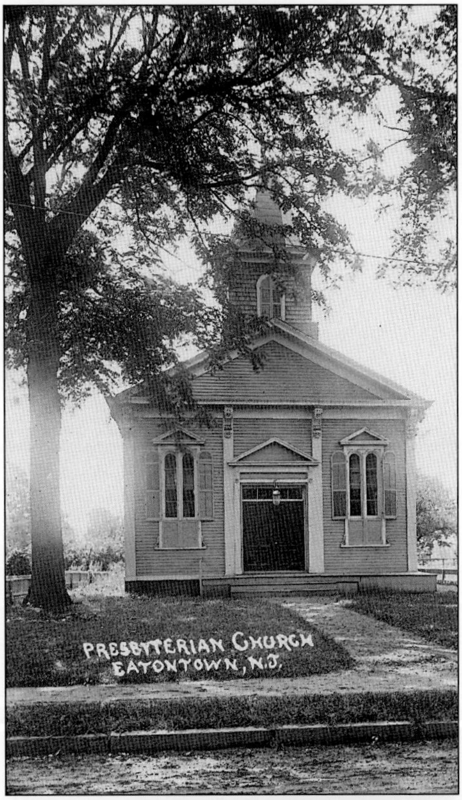

The cornerstone of the First Presbyterian Church of Eatontown village was laid in 1873 on Broad Street, but the actual building once stood in Manhattan. The wood-frame edifice was shipped by barge to Middletown and then by wagon to Eatontown. Today the building serves as Eatontown's Community Center while the Presbyterians have moved to Tinton Falls.

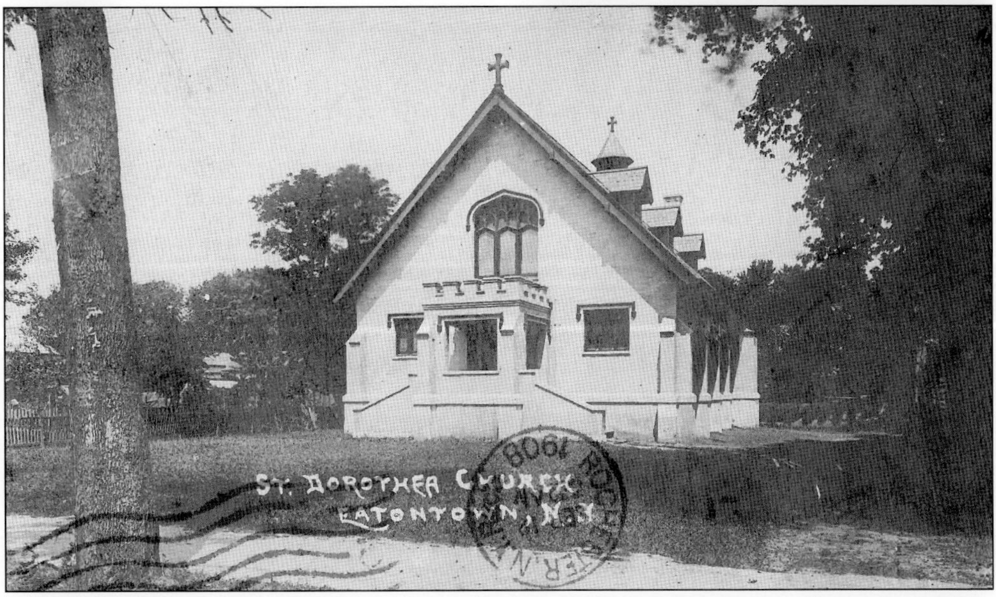

In 1905 magazine magnate Peter F. Collier, who had a country estate in the village, donated the first funds to build St. Dorothea's Roman Catholic Church on Broad Street where the firehouse stands today. In 1929 the church was moved to the southeast corner of Broad and White Streets. In the 1960s, St. Dorothea's congregation built a large modern church about half a mile south on Broad Street. The original edifice is currently a Korean catholic mission.

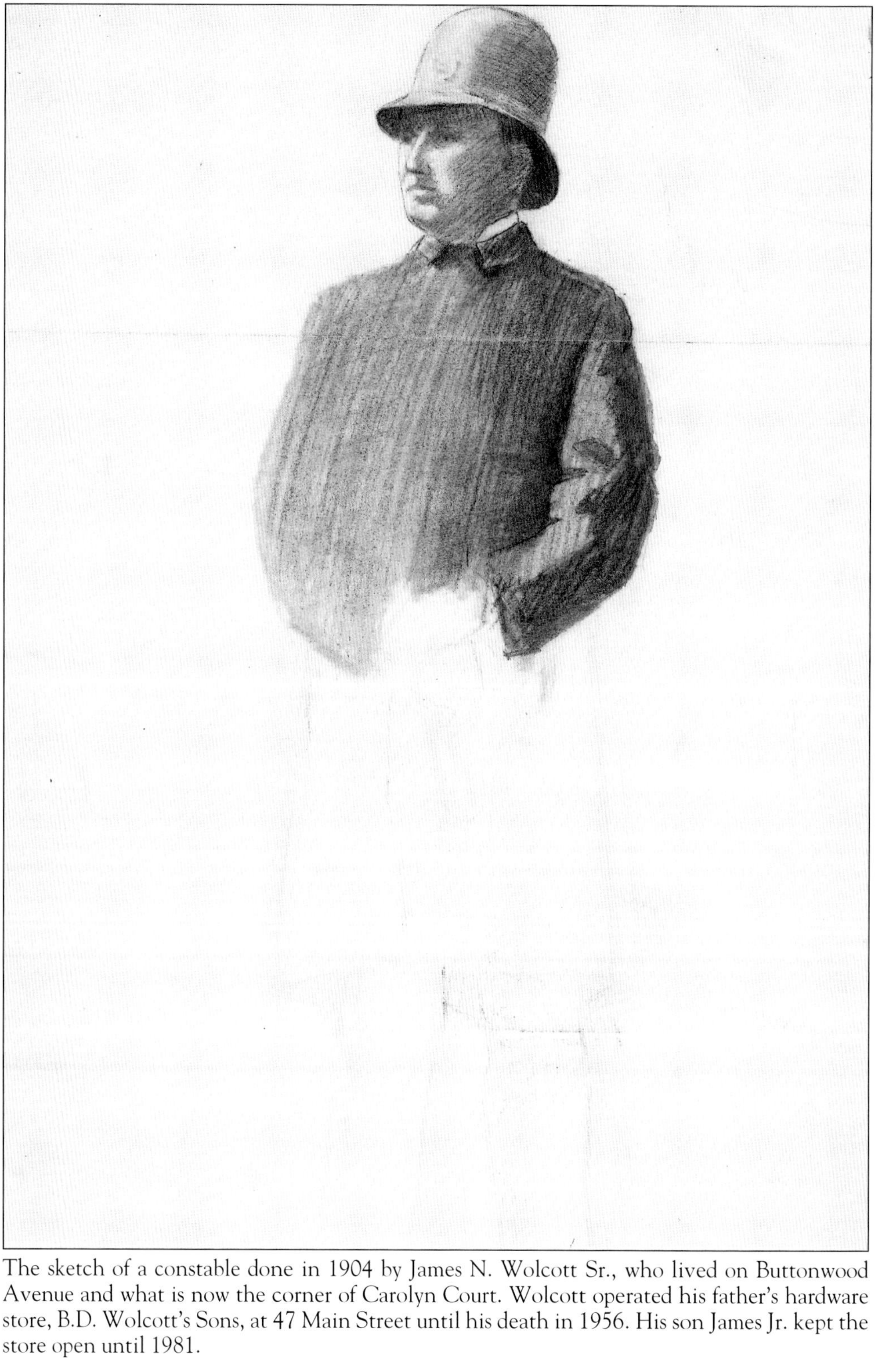

The sketch of a constable done in 1904 by James N. Wolcott Sr., who lived on Buttonwood Avenue and what is now the corner of Carolyn Court. Wolcott operated his father's hardware store, B.D. Wolcott's Sons, at 47 Main Street until his death in 1956. His son James Jr. kept the store open until 1981.

Three

Community

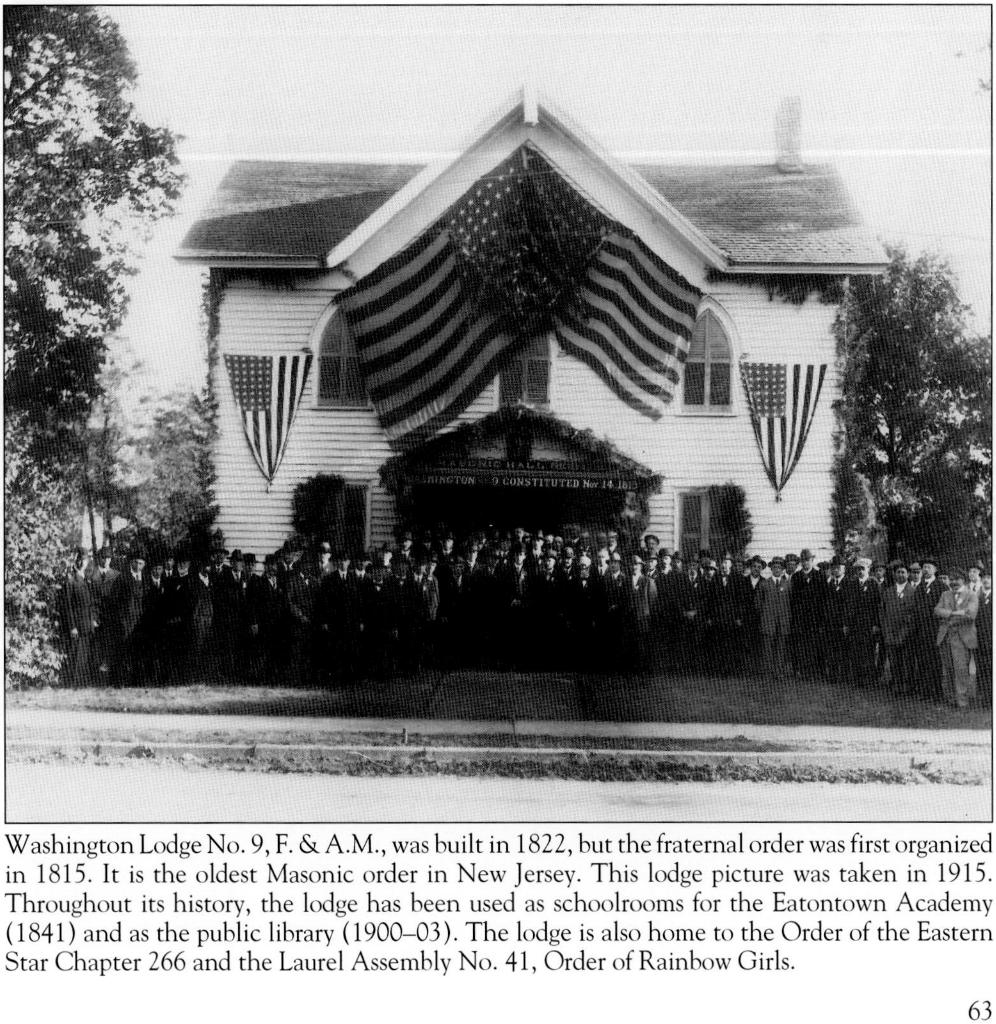

Washington Lodge No. 9, F. & A.M., was built in 1822, but the fraternal order was first organized in 1815. It is the oldest Masonic order in New Jersey. This lodge picture was taken in 1915. Throughout its history, the lodge has been used as schoolrooms for the Eatontown Academy (1841) and as the public library (1900–03). The lodge is also home to the Order of the Eastern Star Chapter 266 and the Laurel Assembly No. 41, Order of Rainbow Girls.

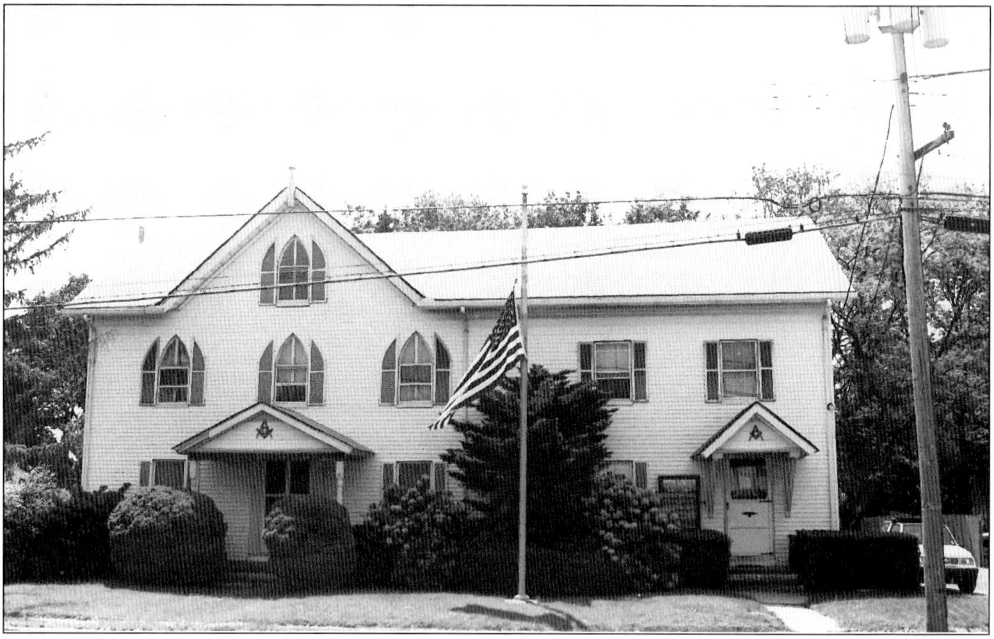

In 1924 an extension was added to the Masonic Lodge. The American Legion Post No. 325 also meets here; its previous hall on Neptune Highway (Route 35) is where Eatontown T.V. is today. In 1994 the flag was at half mast in mourning for Richard M. Nixon.

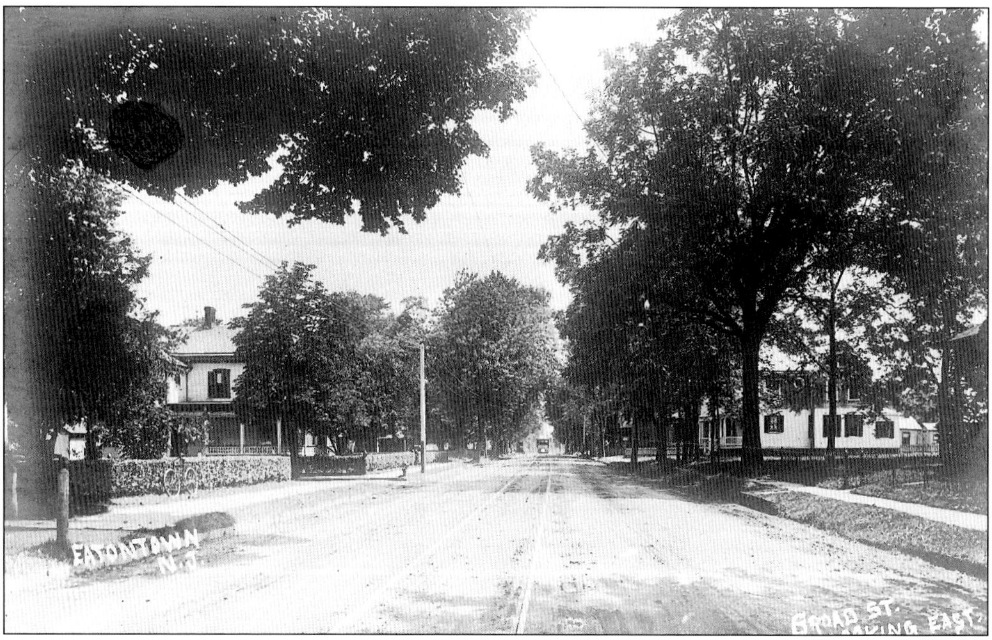

Broad Street looking east from in front of the Masonic Lodge, c. 1908. In the distance is the trolley coming from Oceanport.

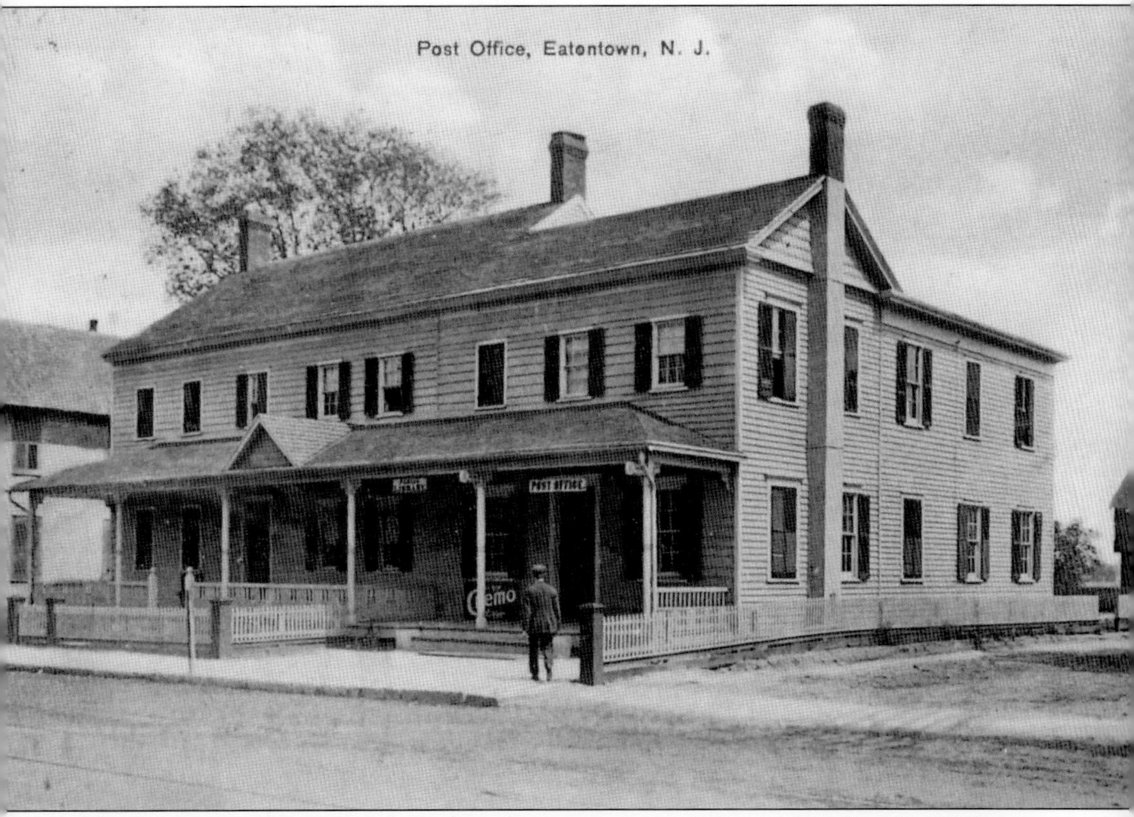

Dr. John P. Lewis was Eatontown Township's first postmaster in 1830. In 1896, President William McKinley appointed resident Ada B. Nafew as postmistress, the only woman singled out in New Jersey that year. By 1911, the post office was located on Broad Street in the former Columbian Hotel. Newspapers, magazines, stationery, and cigars were also sold by her crippled son.

Mrs. Nafew started the town's first circulating library in the back of her husband's Main Street drugstore. When Peter Collier donated 500 volumes, the library was temporarily housed in the Masonic Lodge. It then moved to the back of the post office, and eventually made its way to Borough Hall on the corner of Broad and Main Streets.

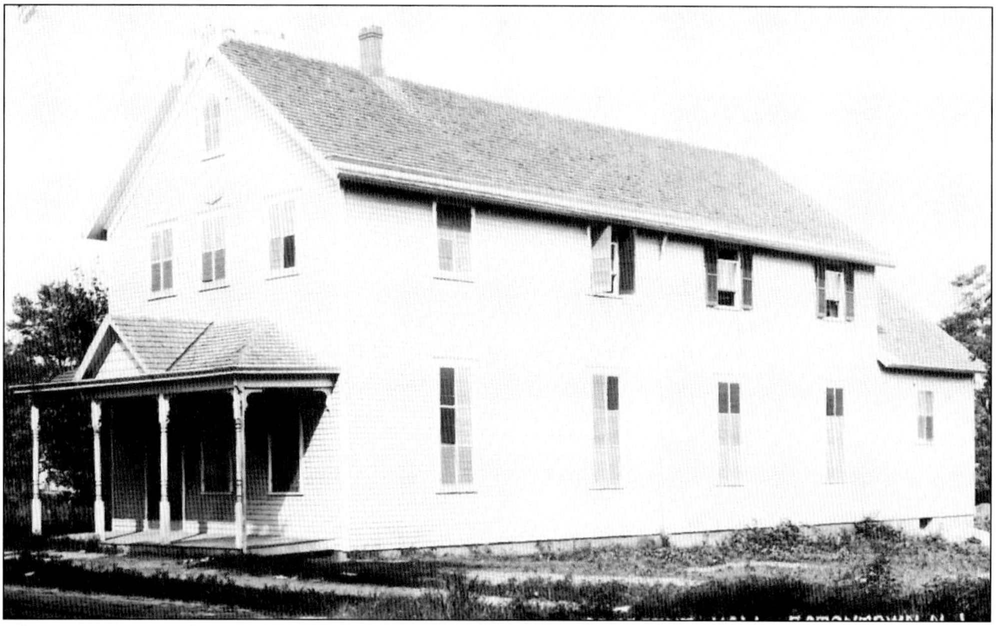

The Crescent Hall Association in the village of Eatontown was established on March 24, 1892, as a patriotic and fraternal organization known as the Order of United American Mechanics. Located on Lewis Street, the building had a bowling alley and theater used by the local fire companies to stage minstrel shows. In more recent times Atkinson & Smith operated an electronics supply store in the building.

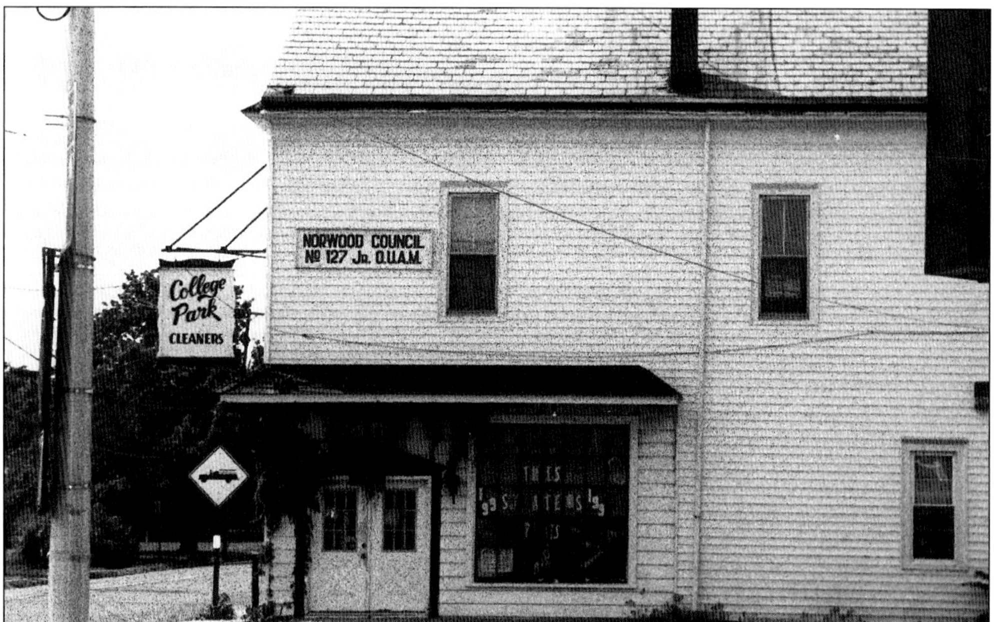

The village of West Long Branch also had a chapter of the same fraternal order that was commonly referred to as the Junior Mechanics. The organization's credo was: friendship, truth, and love. Norwood Lodge No. 127 Jr. OUAM still meets in its original hall on Monmouth Road in what was once the village's wood-frame firehouse.

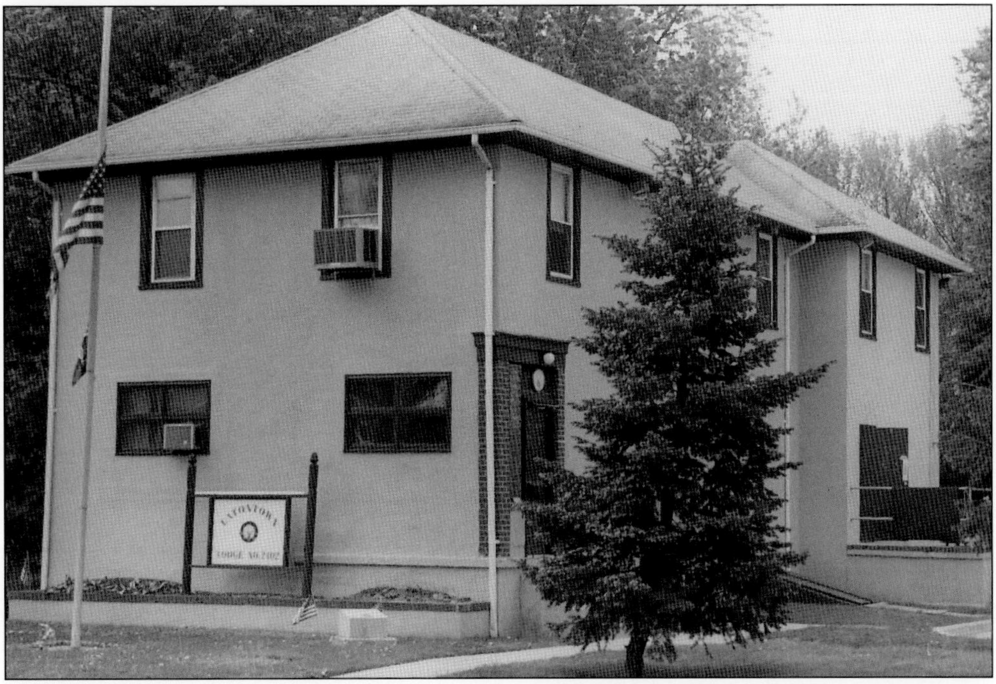

The New York and New Jersey Telephone Co. picked Eatontown as the site of its central switching station in the early 1900s. It put up a building on Broad Street and Cliffwood Avenue. Later, New Jersey Bell would move its operations to Throckmorton Avenue, and Lodge No. 2402 of the Benevolent and Protective Order of the Elks would eventually move in.

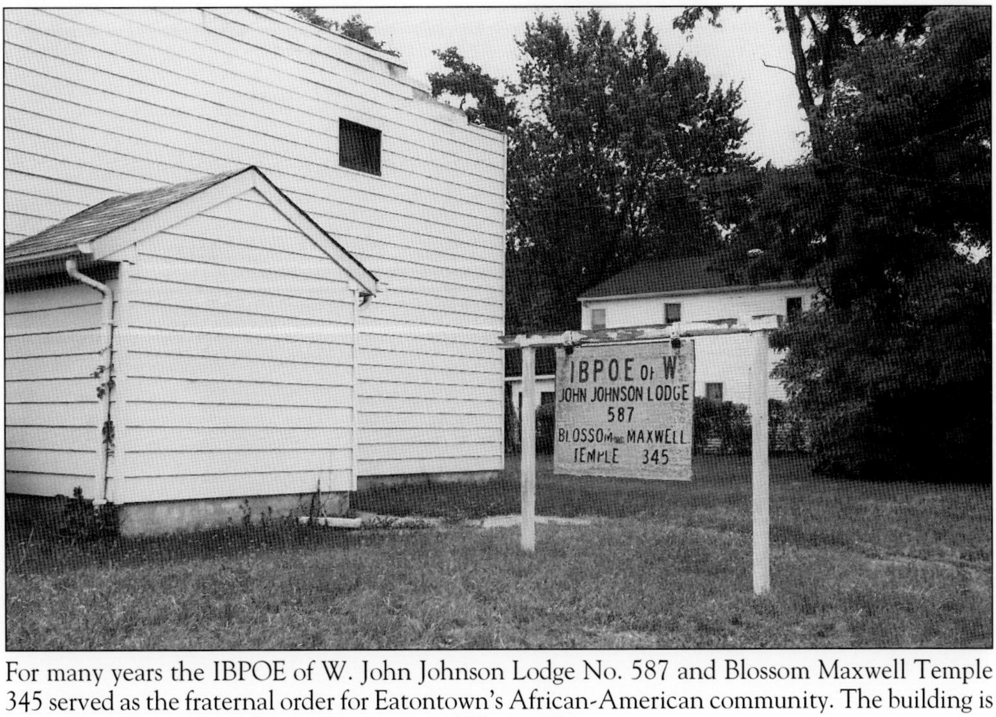

For many years the IBPOE of W. John Johnson Lodge No. 587 and Blossom Maxwell Temple 345 served as the fraternal order for Eatontown's African-American community. The building is located on the corner of Grant Avenue and Victor Place.

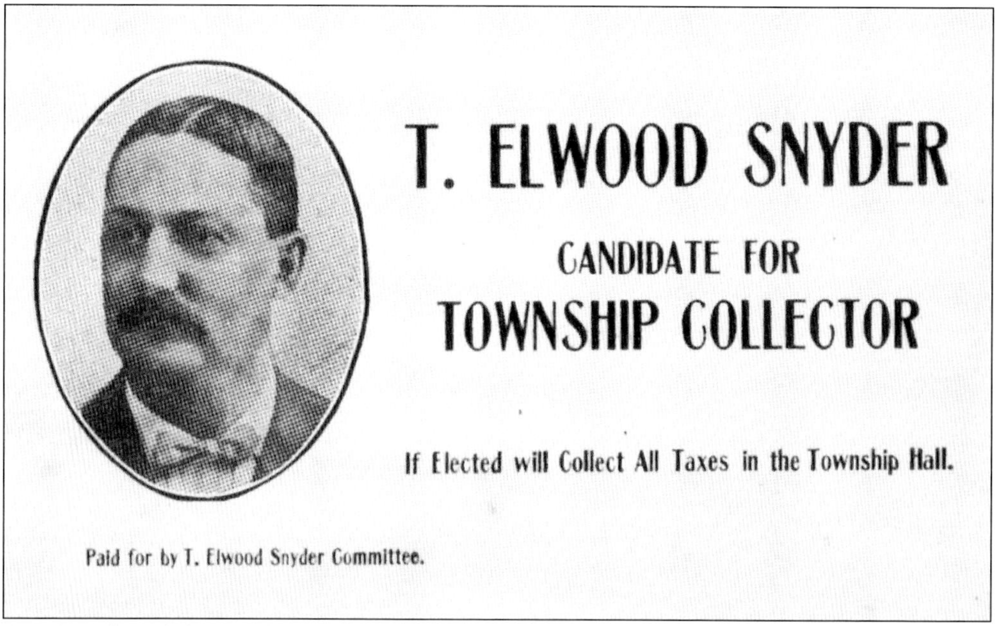

A political card for T. Elwood Snyder Jr., who ran for the position of Eatontown Township tax collector. Snyder was a busy man; as well as being the Metropolitan Hotel proprietor and a prominent member of the Eatontown Improvement Association, he was also a Mason, Red Man, Elk, and Junior Mechanic.

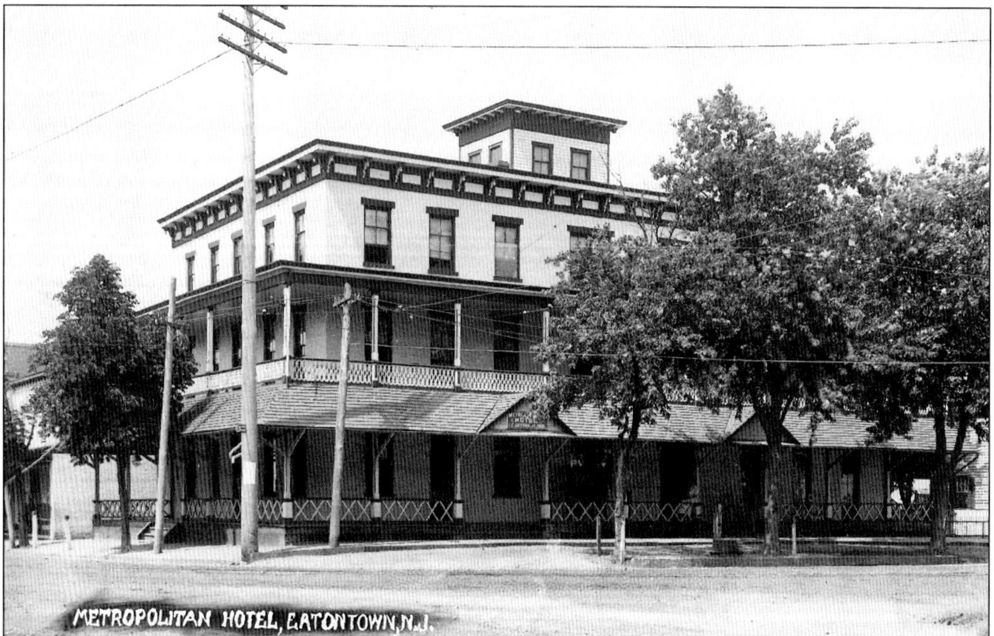

In 1873 the New Jersey State Legislature made the name of Eatontown official. Within ten years of this picture the Metropolitan Hotel would be converted into Eatontown Township's first municipal complex.

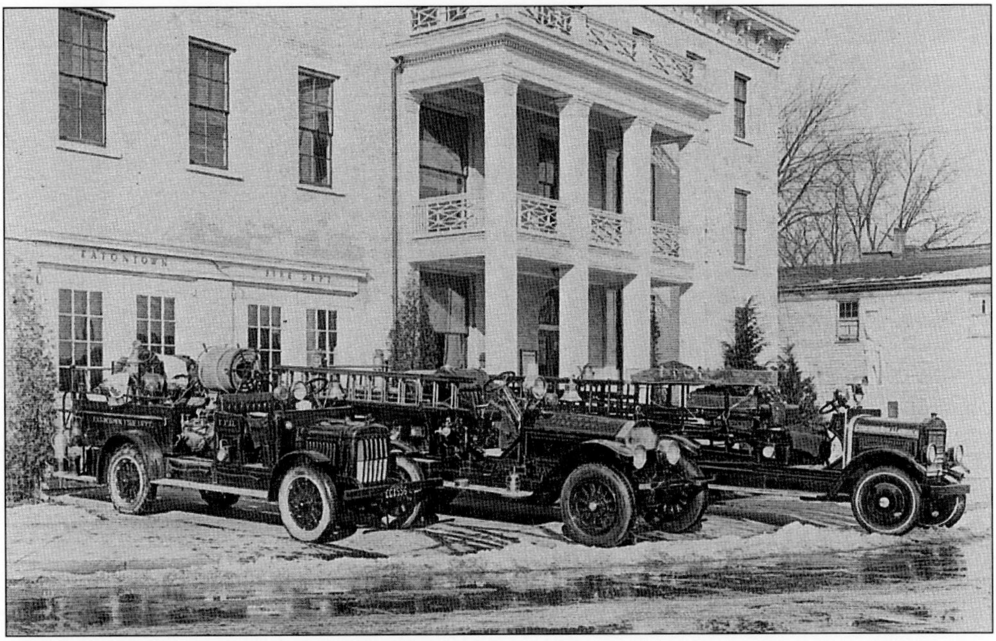

With its porches removed and other modifications made in the early 1920s, the new Eatontown Town Hall housed a Borough Council meeting room, borough offices, the public library, the post office, the fire department's garage, and extra public school classrooms. During World War II residents Jim and Elizabeth Wolcott and Virginia and Norman K. Hammond took turns on the roof scanning the sky for enemy aircraft.

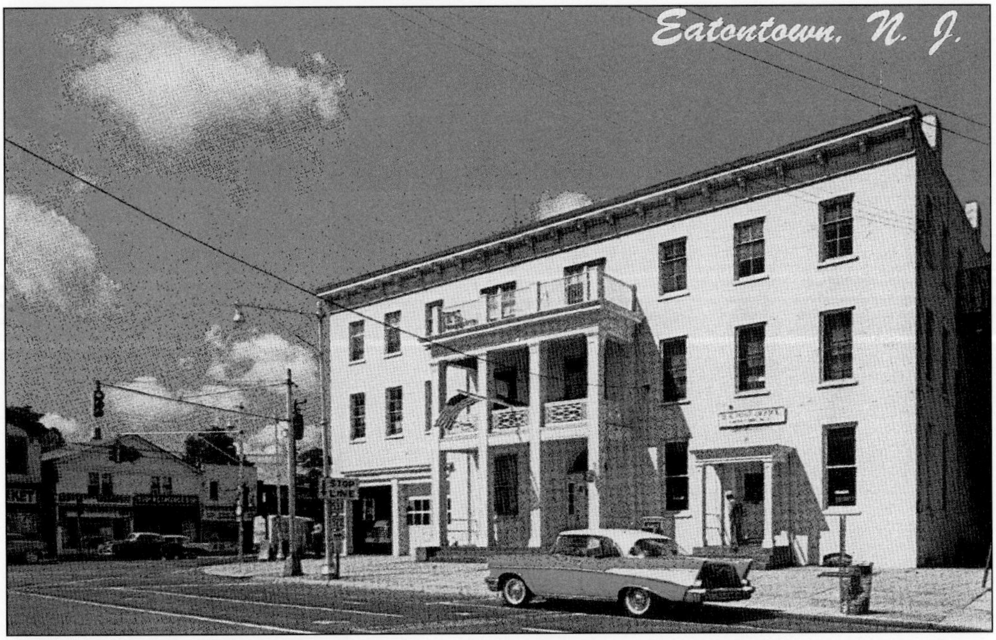

By 1926 Eatontown had reorganized into a borough in the wake of Oceanport and West Long Branch's succession from the township. This picture shows Borough Hall before the Route 71 jughandle was punched through Main Street in 1961. The building was torn down a few years later with the new Borough Hall at 47 Broad Street going up in 1966.

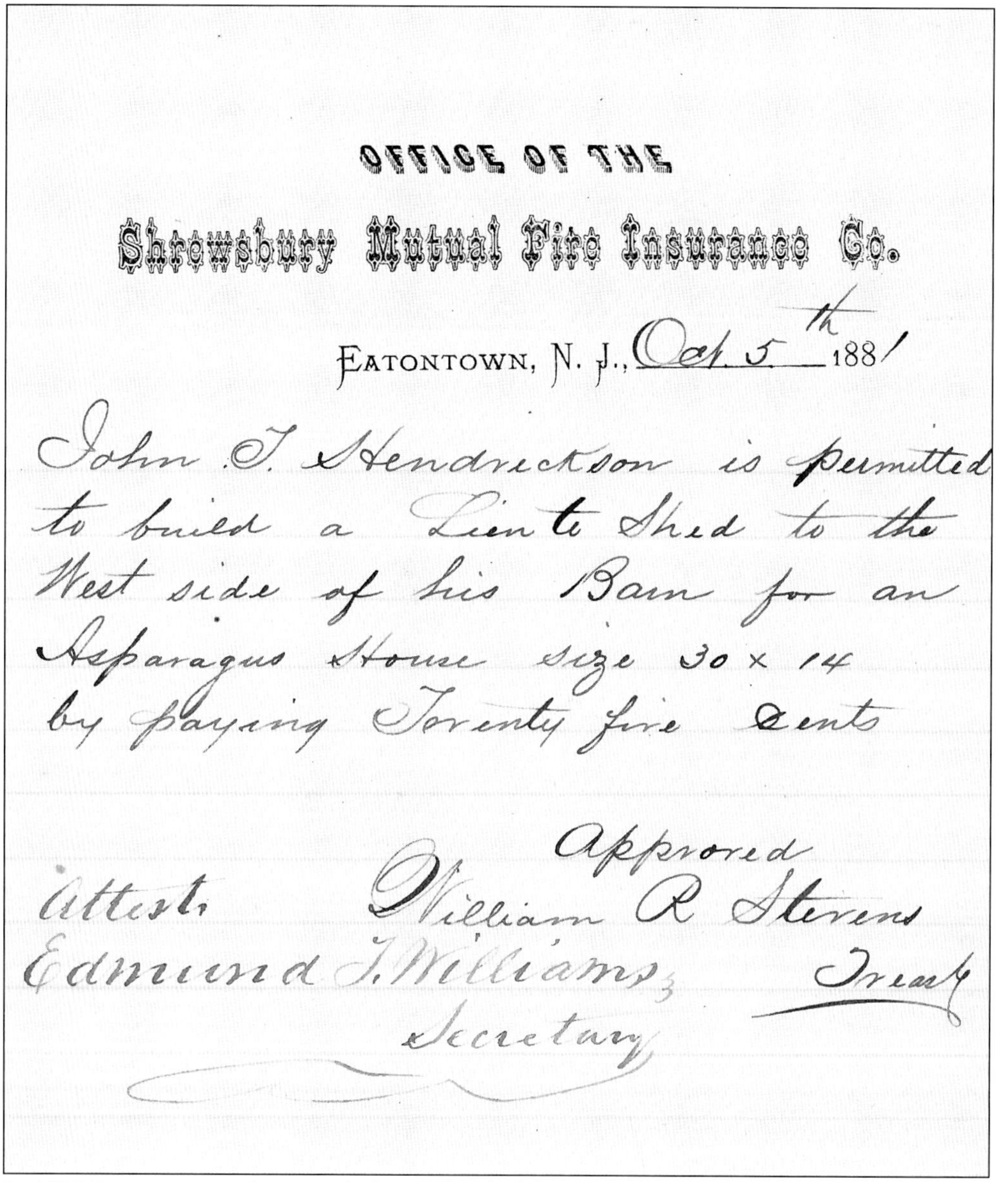

OFFICE OF THE

Shrewsbury Mutual Fire Insurance Co.

Eatontown, N. J., Oct 5th 1881

John T. Hendrickson is permitted to build a Lien to Shed to the West side of his Barn for an Asparagus House size 30 x 14 by paying Twenty five Cents

Approved
William R Stevens
Treas

Attest
Edmund T. Williams
Secretary

In 1838 Eatontown residents could buy individual fire protection from the Shrewsbury Mutual Fire Co. Only those insured buildings identified with SMFC seals on an outer wall would have their fires put out; a building without a seal wasn't touched. This letterhead was one of the last issued in Eatontown to the privately held SMFC.

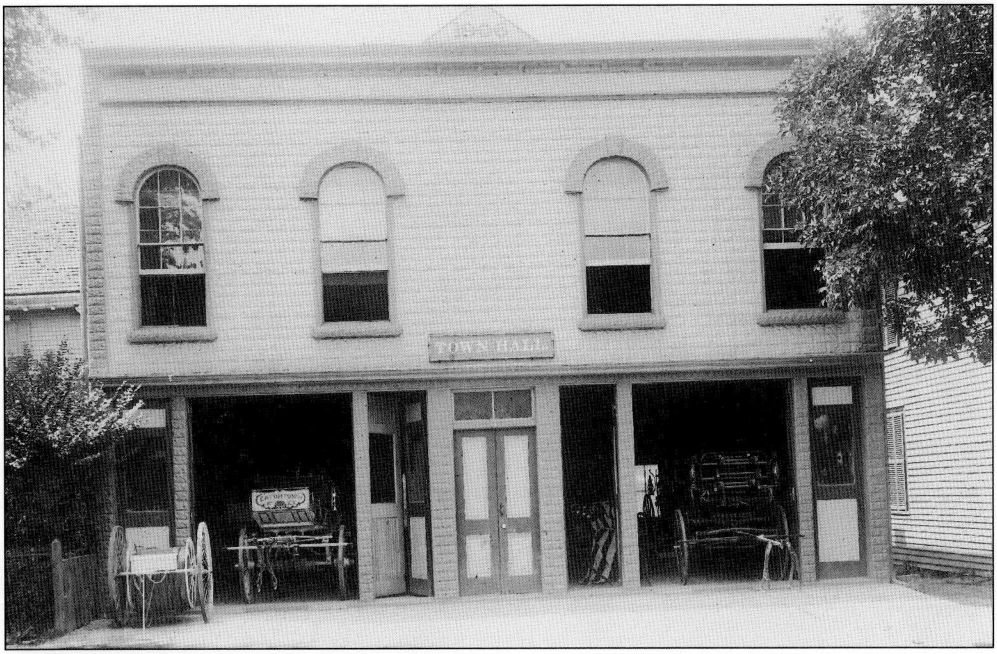

On June 15, 1881, Eatontown village organized its first volunteer fire company, the Perseverance Steam Fire Engine Co. #1, in order that all property owners would have fire protection. In 1888, the Eatontown Hook & Ladder Co. #1 was organized. This picture was taken about 1906 in front of the town hall and fire department on Main Street.

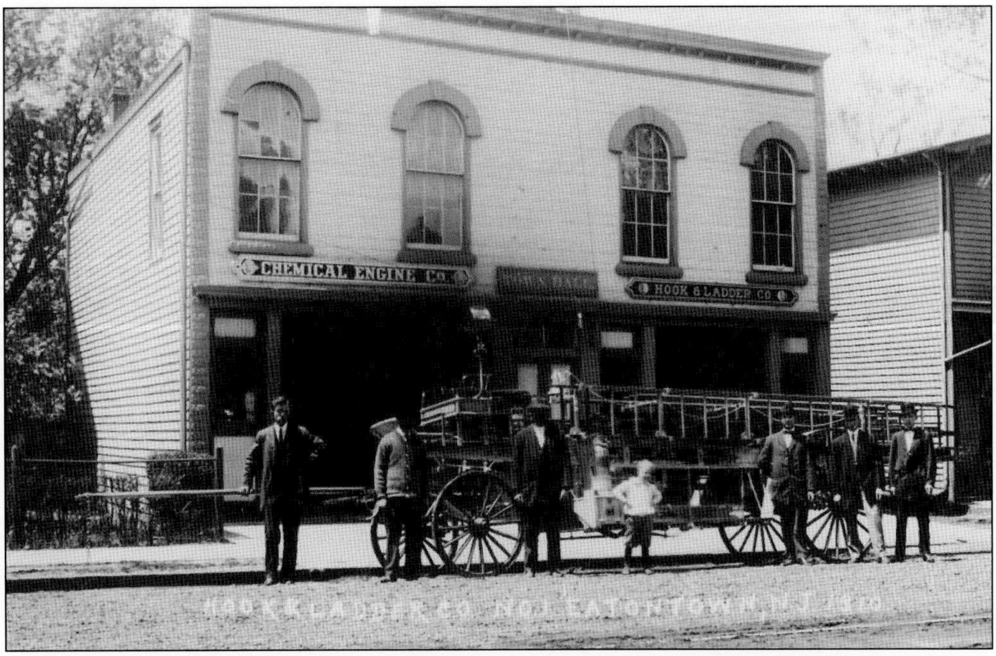

On February 6, 1917, the Hook & Ladder Co. #1 joined forces with Chemical Engine and Hose Co.#1 to form the Engine, Truck, and Hose Co. #1. This picture was taken around 1915 before the two companies merged.

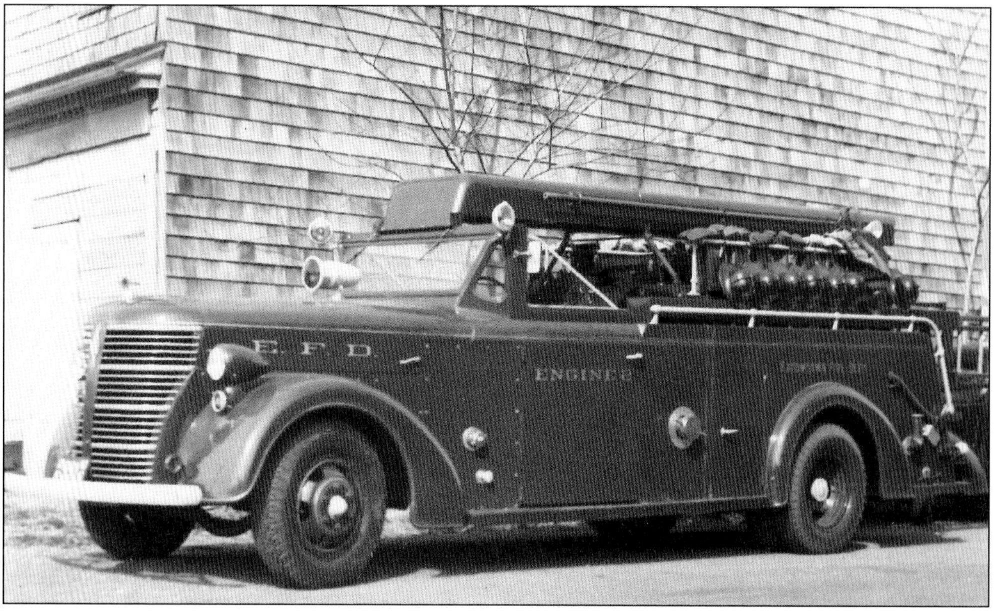

Engine #2 of the Eatontown Fire Co. is a 750-gallon American-LaFrance pumper purchased in 1946.

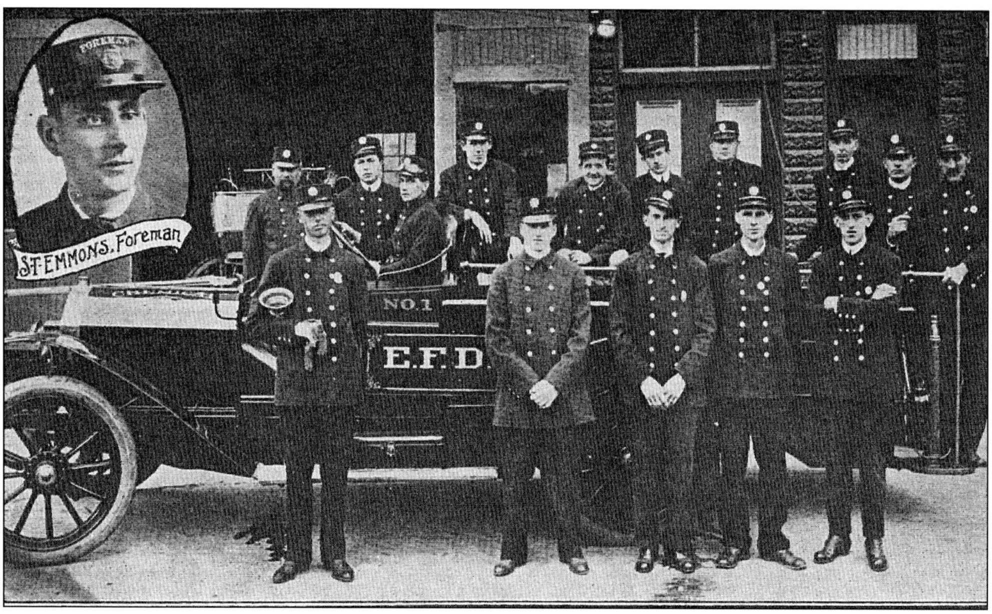

Chemical Engine and Hose Company #1 pictured with its 1917 Locomobile firetruck.

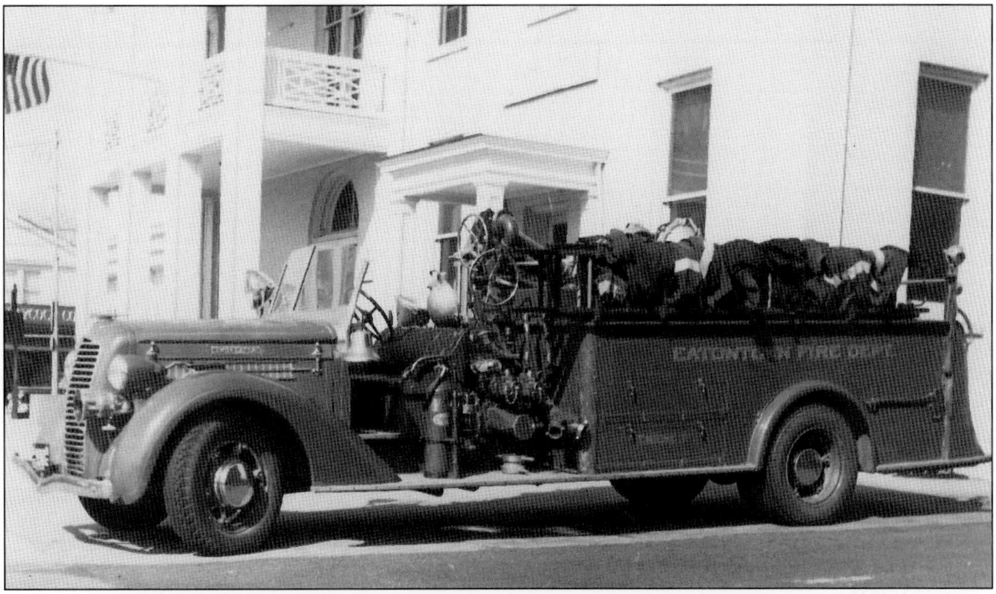

Engine #3 of the Eatontown Fire Co. is a 500-gallon Diamond T. Pirsch.

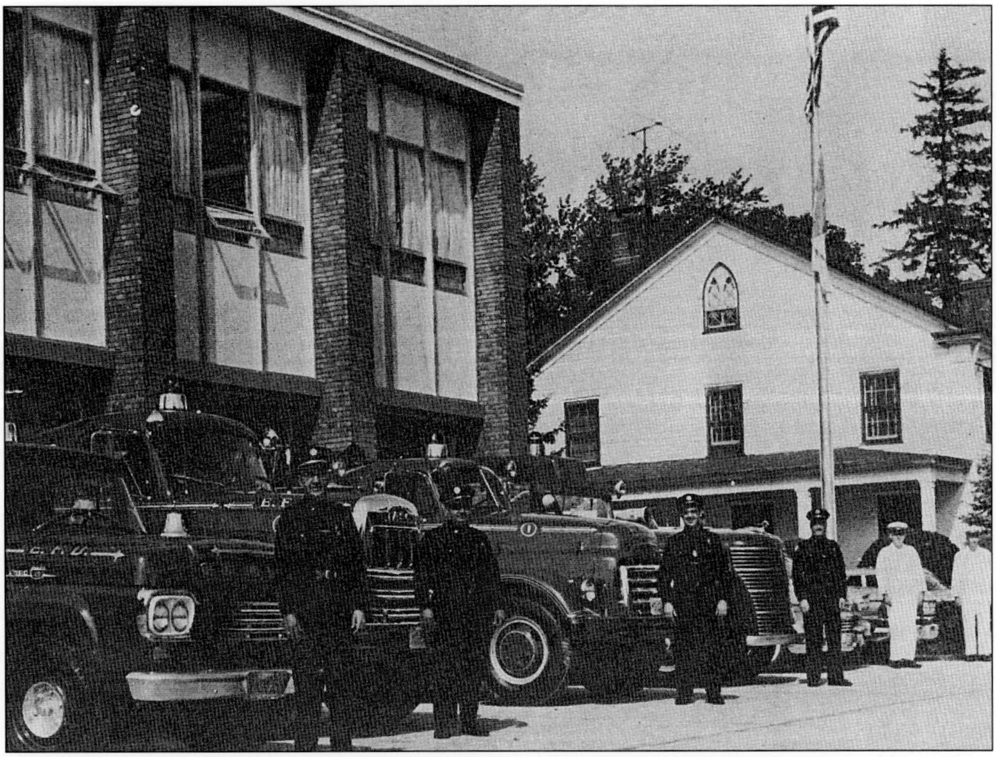

The new, standalone firehouse was dedicated in 1964. The house in the background would be demolished in the next two years to make way for the new Borough Hall.

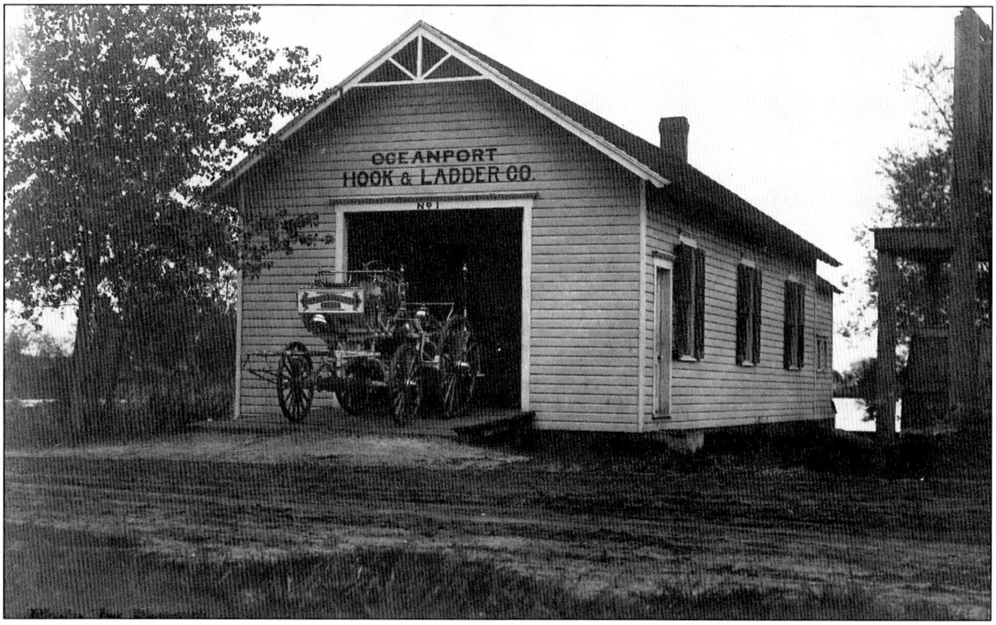

In 1895 the Oceanport Hook & Ladder Co. organized and bought the Fife & Drum Corps building on Oceanport Avenue. In 1909 a second floor was added, and a hose wagon purchased. In 1918 a Model T was purchased to motorize the wagon. In 1920, after Oceanport declared its independence from Eatontown, its municipal offices moved into the second floor.

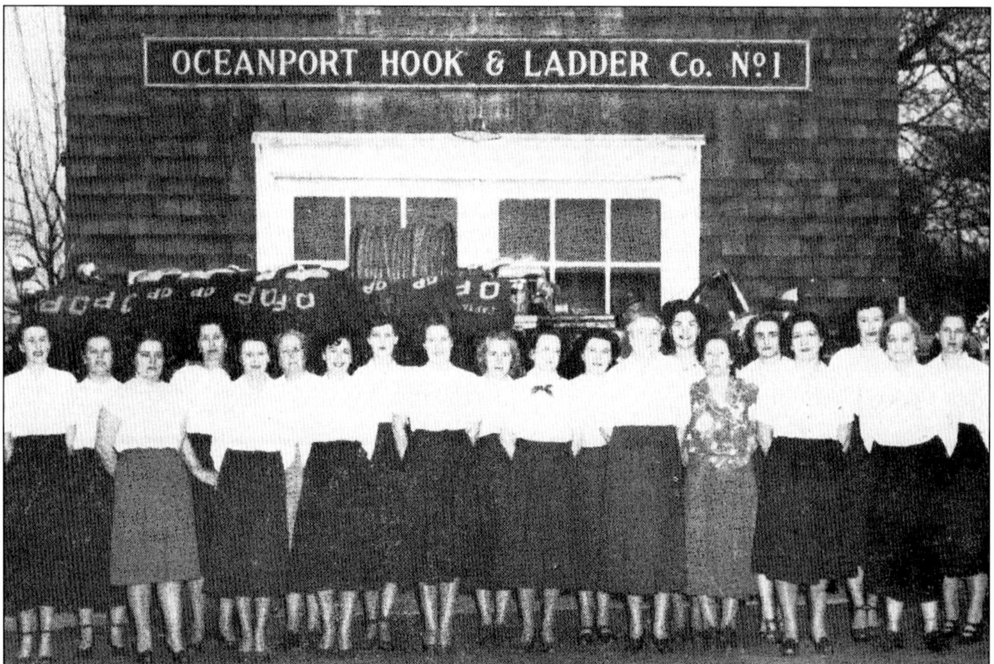

In 1909 a second floor was added, and a hose wagon purchased. In 1918 a Model T was purchased to motorize the wagon. In 1920, after Oceanport declared its independence from Eatontown, its municipal offices moved into the second floor. A Ladies Auxiliary was organized in 1924.

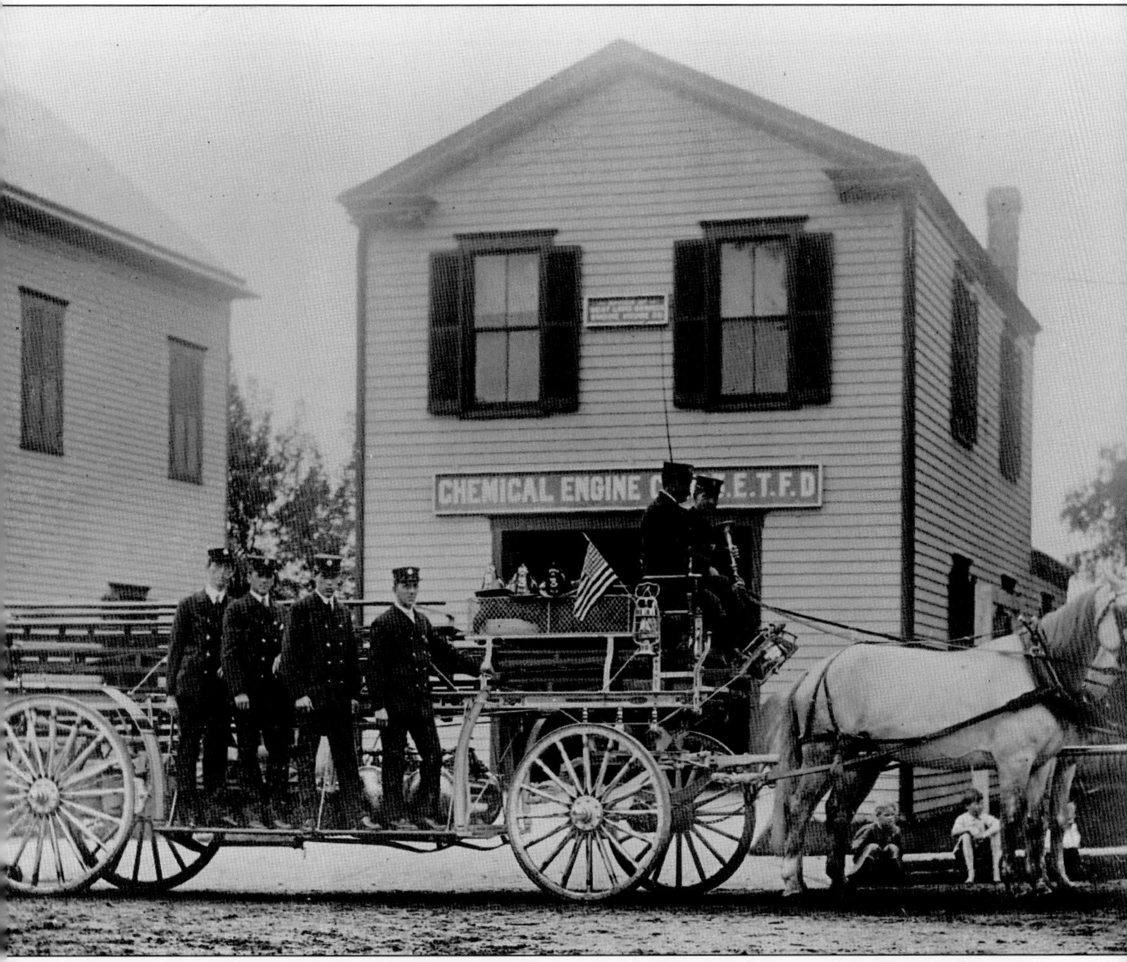

Eatontown Township's Chemical Engine Co. #3 was located in the village of West Long Branch in 1902. This building was located on Monmouth Road at the Cedar Avenue junction.

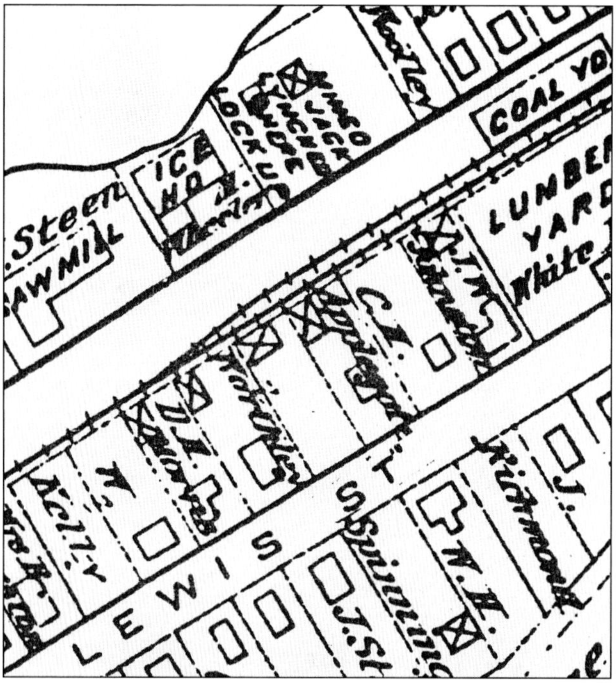

The Eatontown lockup, as shown in the *1889 Wolverton Atlas of Monmouth County*.

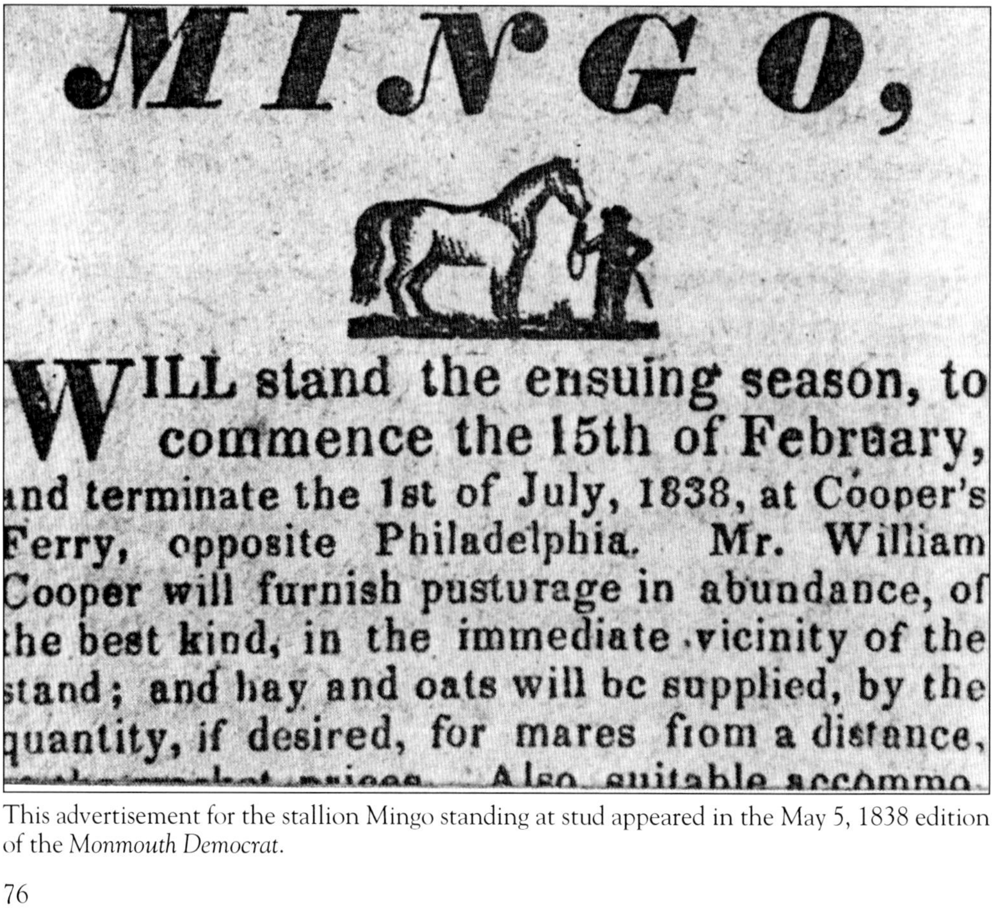

MINGO,

WILL stand the ensuing season, to commence the 15th of February, and terminate the 1st of July, 1838, at Cooper's Ferry, opposite Philadelphia. Mr. William Cooper will furnish pusturage in abundance, of the best kind, in the immediate vicinity of the stand; and hay and oats will bc supplied, by the quantity, if desired, for mares fiom a distance,

This advertisement for the stallion Mingo standing at stud appeared in the May 5, 1838 edition of the *Monmouth Democrat*.

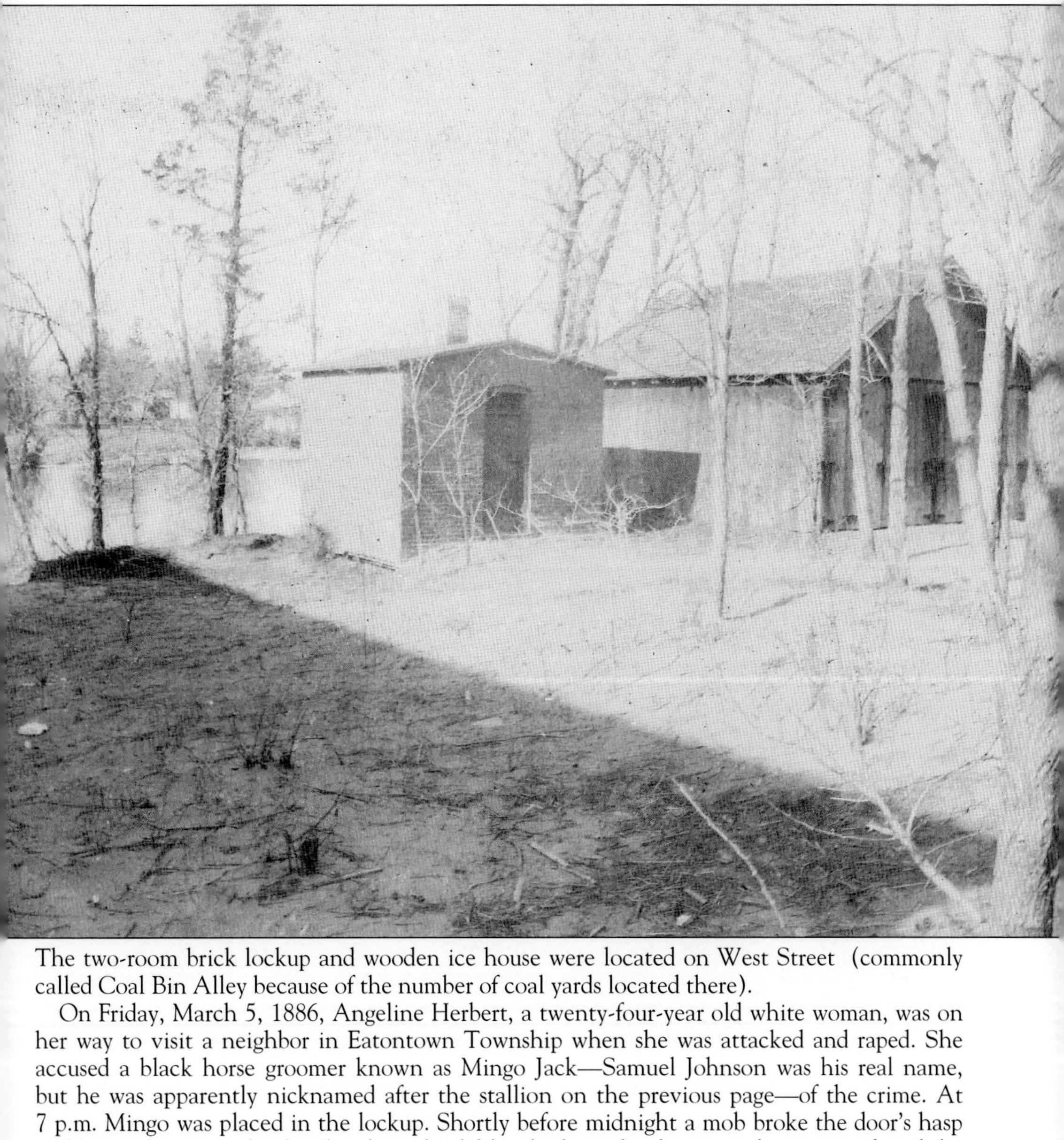

The two-room brick lockup and wooden ice house were located on West Street (commonly called Coal Bin Alley because of the number of coal yards located there).

On Friday, March 5, 1886, Angeline Herbert, a twenty-four-year old white woman, was on her way to visit a neighbor in Eatontown Township when she was attacked and raped. She accused a black horse groomer known as Mingo Jack—Samuel Johnson was his real name, but he was apparently nicknamed after the stallion on the previous page—of the crime. At 7 p.m. Mingo was placed in the lockup. Shortly before midnight a mob broke the door's hasp and beat Johnson to death. They hung his lifeless body in the doorway where it was found the next morning.

During the six-day inquest held at Hall's Hotel no one came forward to identify the assailants. A year later Richard Kearney, in prison for the murder of another local woman, confessed to Herbert's rape. In 1886, John Miller, a sailor dying of typhoid fever, confessed to the same crime.

No one appears to have made any great effort to get at the truth of the original accusations. Herbert died in 1893. Mingo Jack's ghost is said to have haunted the Eatontown jail while it remained on West Street.

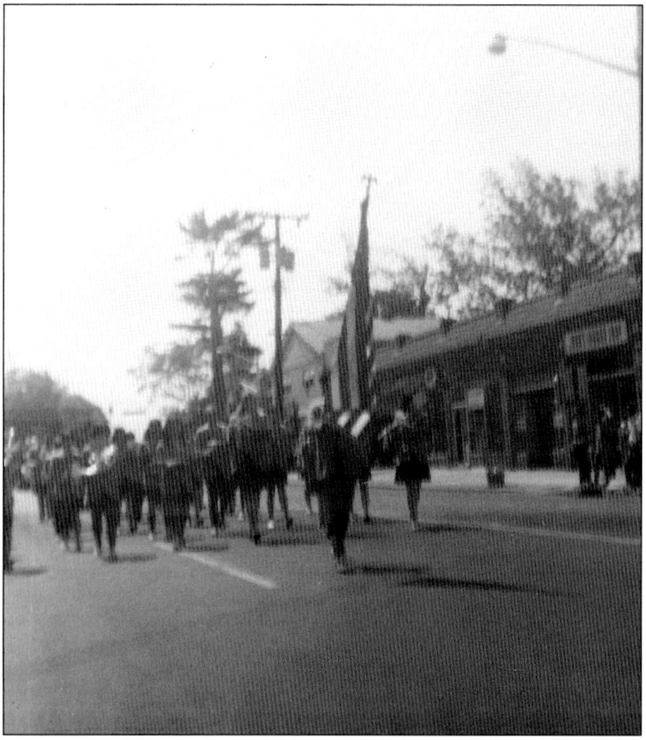

The June 1969 Memorial Day Parade, with the Memorial Junior High School's marching band heading south on Main Street to what was then called Memorial Park on the site of Eaton's mill.

The Society for the Prevention of Cruelty to Animals was located on a former chicken farm on Wall Street. This picture was taken in 1954. Note the medals.

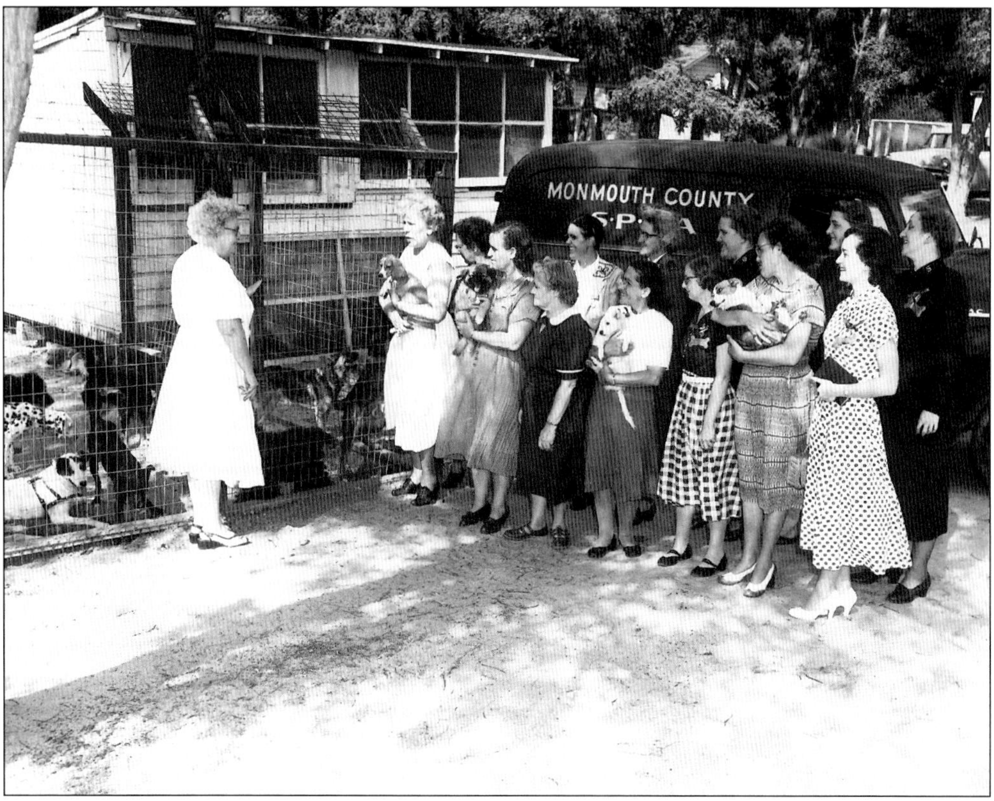

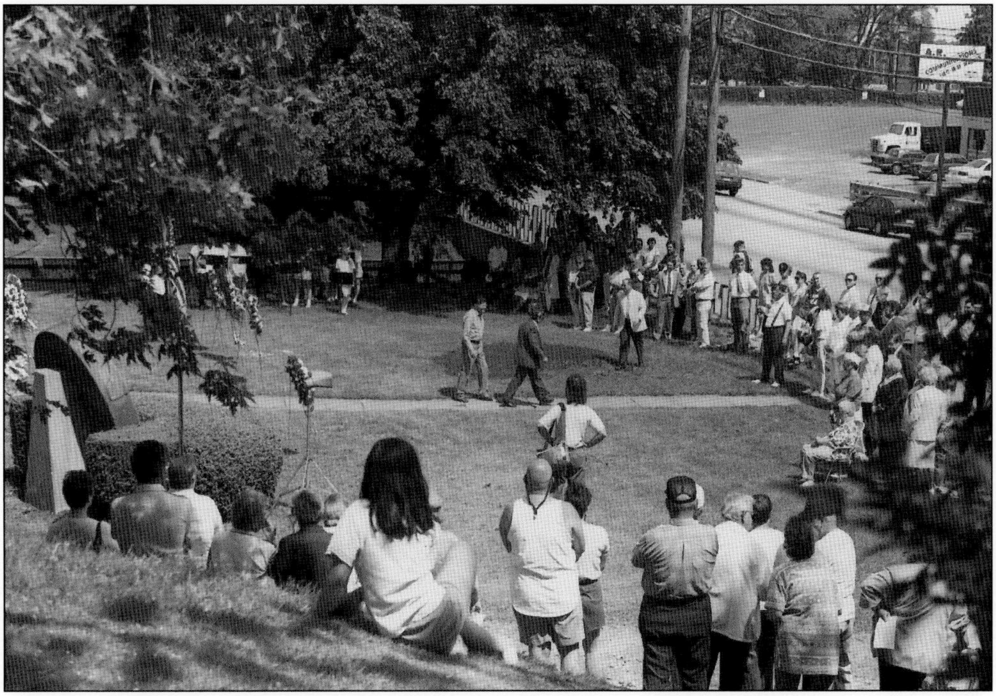

The June 1994 Memorial Day observance at Wampum Park, where the Eatontown community honors its soldiers who bravely gave their lives to defend the nation's freedoms. Among those residents to volunteer for the Civil War were Methodist minister Reybold of the 8th New Jersey Chaplaincy.

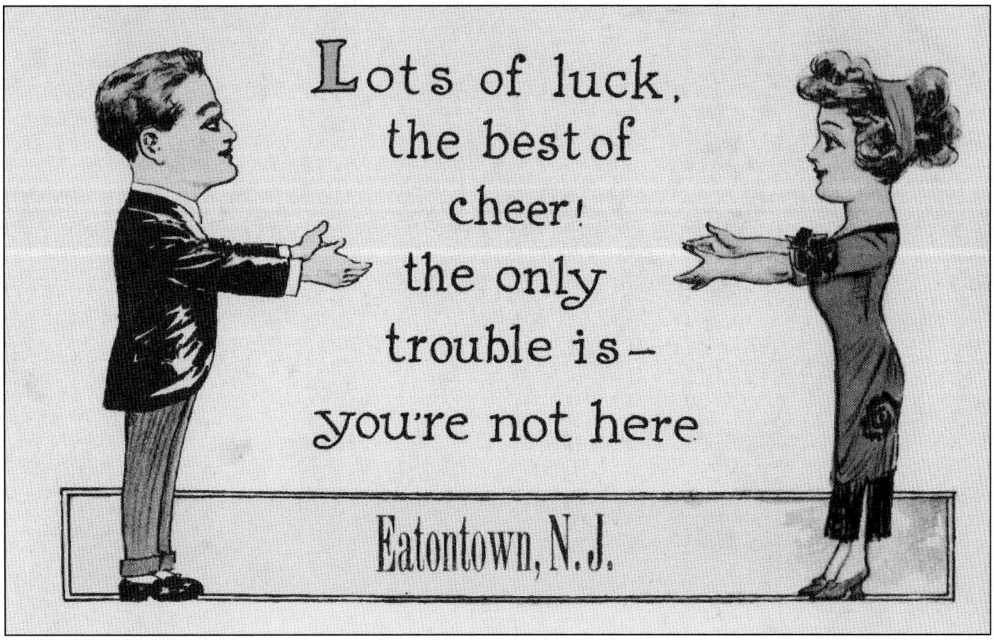

A greeting card expressing an oft-repeated sentiment.

Buy a Lot or Plot in Eatontown

The Monmouth Park Villa Site Co.

Will sell you a lot at surprisingly low prices---and give you a big discount if you build within a year.

Sixty Per Cent. Can Remain on Bond and Mortgage if desired

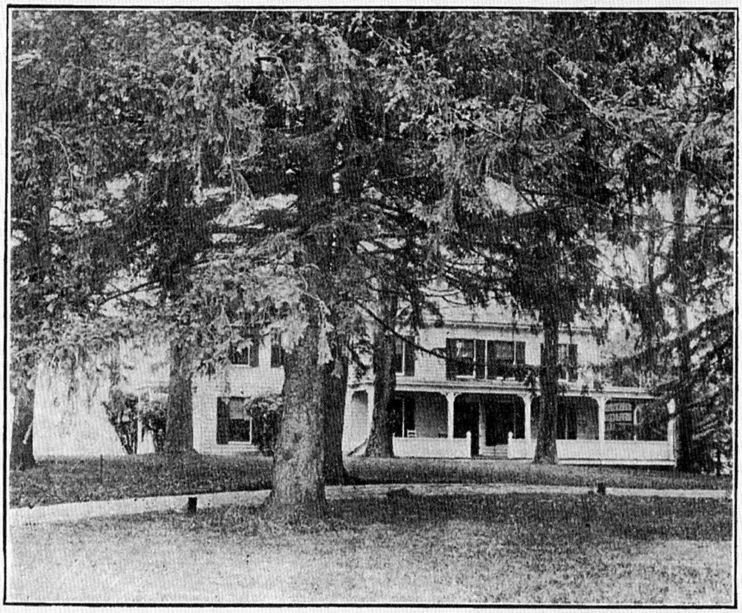

RESIDENCE OF M. R. VAN KEUREN

Restricted against nuisances and annoyances. Private streets and Parks, so that the little folks can have some place to play without the attendant dangers from Automobiles, Trolleys, Etc.

Look it up---the best inducements offered in the country---but you have to get *aboard quick*---as this offer won't stand open very long.

M. R. VAN KEUREN, President, EATONTOWN, N. J.

Four

Houses and Horses

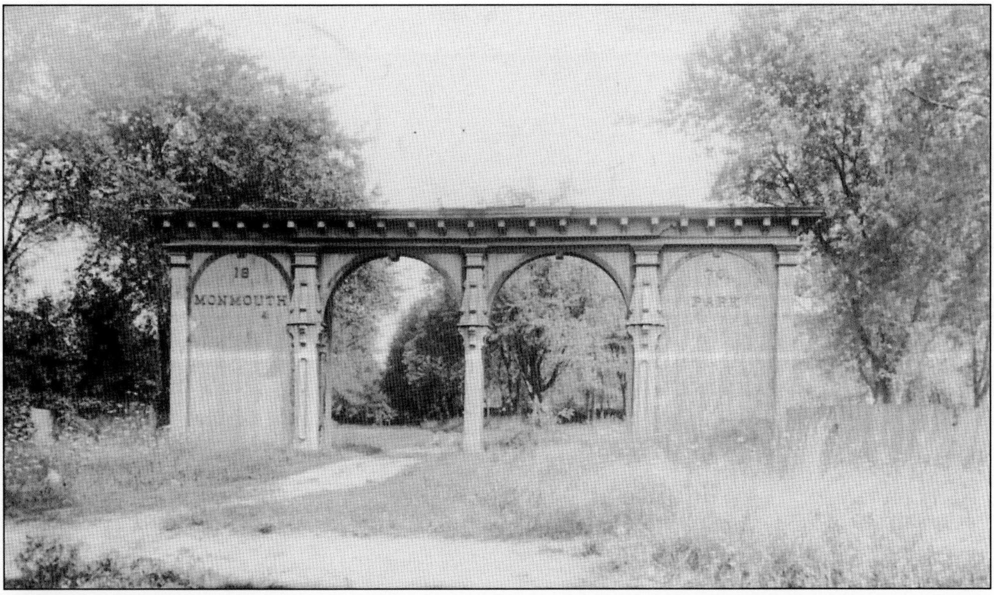

Promoters built the first Monmouth Park in 1870 on Eatontown farmland owned by the Corlies and Fielder families. As the nineteenth century began drawing to a close, Mark Twain dubbed this era "The Gilded Age." Racing enthusiasts such as Diamond Jim Brady, stage actresses Lillian Russell and Lillie Langtry, and short story writers such as Bret Harte and Alfred Lord Tennyson came to Eatontown to see and be seen. The arched wooden entrance gate shown above stood at what is today Broad Street and Park Avenue.

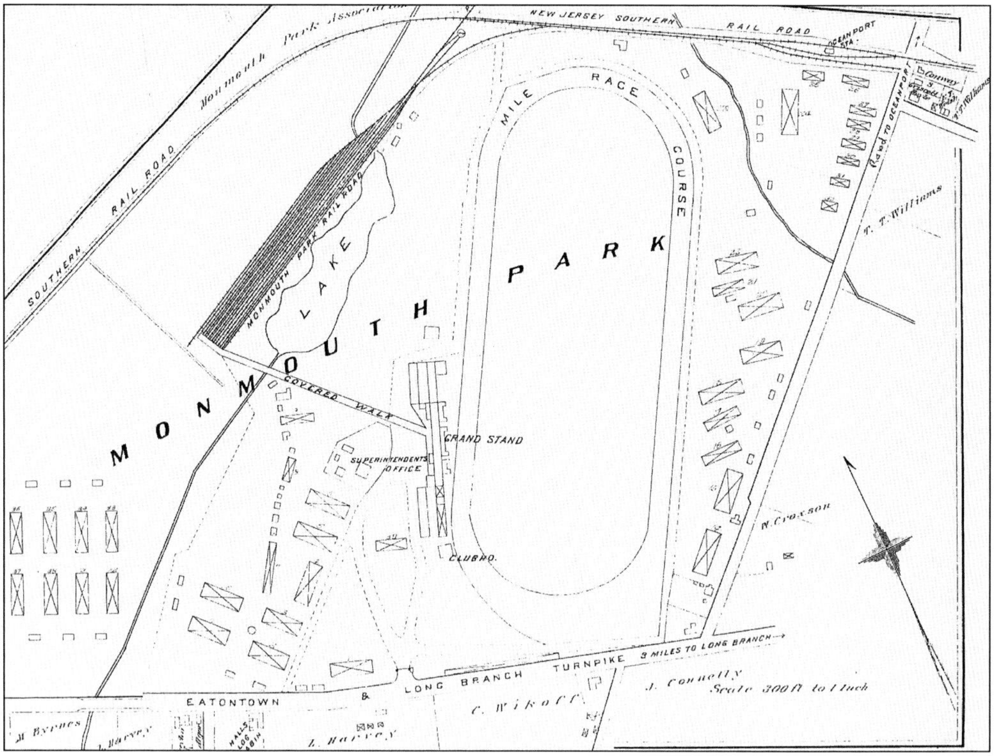

An 1889 map for the original location of Monmouth Park. The Eatontown & Long Branch Turnpike is now Broad Street and the road to Oceanport is now Main Street.

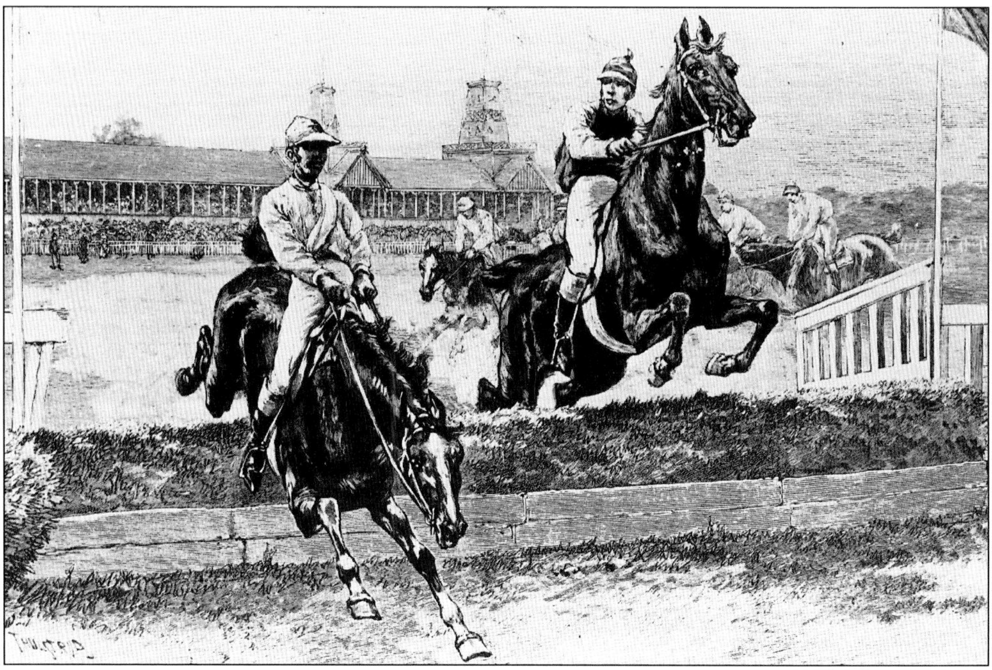

This lithograph, done from a July 25, 1885 woodcut, shows some of the course horses took when competing in a steeplechase. It first appeared in *Harper's Weekly*.

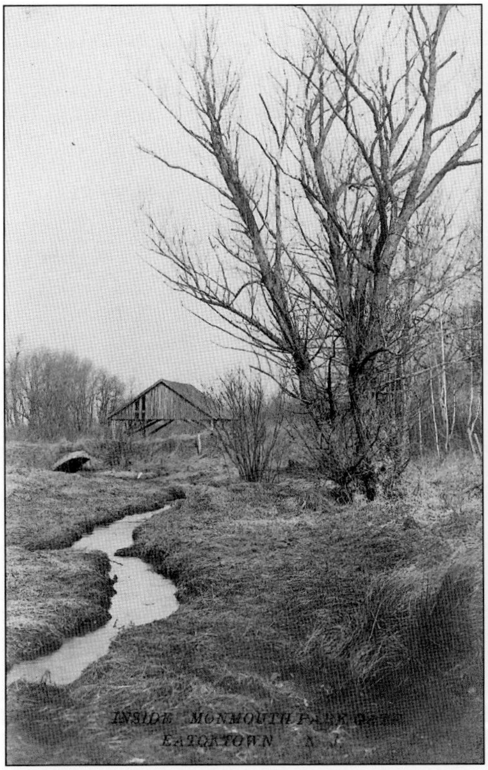

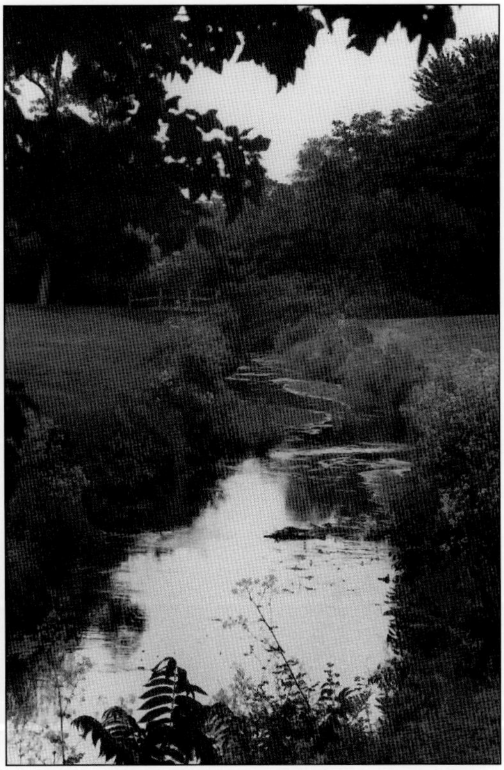

Left: This *c.* 1908 photograph shows the remnants of the racetrack's cooling shed, used to cool the horses' hooves and legs after a race on the mile-long oval track.
Right: The water for the cooling shed came from Huskey Brook, as shown in this modern photograph.

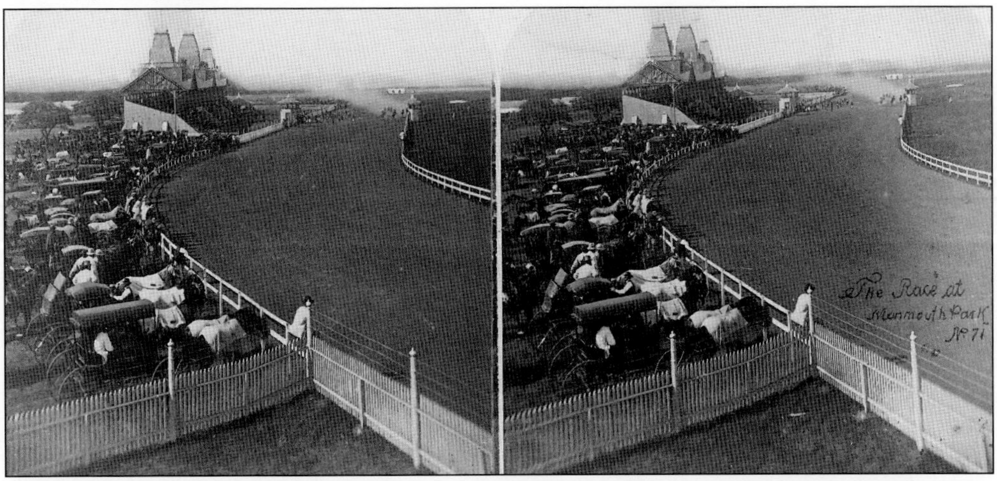

This stereoview of the first race on opening day, July 4, 1870, shows the famous 700-foot iron grandstand. On July 4, 1890, the new larger track was built a few hundred feet away. The racetrack's promotional literature listed the track's location as Long Branch though the famous seashore resort was 3 miles away. Monmouth Park's demise began 1894 when Congress passed an anti-gambling act. By 1897 a constitutional amendment outlawed gambling in general, and book-making in particular.

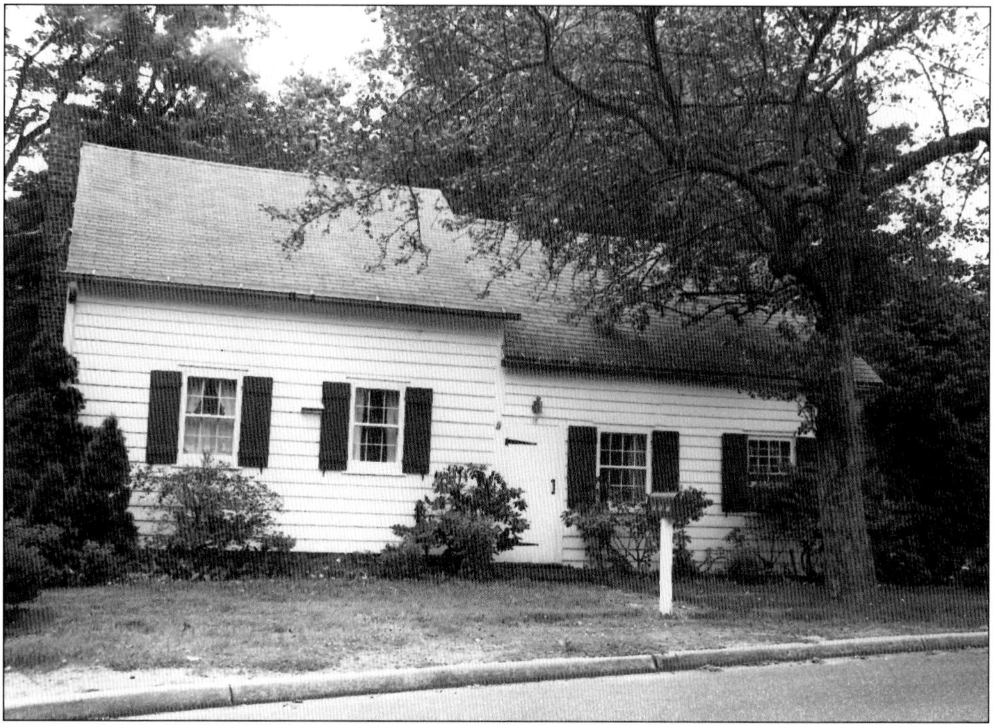

A Wolcott homestead on Buttonwood Avenue dating from the late 1600s.

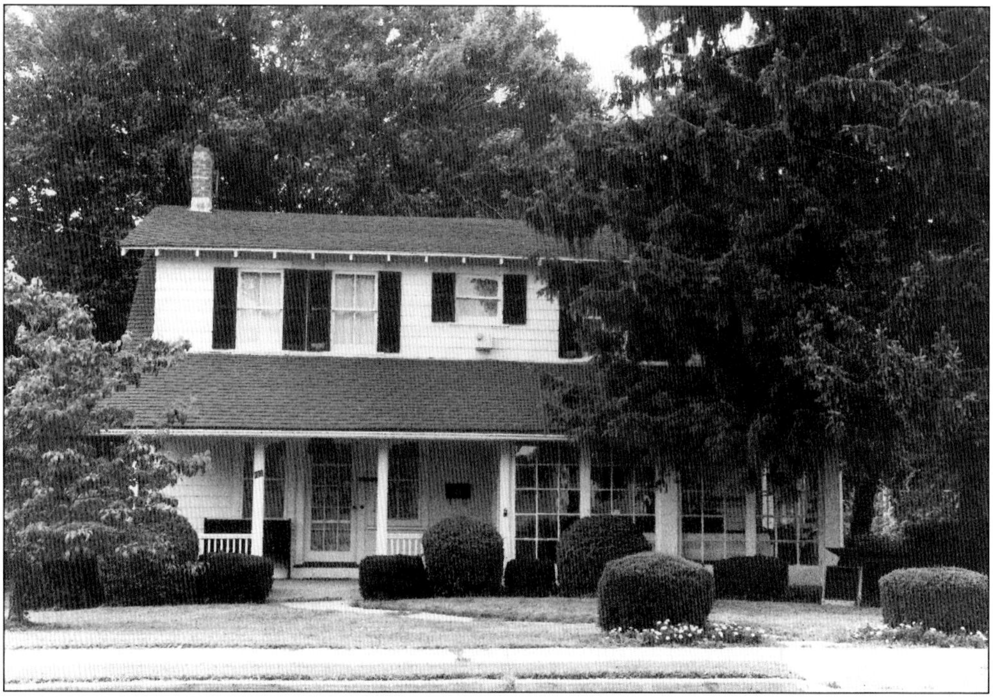

Ownership of the Eatontown Historical Museum, located on Broad Street, has been documented as far back as 1805. Known as the Read House, part of its sandstone foundation is believed to have come from the Stony Hill section of town off Grant Avenue.

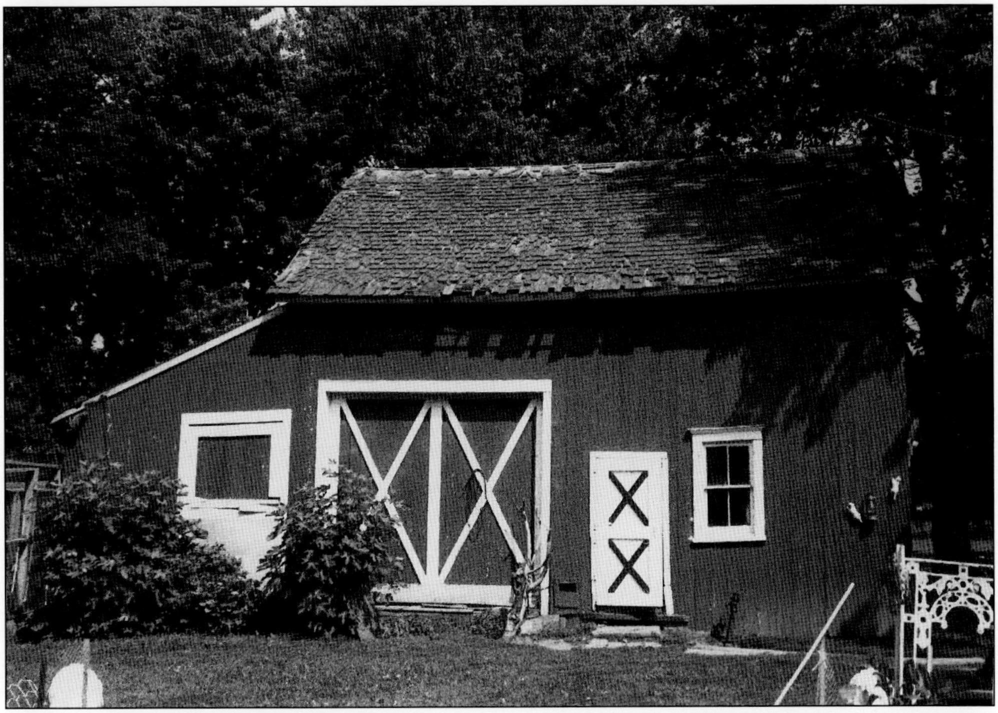
The 1875 barn from the Coventry Farm at the corner of Monmouth Road and Reynolds Drive. The property once extended down Reynolds Drive to the Polhemus Farm just before latter-day Pine Street.

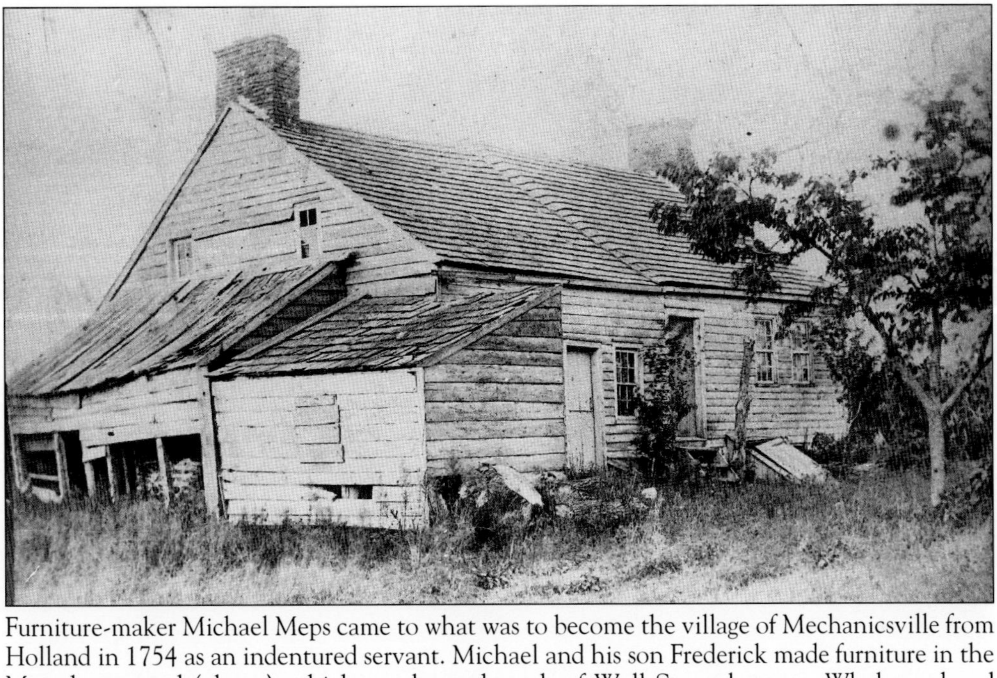
Furniture-maker Michael Meps came to what was to become the village of Mechanicsville from Holland in 1754 as an indentured servant. Michael and his son Frederick made furniture in the Meps homestead (above), which was located south of Wall Street between Whalepond and Monmouth Roads. The Meps name eventually became Maps.

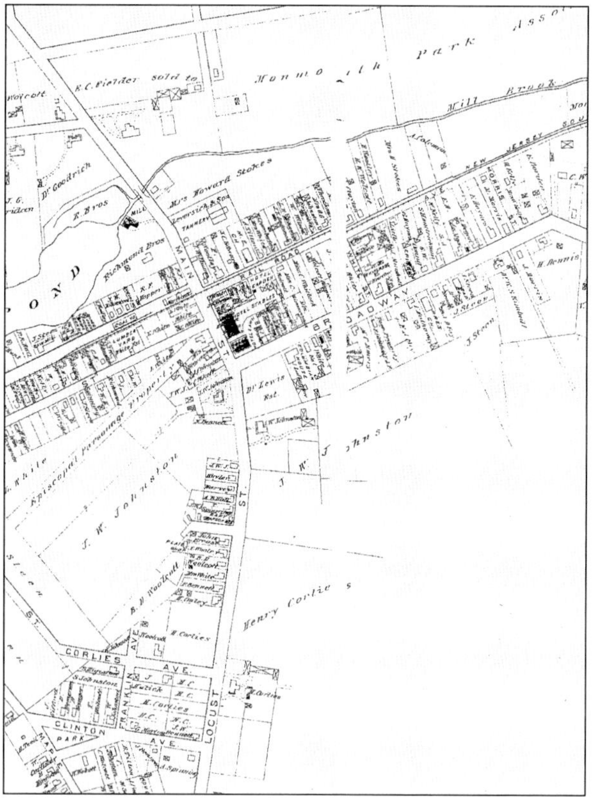

The 1889 Wolverton map details Eatontown village properties. Locust Street is South Street today, Broadway is Broad Street, and Railroad Avenue is Throckmorton Avenue. This view is looking north.

In 1873 this was the J. Morris house on Broadway and Byrne's Lane. Edgar Caffyn stands out front, while his wife Helena is sitting on the porch steps, *c.* 1900. In the 1960s it served as the St. James Rectory; it is a private residence today.

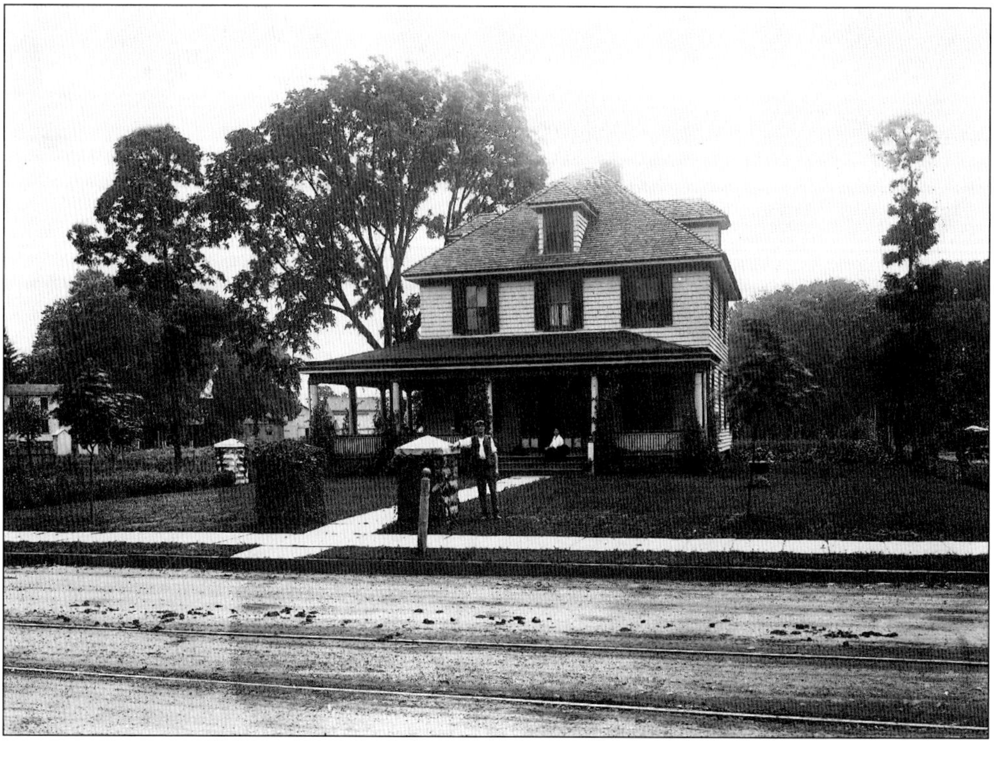

DR. H. T. PARTREE, Physician and Druggist

Eatontown's only drug store came under control of its present owner, Dr. Homer T. Partree, about seven years ago and in a way it was fortunate that it fell in such excellent hands. Dr. Partree came here from Massachusetts and is both a practicing physician and pharmacist. Dr. Partree is a graduate of the Academic and Medical departments of Yale University and has also successfully passed the examination required by the New Jersey State Board of Pharmacy. The store contains a complete line of sick-room necessities, druggists' sundries, pharmaceutical specialties and prescription requisites. The compounding of prescriptions is done personally by Dr. Partree himself and his experience in both medicine and pharmacy proves especially valuable, inasmuch as he is assured that his prescription ingredients are as pure and fresh as money, skill and experience can secure. Since locating in Eatontown, Dr. Partree has developed a very lucrative practice and has been successful in every way. He is thoroughly progressive, has affiliated himself with the Improvement Association and although here but seven years is to-day classed among the leading and prominent citizens of Eatontown.

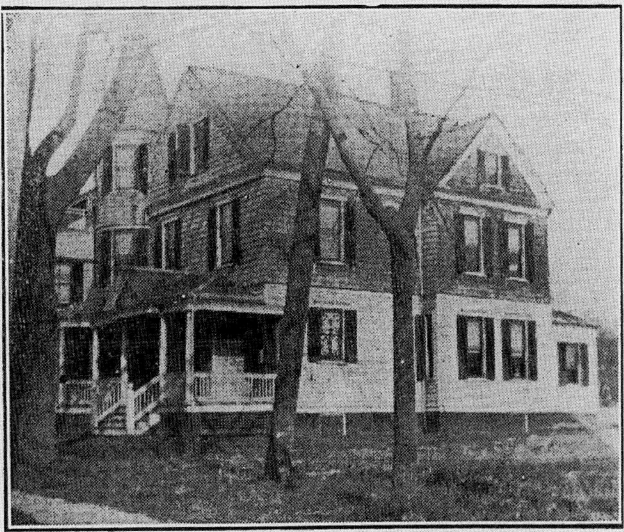

DR. H. T. PARTREE'S RESIDENCE

Beginning in the 1930s Dr. Partree's house has served as the rectory for St. Dorothea's and successive Roman Catholic parishes.

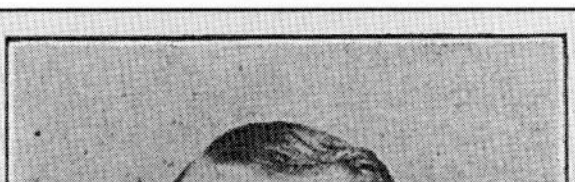

J. W. JOHNSTON, Real Estate

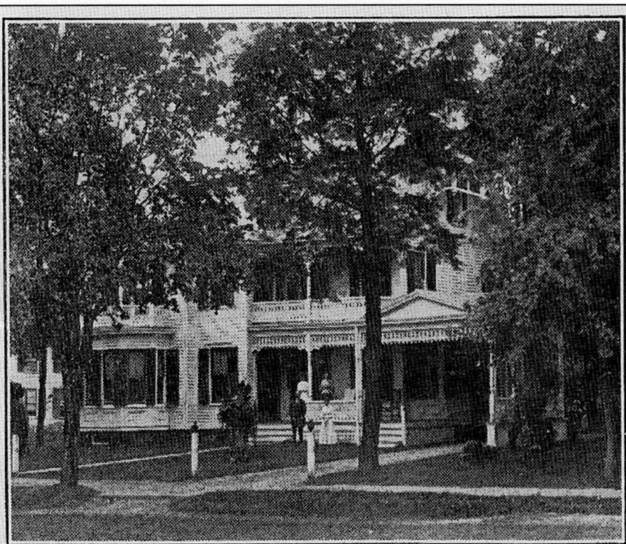

J. W. JOHNSTON'S RESIDENCE

The name of Joseph W. Johnston has been an influential factor in the commercial life of Eatontown for many years, and no citizen has been more closely identified with the town's development or done more to improve it. For 35 years Mr. Johnston was engaged in the mercantile business here, retiring in 1890 to attend to his large property interests, which are by far the largest of anyone in this section. At the present time he owns about 47 houses in Eatontown and Red Bank, and is buying and selling all the time. Those interested in securing either homes or farms will find him in a position to supply their needs. Mr. Johnston has himself built about 20 houses in Eatontown, and is regarded as an authority on land and property values here. Few citizens in this end of the county are more widely known than he, and certainly none enjoy a higher personal standing. Mr. Johnston has always been a prime mover in supporting anything having for its object the benefiting of Eatontown. He is at present township collector, president of the Shrewsbury Mutual Fire Insurance Company, is the sole owner of the nearby town of Maxwell, and is regarded as one of Eatontown's solid and most successful citizens. In a general review of Eatontown and its representative citizens the name of J. W. Johnston will naturally occupy a foremost position.

J.W. Johnston was a sizeable landowner in town. McDonald's, on the corner of Main Street and the Route 71 jughandle, is now located on the site of his house.

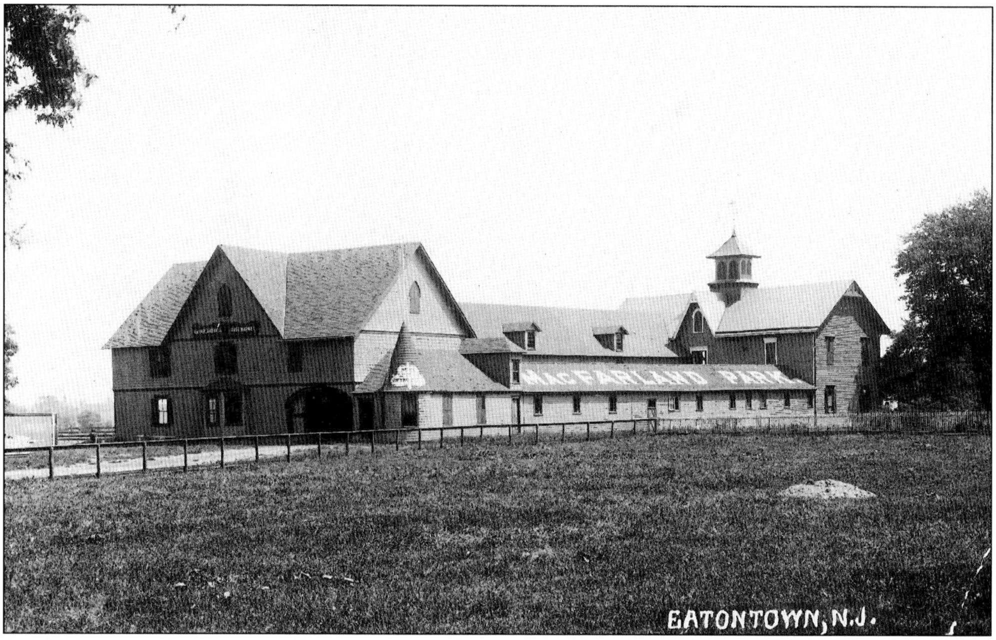

In the late nineteenth century MacFarland Park was built off Locust Street. MacFarland was a horse trader dealing in high-stepping singles and pairs, hunters, hacks, polo ponies, and gentlemen's show roadsters. Today the stables are the site of Twin Brook condominiums on White Street.

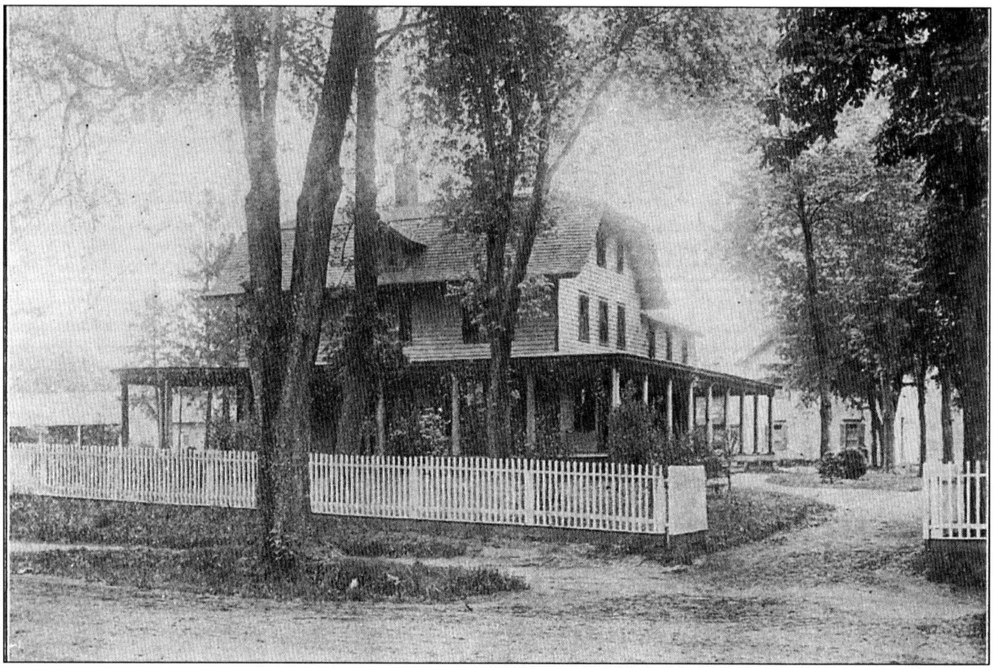

By 1911 M.F. McDonald bought MacFarland's Park, and operated a branch stable at 233 W. 50th in Manhattan. Doris Angelbeck, a Wolcott descendent, and her husband Christopher Angelbeck Jr., who was a councilman from 1937 to 1940, lived in the McDonald's farmhouse. Today the empty lot is south of the Route 35 Wendy's.

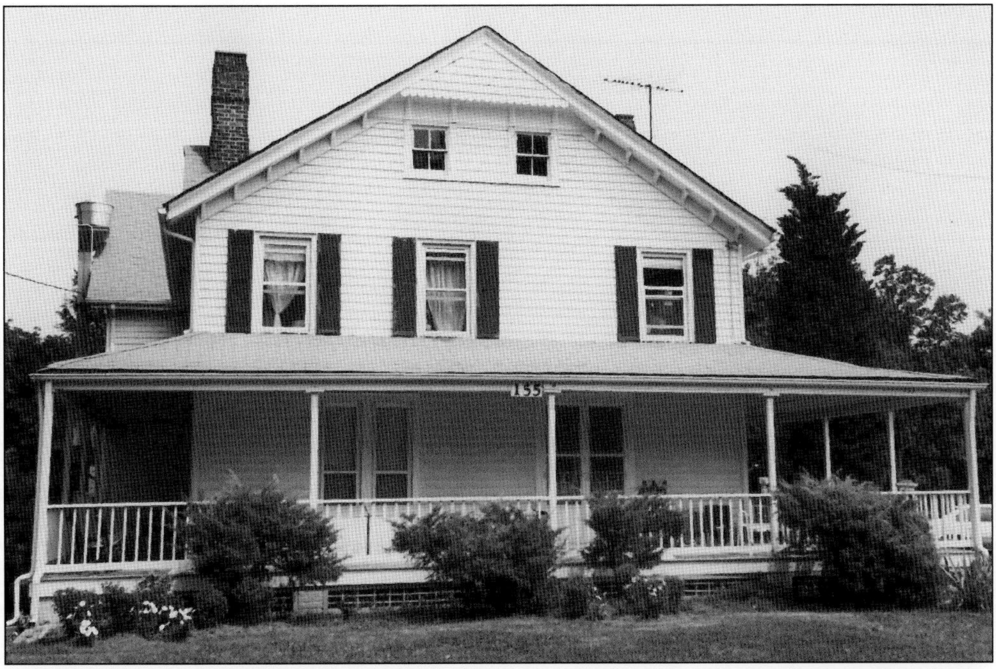

Jeter Walden owned stables and a half-mile horse track on his South Street farm in 1889. By the late 1940s Don Phillips operated the farm as Shoe String Stables. When a fire broke out, one horse ran all the way to Red Bank, its tale aflame. In 1950 Bendix Corp. bought the part of the farm property that fronted on Route 35.

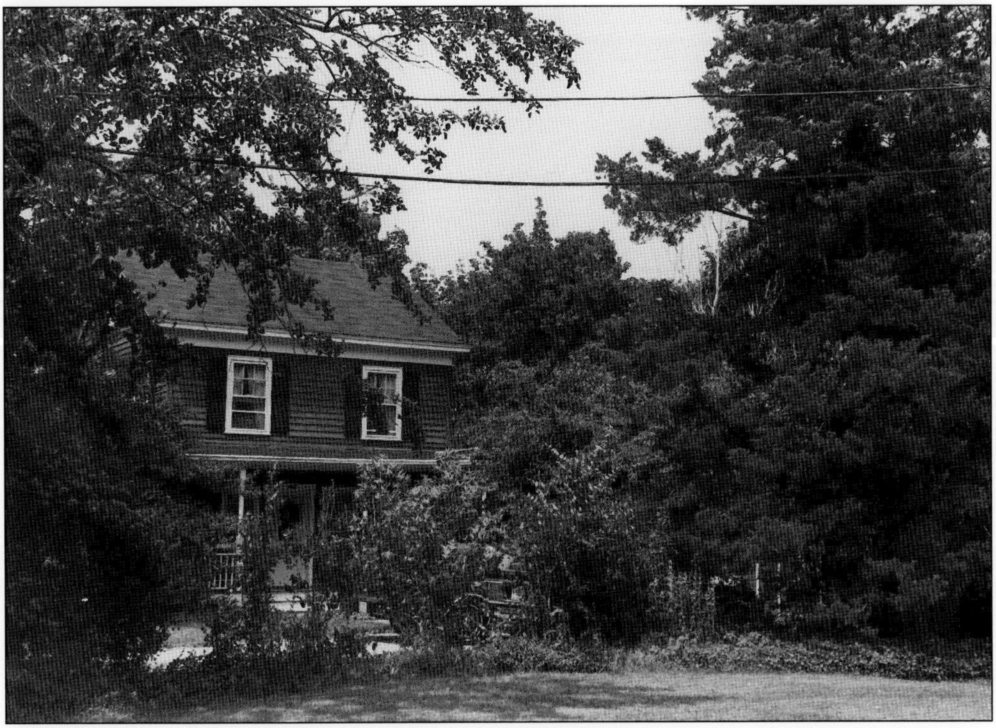

The trainer's house for the Walden stables on South Street.

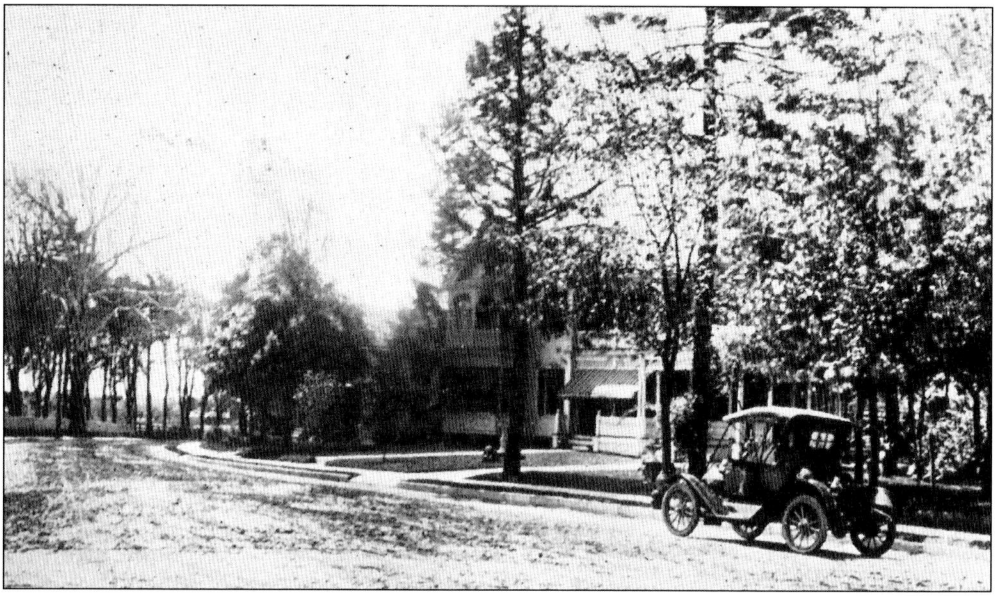

South Street, *c.* 1912, showing J.W. Johnston's estate house.

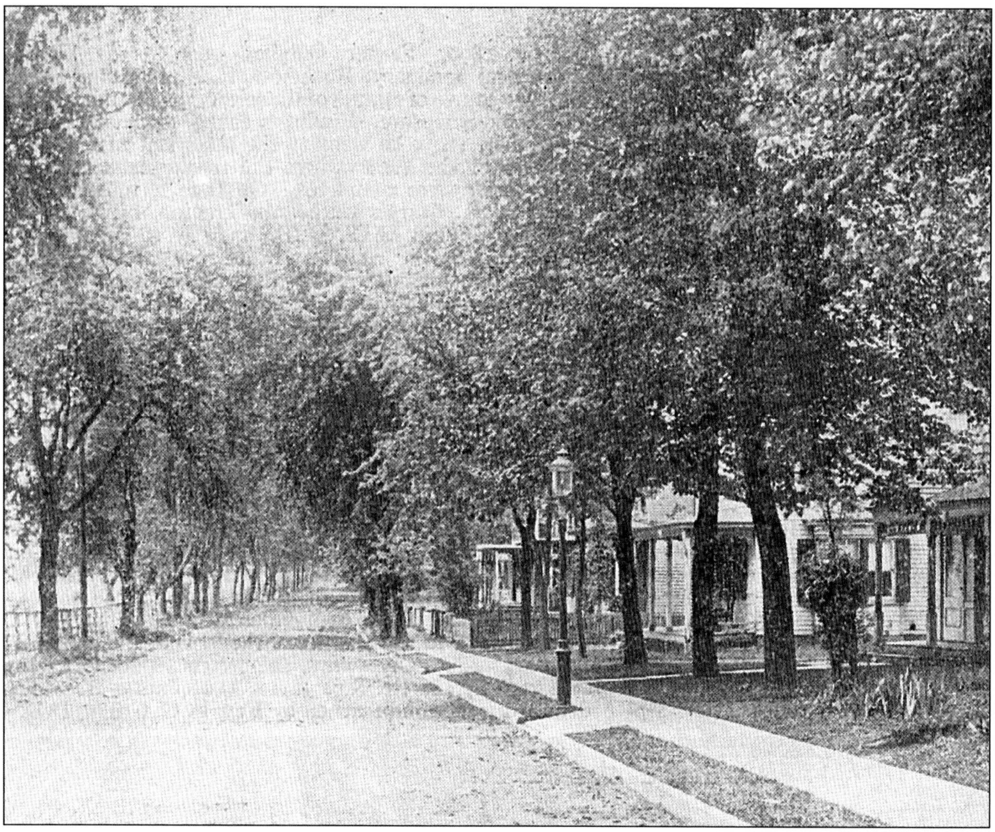

Further down South Street more modest houses were built.

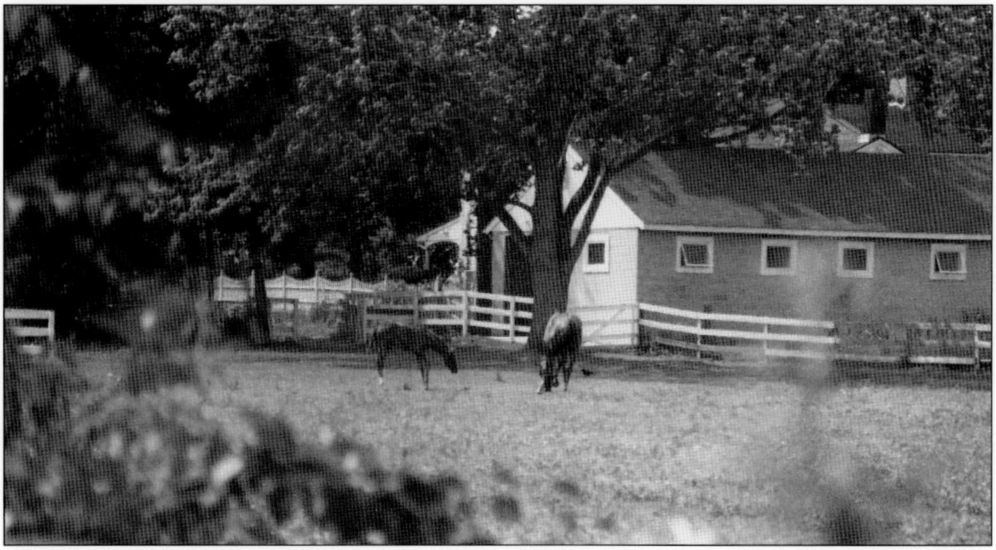

The property originally owned by one of Eatontown's earliest settlers, Henry Corlies, is today the last remaining horse farm in town at the corner of South Street and Clinton Avenue.

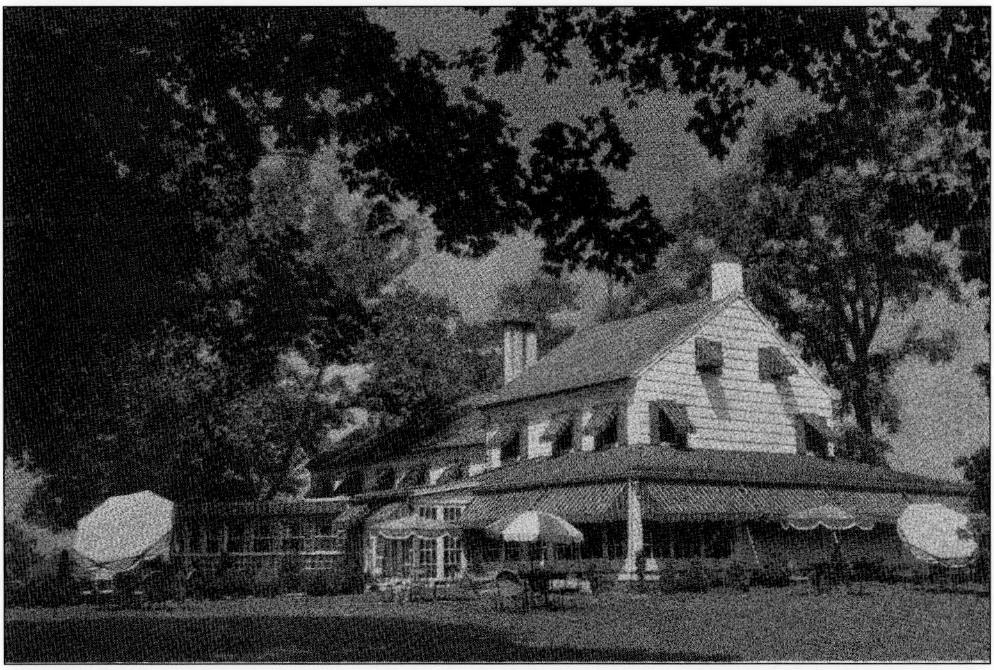

The Crystal Brook Farm Inn on Route 35 at the Eatontown-Shrewsbury border was the scene of a suspicious fire in the late 1940s, when it was a popular nightclub. Five people perished in the early morning blaze including the owner, three members of his family, and a crippled musician. Today the site is Hannah's Restaurant.

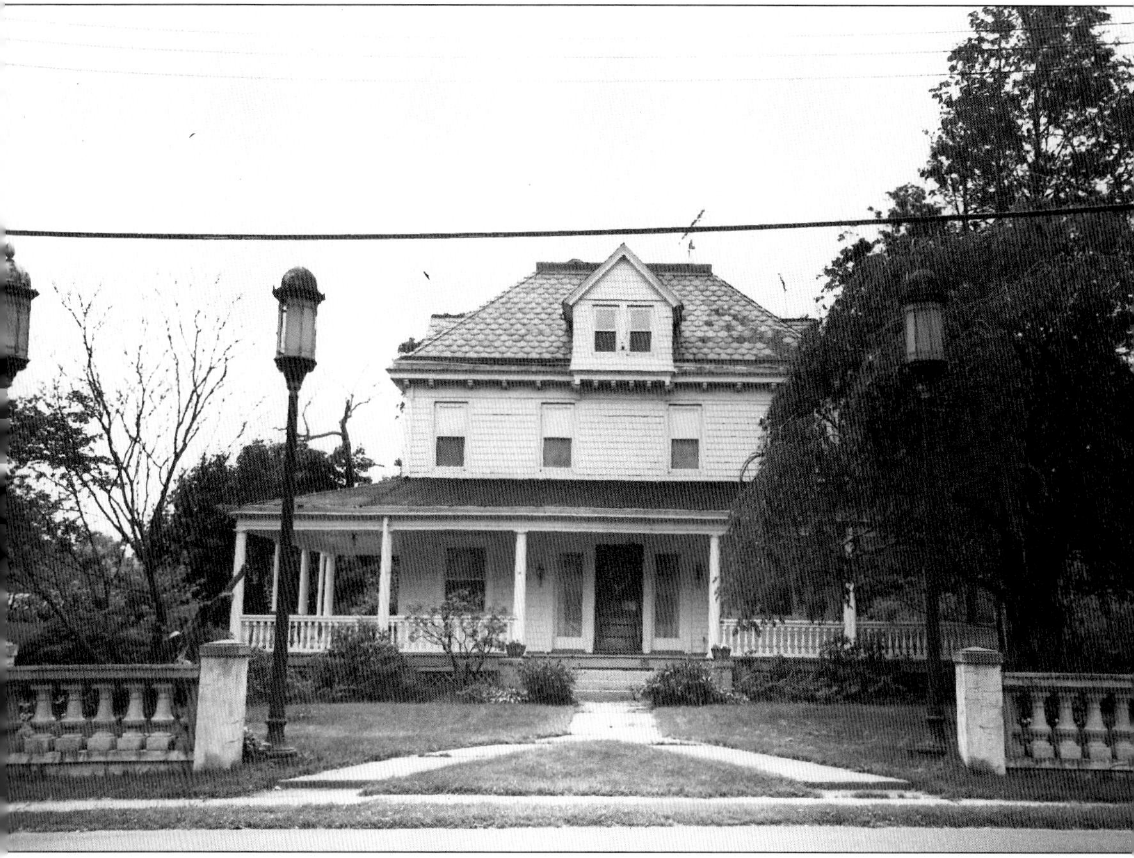

Herbert Werner, who came to Eatontown in 1939, was a Republican mayor from 1961 to 1975. Before he retired, he was the executive director of the YMCA of Greater New York, when it was then located in the original Pennsylvania station in Manhattan. He tried everything he could to save artifacts from the station when it was being torn down. He managed to save four gas lamps, and placed them in front of his Tinton Avenue home. Werner was a member of the New York Railroad Club and was a 32nd degree Mason. He was also an elder in the Presbyterian Church in Red Bank.

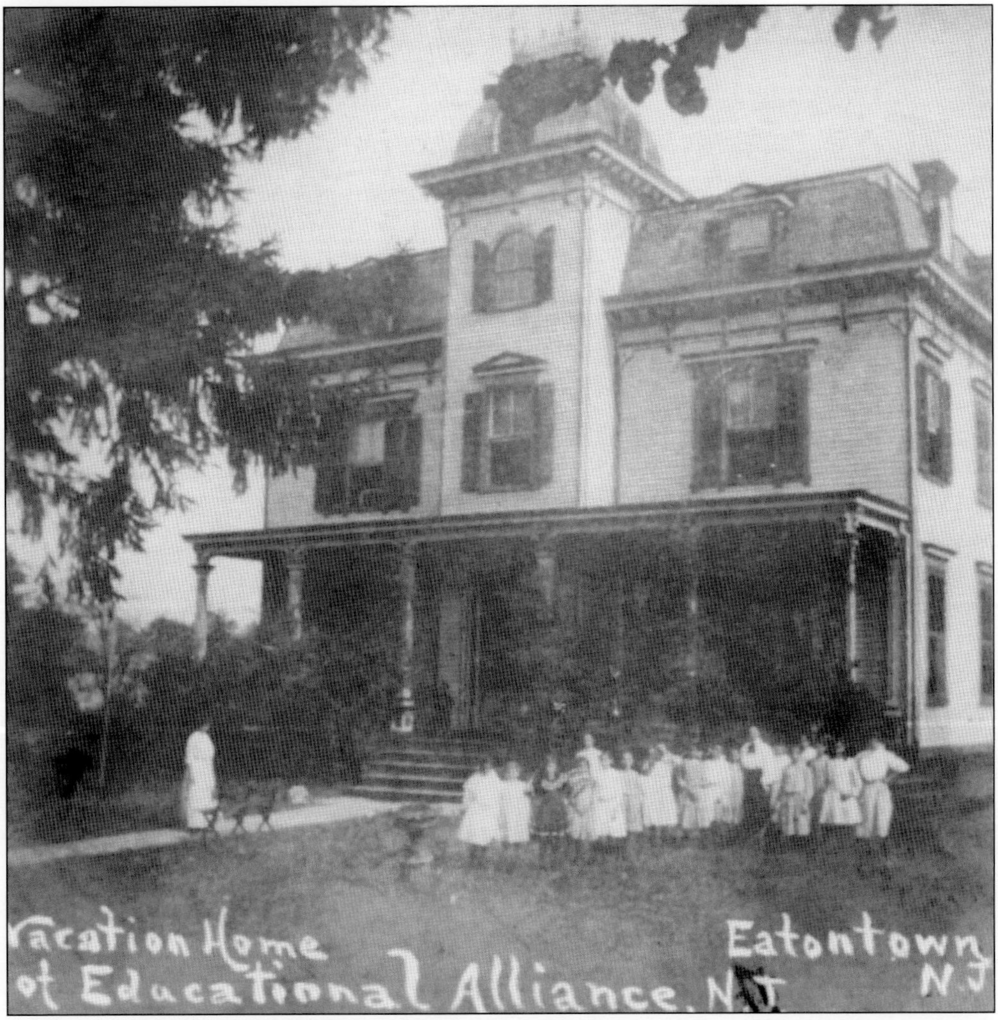

The vacation home of the Educational Alliance on Tinton Avenue, *c*. 1906, became the home of George A. Steele, who operated Shrewsbury Nurseries on the northwest corner of Tinton Avenue and Hope Road on Dr. Lippincott's old farm. Among his contracts for evergreens were City Hall Park in Manhattan. Other clients included Senator Simon Guggenheim of Elberon, A.N. Beadleston of Seabright, and Ira Barrows of Rumson.

WILLIAM H. FOSTER

William H. Foster is a veteran of the Civil War. Born in New York City December 5, 1841, attended school in New York City and came with his father to a farm at Scobeyville, N. J., and has lived on a farm continuously, with the exception of a three years' service in the army from 1862 to 1865 in the war of the rebellion, with the 14th N. J. Volunteer Infantry, serving in almost all capacities from private to first lieutenant and adjutant of the regiment and was later commissioned by President Johnson as Brevt., Capt. and Major. He came to Eatontown in April, 1910, starting an office in the town as a Real Estate and Insurance Agency.

William H. Foster

REAL ESTATE, COLLECTIONS, LOANS AND INSURANCE

Commissioner of Deeds, Notary Public

EATONTOWN, N. J.

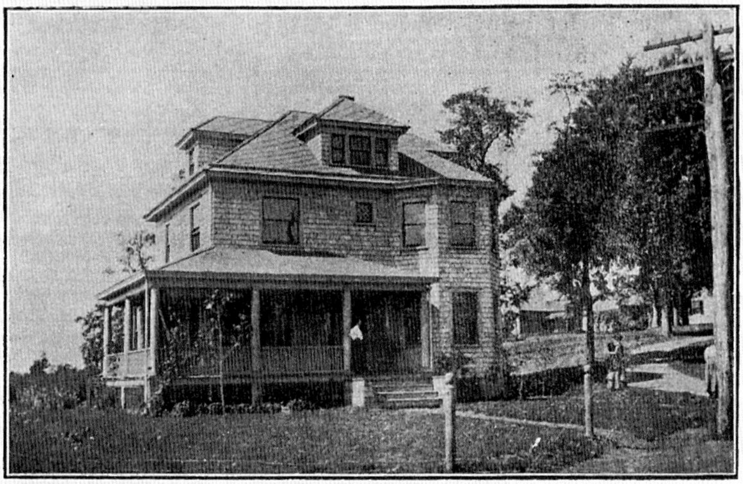

WILLIAM H. FOSTER'S RESIDENCE

Foster's two maiden daughters lived here until they died. Today this is 134 Main Street (Route 35) located between the Exxon service station at the Tinton Avenue corner and the Kentucky Fried Chicken.

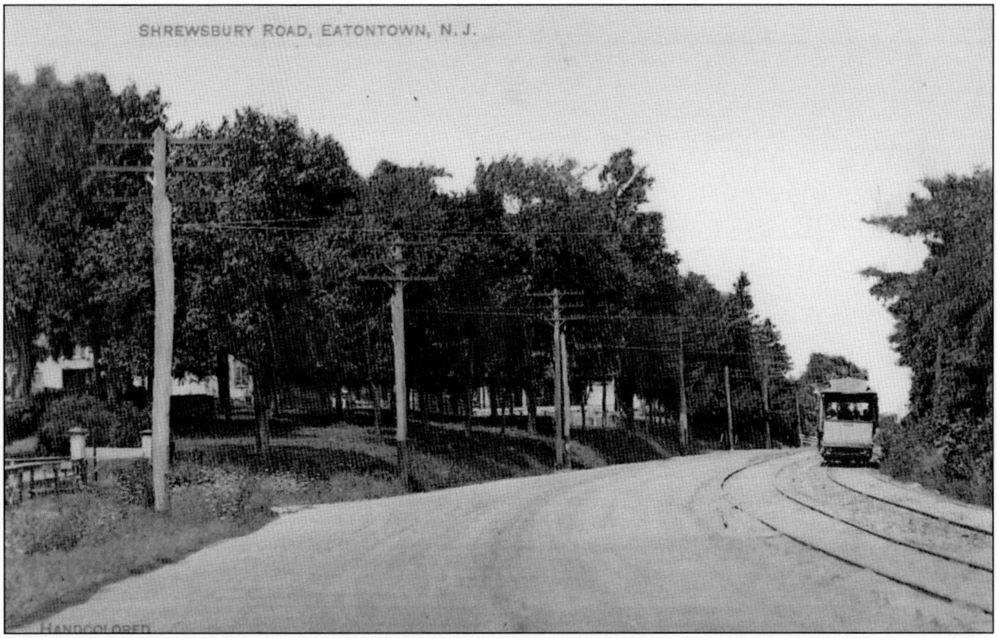

The Red Bank Turnpike, *c.* 1910, looking north to Shrewsbury with the Monmouth County Electric Co. trolley heading into Eatontown.

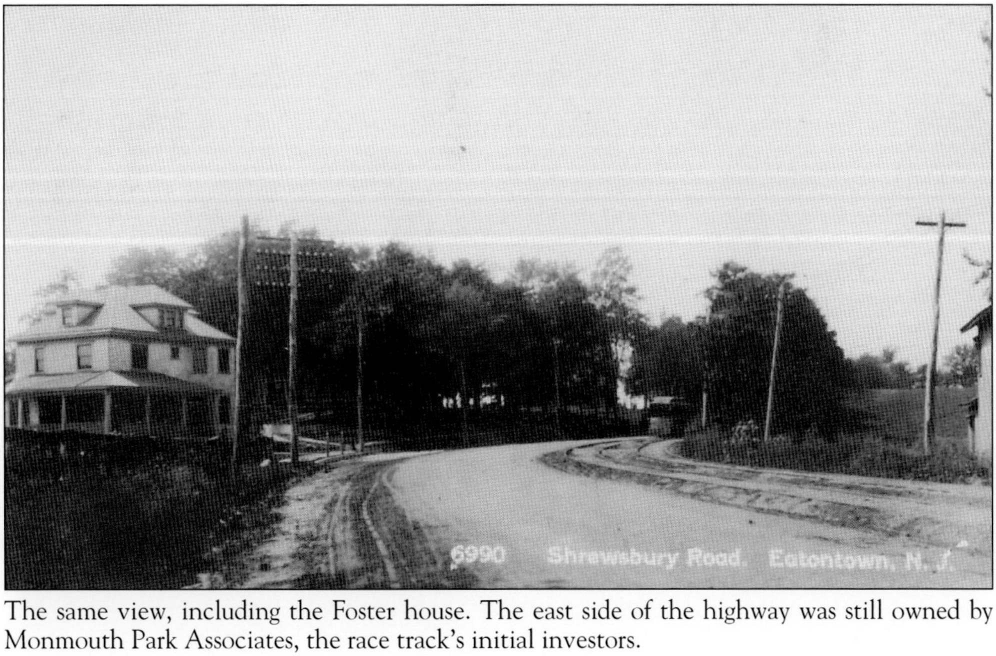

The same view, including the Foster house. The east side of the highway was still owned by Monmouth Park Associates, the race track's initial investors.

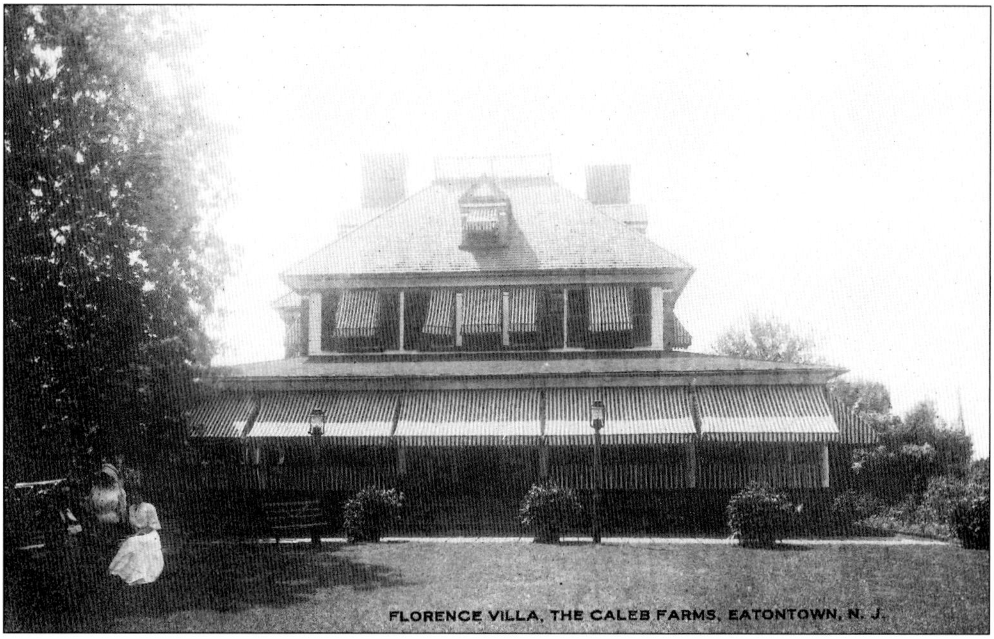

The country house on the estate known as Florence Villa, located on Tinton Avenue.

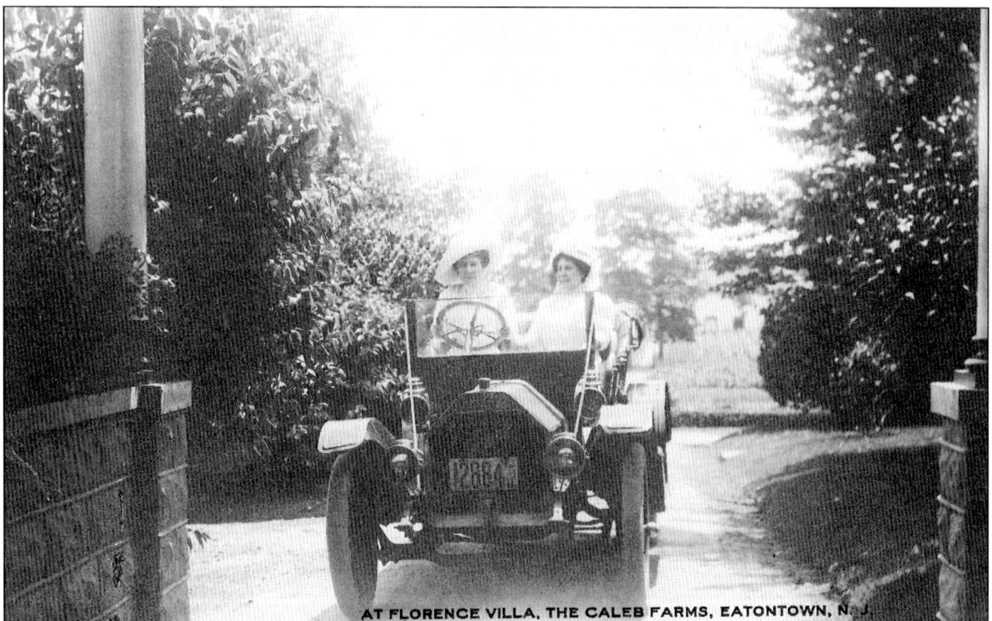

Florence Villa and the G.M. Caleb Farms were one and the same property listed in the 1914 Farm and Business Directory of Monmouth County. The women are driving an Oakland automobile registered in 1911.

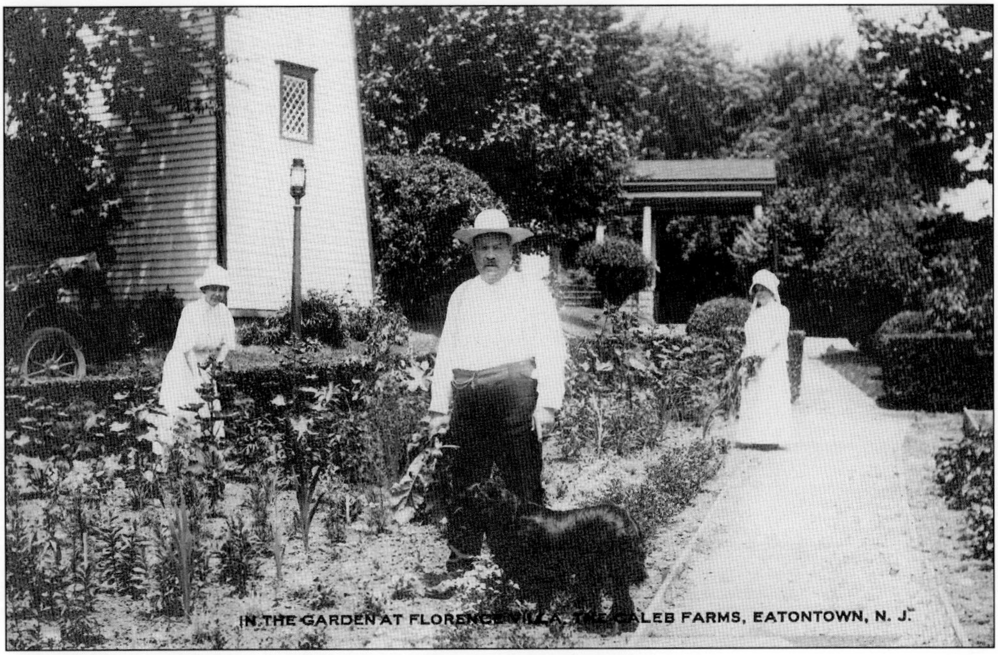

G.M. Caleb in the garden at Florence Villa.

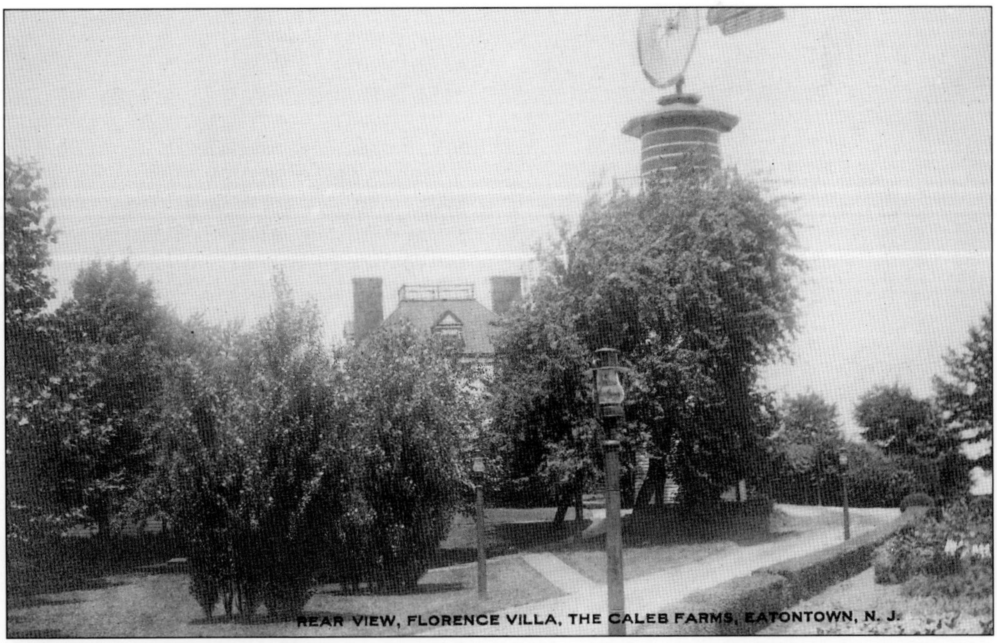

A rear view of Florence Villa.

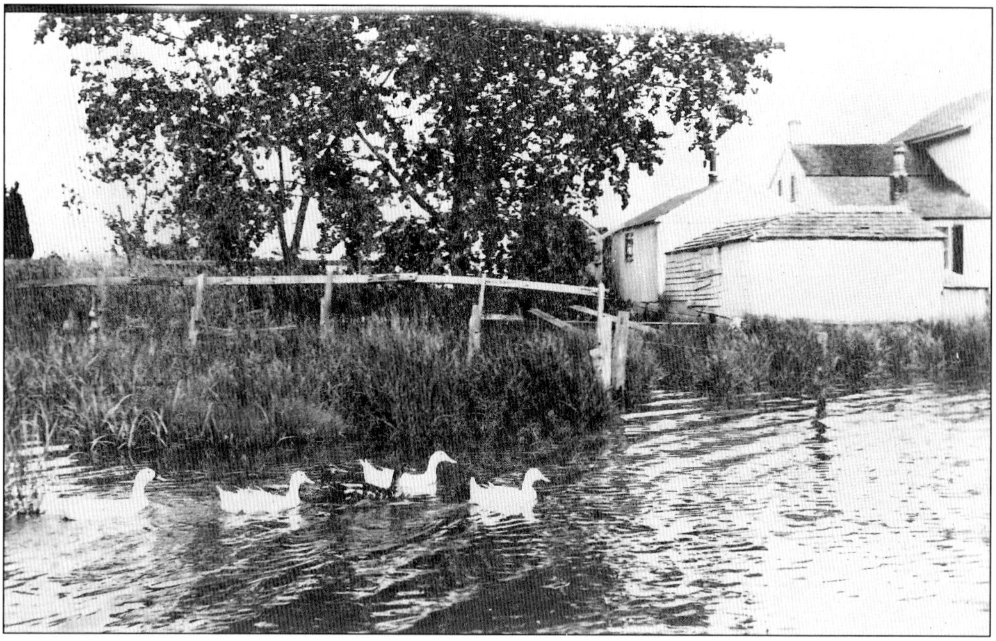

More than half of Monmouth County's 300,000 acres were devoted to farming, dairying, and the raising of flowers and nursery stock.

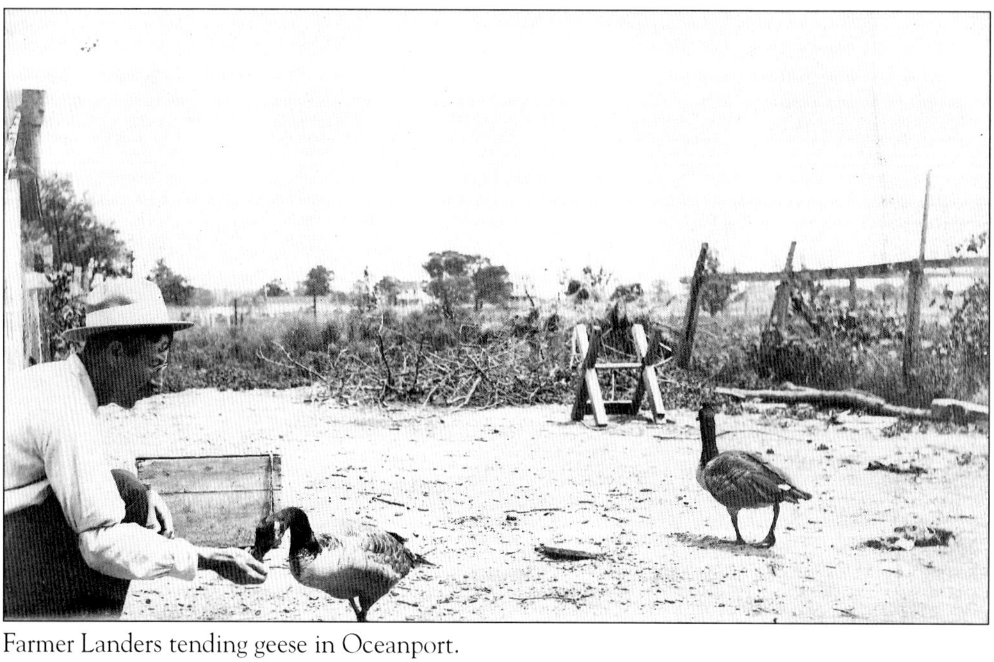

Farmer Landers tending geese in Oceanport.

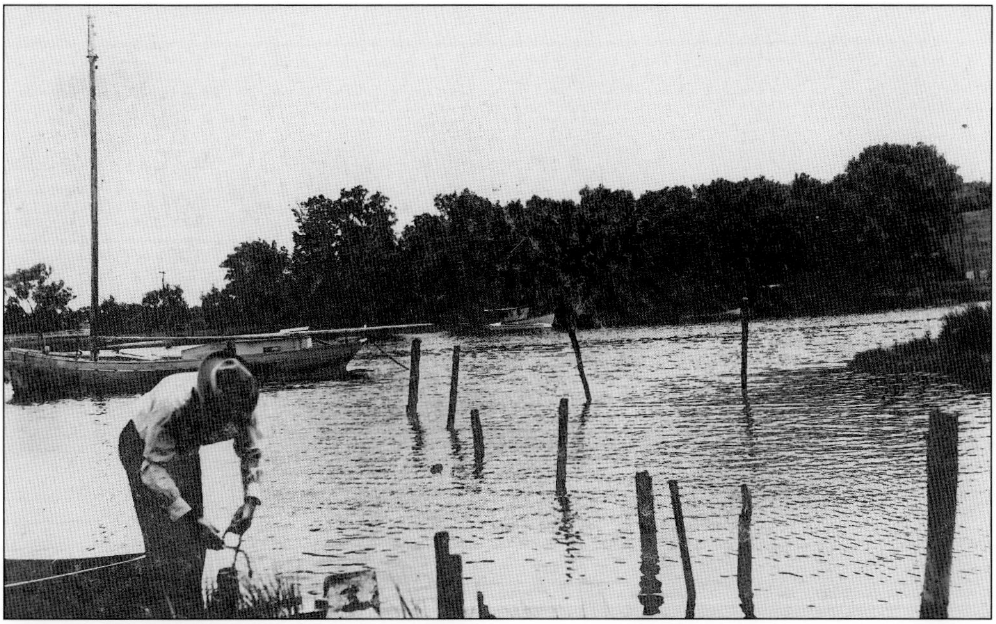

Casting off on the South Shrewsbury River.

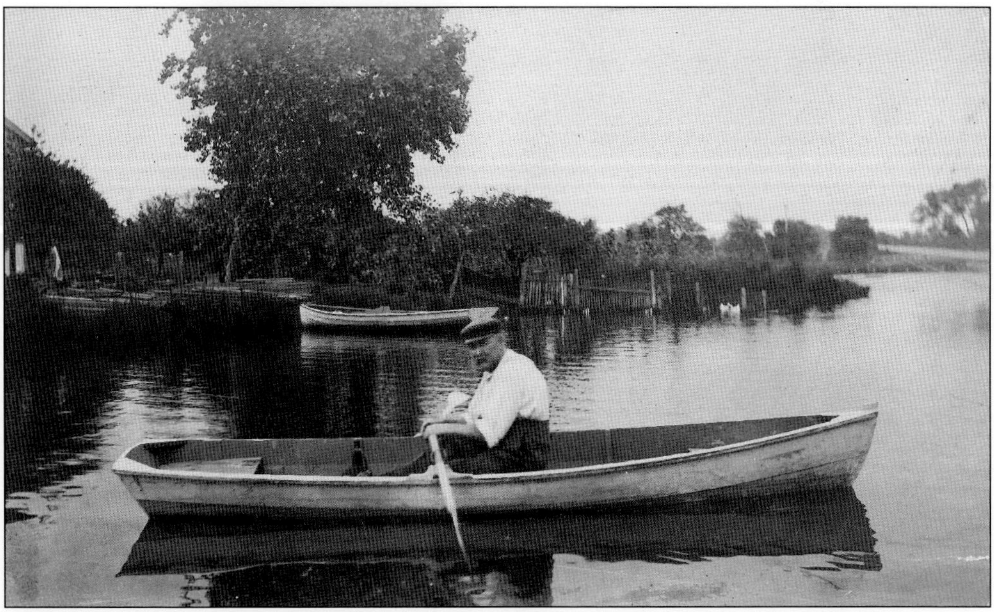

Out for a row on Oceanport Creek.

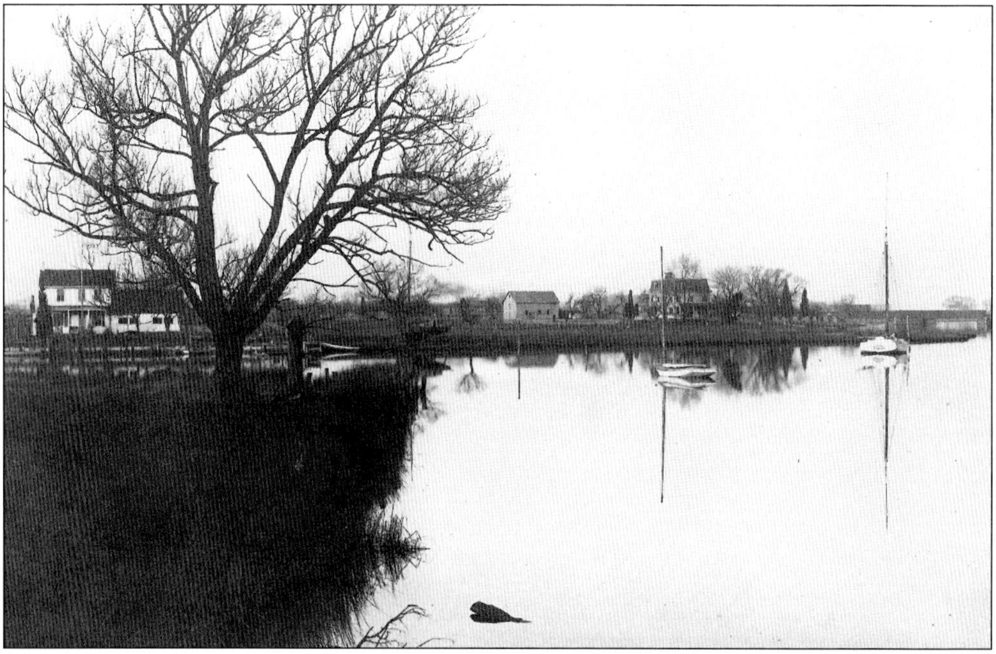

The 1800s farmhouse fronting on Oceanport Creek from Riverside Avenue is still standing today, and can be seen across the water from Old Wharf Park.

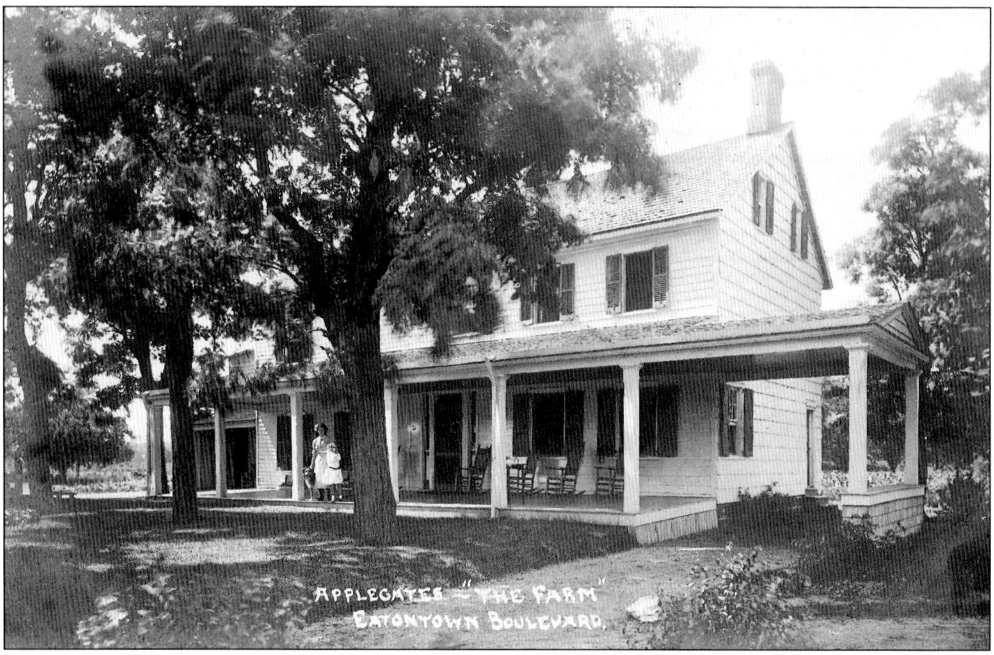

The Applegate Farm, identified by the postcard as being on Eatontown Boulevard, structurally resembles an 1800s farmhouse on Wyckoff Road.

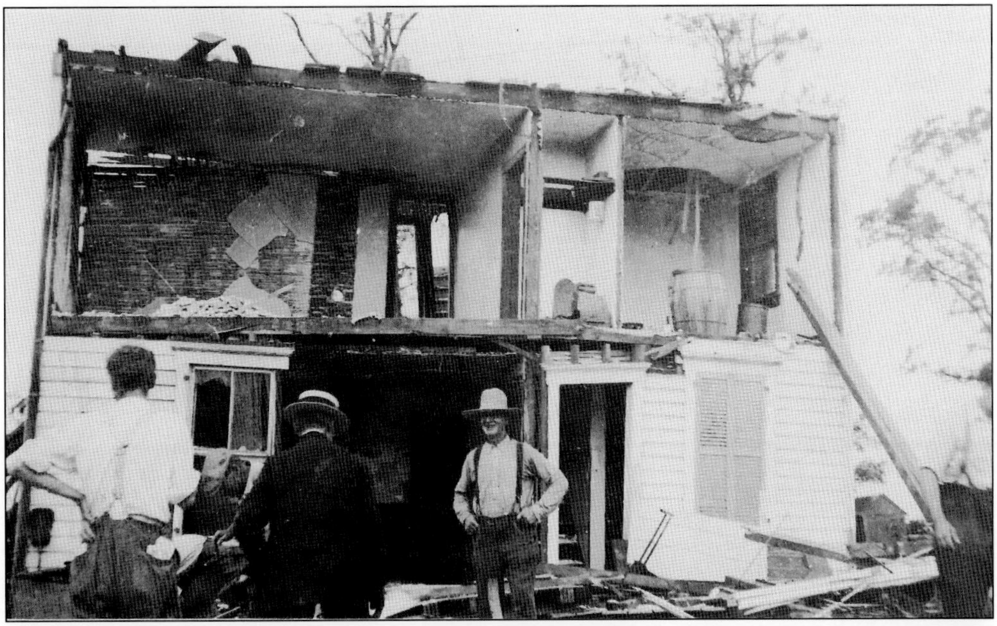

Joel Fields (facing the camera) owned a 300-acre farm off Wyckoff Road by Smock's Hill. The entrance to the colonial home was off West Grant Avenue. A cyclone split the farmhouse in half in July 1921. Fields was sixty years old when this photograph was taken. Dr. Anthony DeVito of Eatontown subsequently bought the property where the Boy Scouts were allowed to camp. The property is now the site of Deepwood Estates.

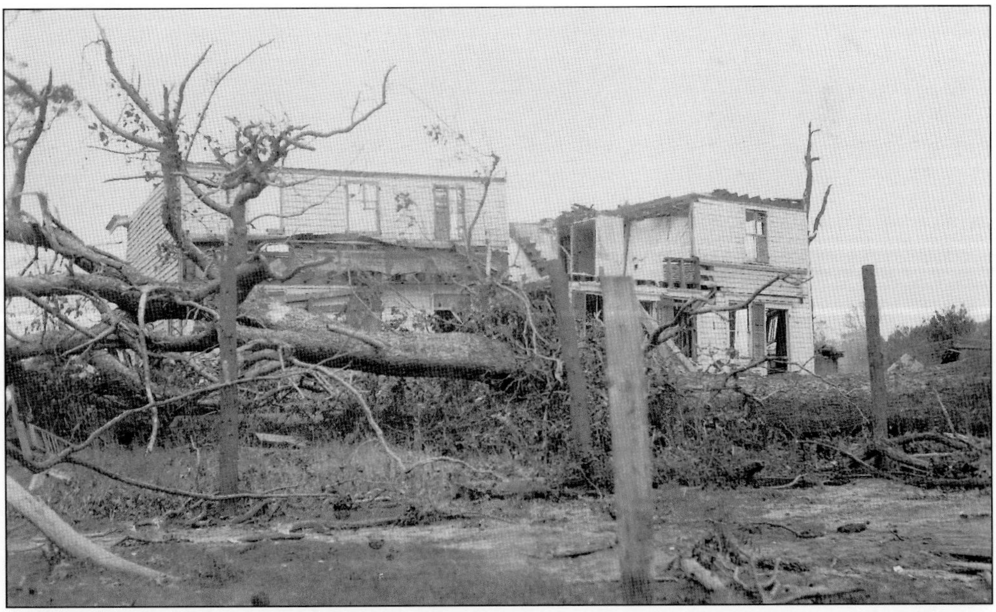

Fields named his farm Gold Hill after gold particles were found at the bottom of a water bucket used to wash his sheep. Cuff links were made of the gold. No one knows why gold came up with the water. During World War I the War Department offered Fields $100,000 to use part of his farm as a wireless site; Fields refused the offer.

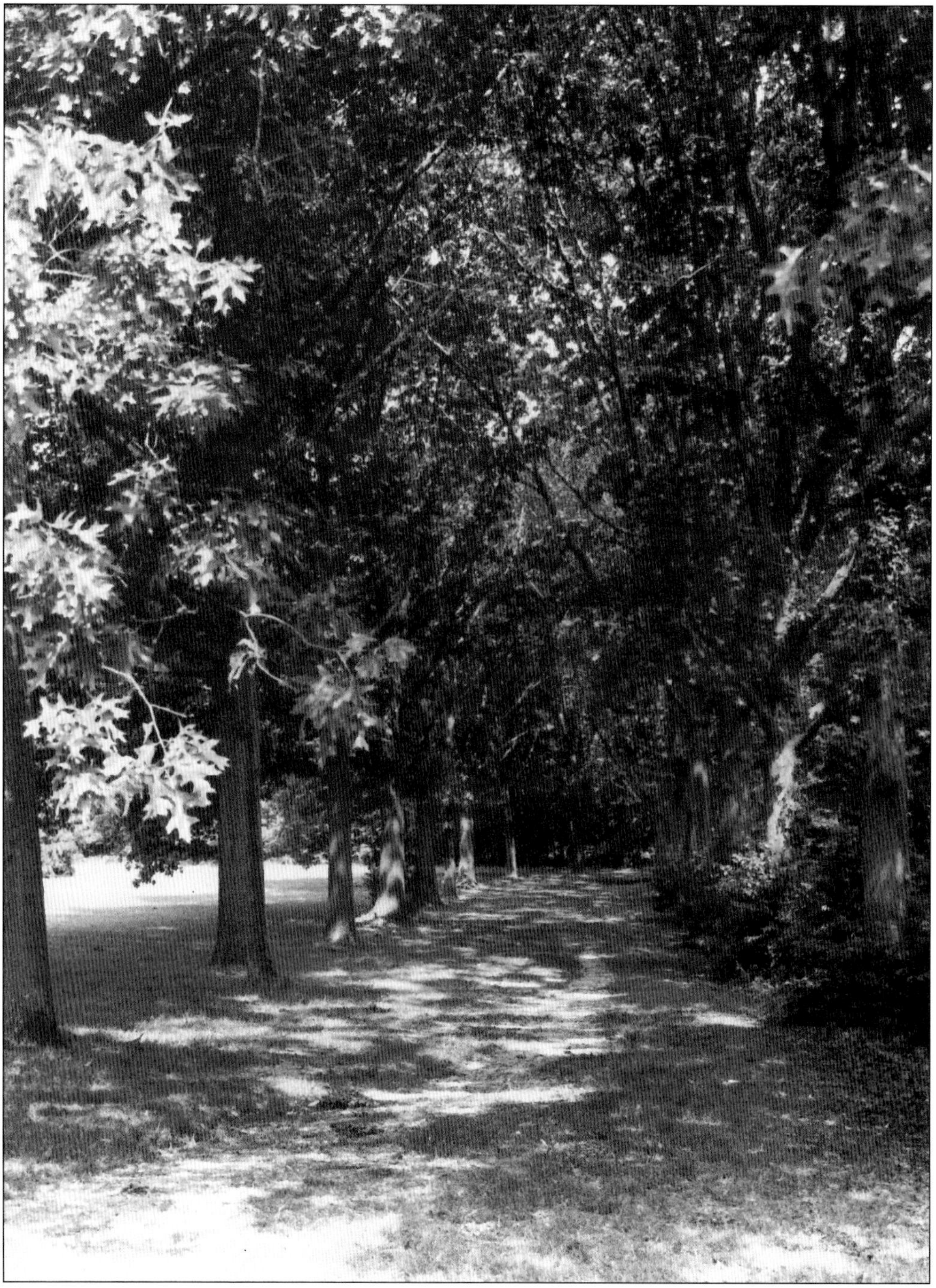

The tree-lined drive into the country estate of Peter F. Collier, magazine and school book publisher, at the foot of Byrne's Lane. It used to be lined with gas lamps. Collier, who once studied for the priesthood, was the first contributor to the building fund for St. Dorothea's Roman Catholic Church. He was born in Ireland in 1849 and came to America when he was age seventeen. A watercress pond grew just outside the drive. It was eventually filled in, and evergreens grow there now.

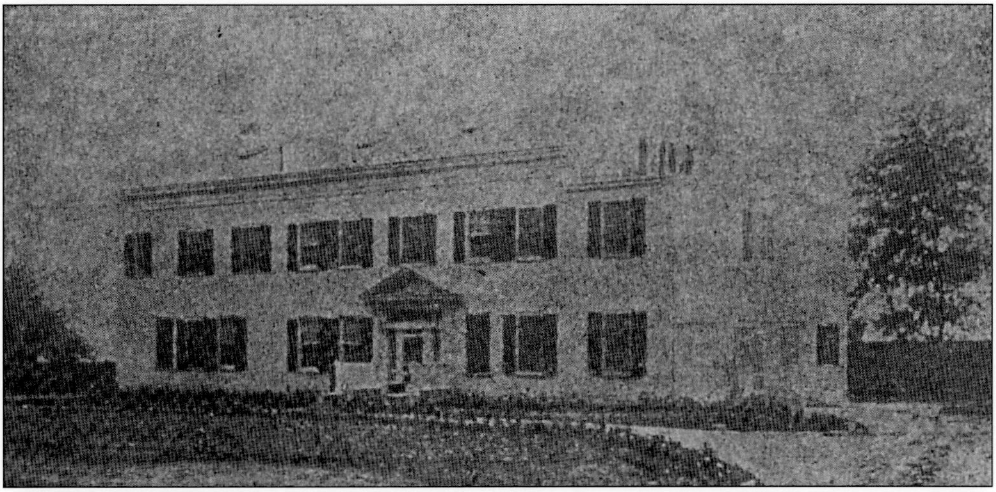

Collier's house after it was moved from his country estate to Byrne's Lane between Lafetra Avenue and Shubert Place. A row of Cape Cod homes occupies the land today.

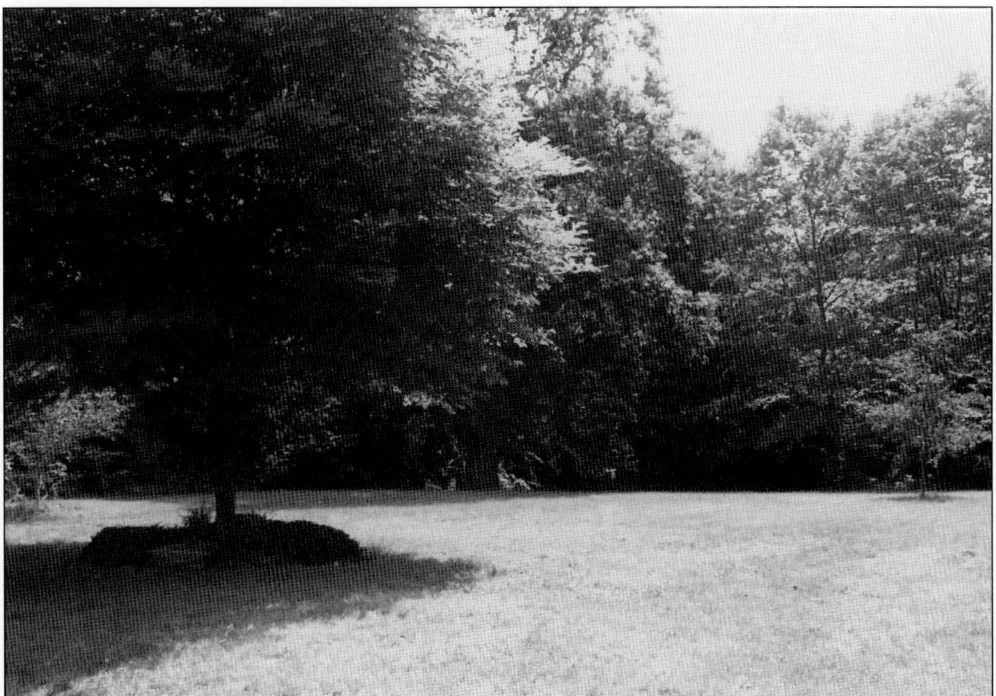

The original site of Collier's house is today occupied by the F. Bliss Price Arboretum, named after Eatontown's first Democratic mayor, who served between 1949 to 1960. The tree in the lower left was planted in honor of Eva Falkenburg, Eatontown's long-time Registrar of Vital Statistics.

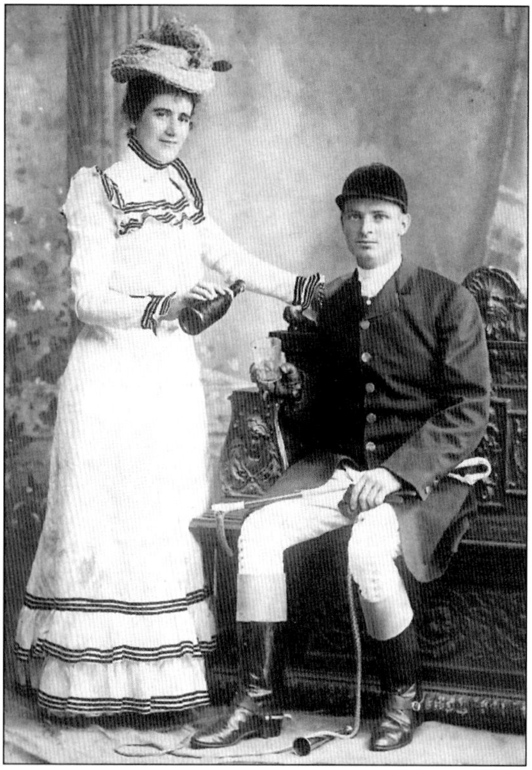

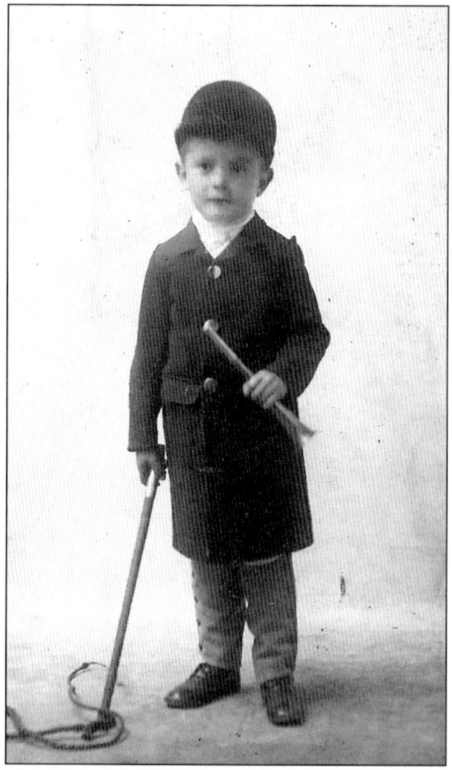

Left: Helena and Edgar Caffyn, who was head huntsman and a horse trainer for Collier, *c*. 1900. The Canadian-born Helena brooked no nonsense: she was known to have scolded Mark Twain, a guest of Collier's, when he flicked ashes on the parlor rug.
Right: Edwin Caffyn, their son, about 1908.

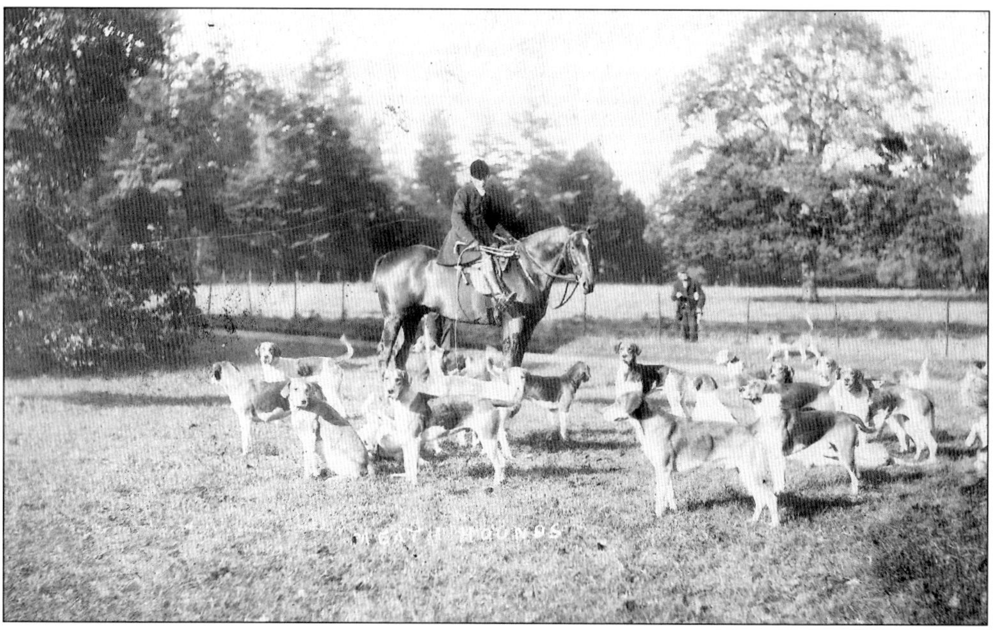

A horse and hounds on the Collier estate in a section of the village known as Chestnut Grove.

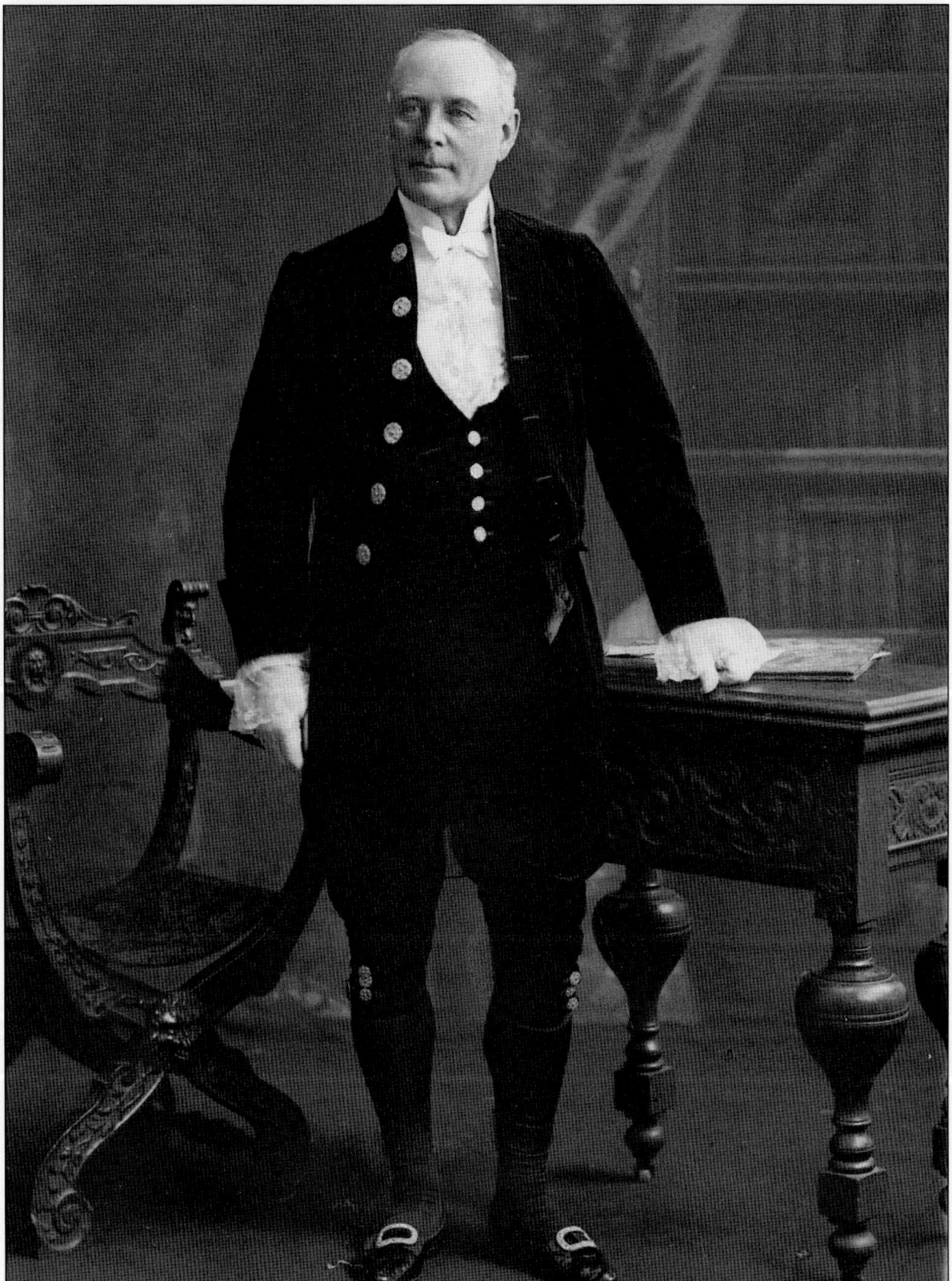

Collier, who launched *Collier's Weekly* in 1896, was known as an "out-of-doors" man. For years he was master of the Meadowbrook Hunt on Long Island and later was active in New Jersey hunting clubs that included rides in the North American Phalanx in Colts Neck. He was also a polo enthusiast.

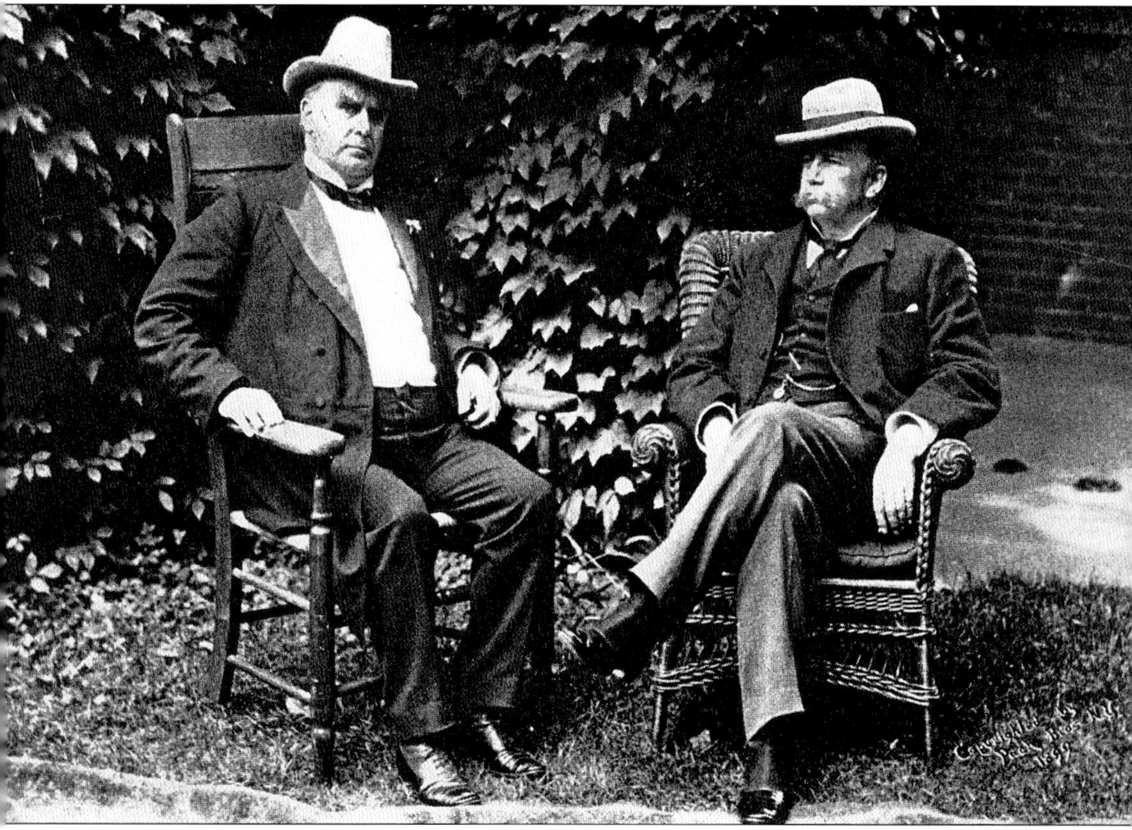

President William McKinley (left) and Vice President Garret A. Hobart (right) in the late summer of 1899, at Normanhurst, Hobart's summer home in Eatontown Township's seashore village of West Long Branch.

Hobart was born in 1844 on the north side of Broadway near Oceanport Avenue in West Long Branch, and he grew up in Paterson.

While in office in Washington he maintained a summer home on the northeast corner of Cedar and Norwood Avenues on what had been a colonial farm. Normanhurst was described as "commodious, the grounds were ample and well shaded . . . (and Hobart) fed the goldfish swimming in the pool on the grounds. He knew them separately, and gave to each one the name of some distinguished friend."

In his biography of the 24th president of the United States, David Magie also described the Jersey Shore as "thronged with people seeking the relief of ocean breezes from the heat of adjoining cities."

Hobart came here one last time on August 25, 1899. He died in November in Paterson, a scant two years in office.

Normanhurst was destroyed by fire in 1902.

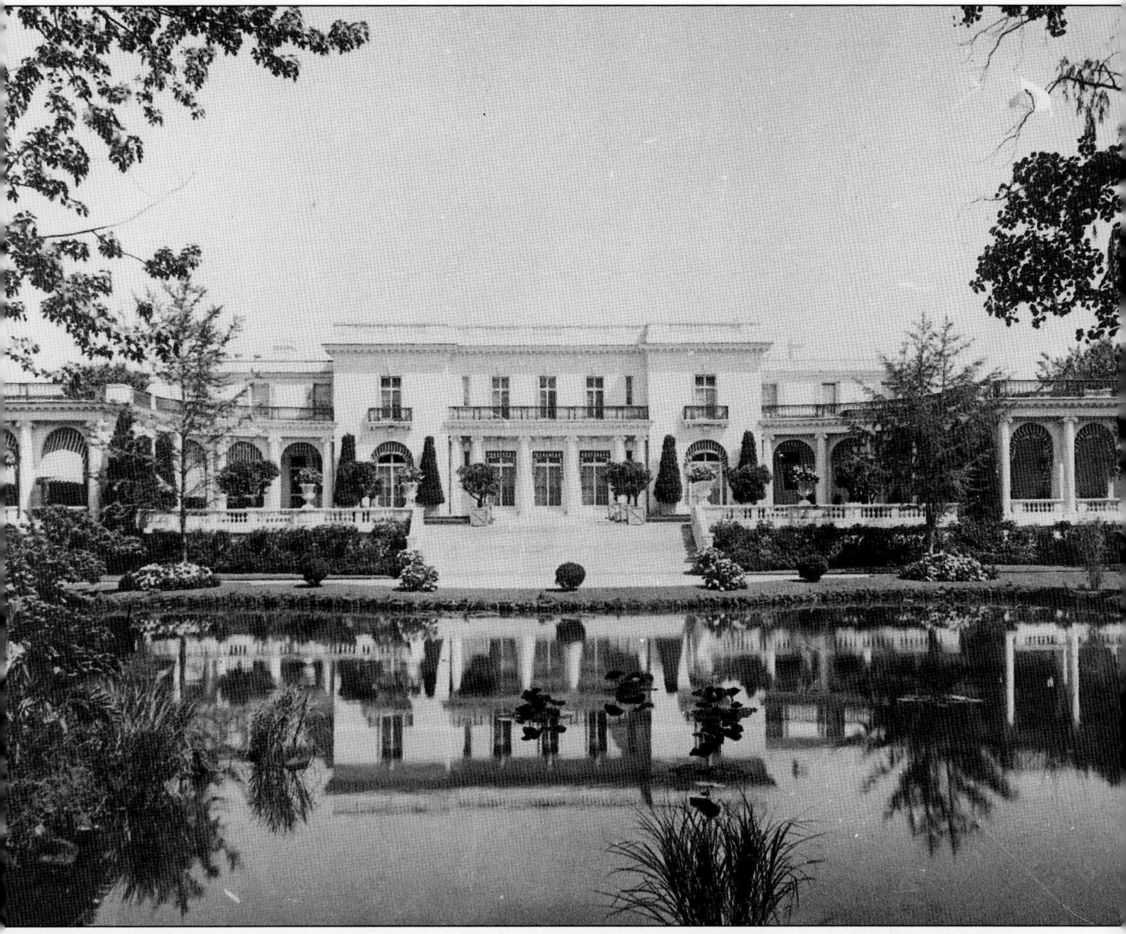

New York philanthropists Murry and Leonie Guggenheim subsequently bought Hobart's property. Between 1903 and 1905 they had a thirty-five-room French renaissance mansion built by the architectural team of Carrere and Hastings. This design, based on the Grand Trianon at Versailles, won them the gold medal of the New York Chapter of the American Institute of Architects. They went on to design the New York Public Library.

This photograph of the 9-acre estate and "cottage" was taken about 1920. The Guggenheims summered here for more than fifty years, and would frequently arrive from New York in a caravan of four limousines.

In 1960 the Guggenheim Foundation donated the mansion, worth 1.2 million dollars, to what was then Monmouth College, a private four-year institution that began as a night school convening in Long Branch High School. Ten thousand residents streamed through the estate the day the college received title to the property. Shortly thereafter, renovation began, and on September 24, 1961, it was formally dedicated as a library.

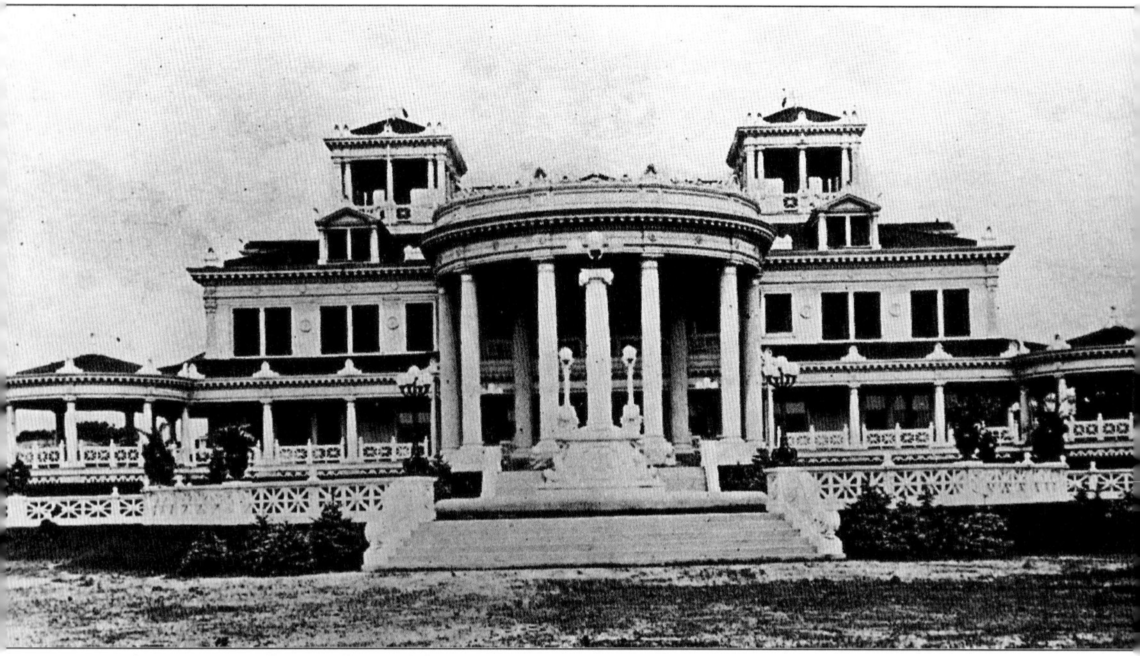

John H. McCall, president of the New Jersey Life Insurance Co., built a fifty-two-room colonial frame mansion on the site of the old Hulick farm on the southwest of Cedar and Norwood Avenues in 1903, when he was still summering with his family in Allenhurst. The architect was Henry E. Cregier. McCall called the estate Shadow Lawn. He died in 1905.

In 1908, West Long Branch voters decided to unify their rather large property tax base and ceded from Eatontown Township. Regardless, some estates continued to identify their locations as Long Branch, a resort popular with New York's entertainers, and a keen competitor to Asbury Park for vacationers' summer money.

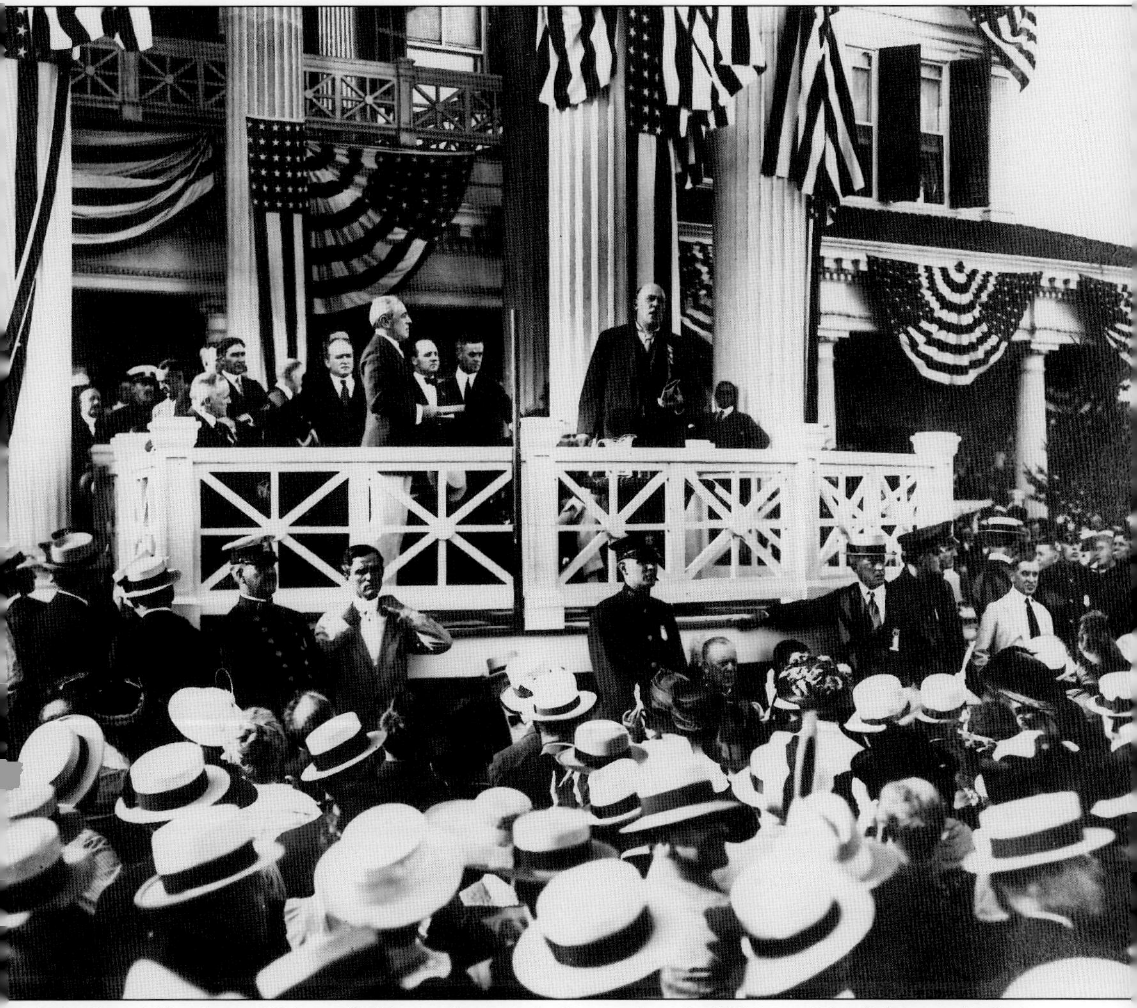

President Woodrow Wilson (left) on the porch September 2, 1916, as Olie Johnson (right) officially notified him of the Democratic Party's nod for his re-election bid.

The wooden summer White House burned to the ground on January 7, 1927. It took weeks to sort through the ash for all the gold melted from the plumbing fixtures.

On its site today, a new Versailles-style mansion, built by yet another department store millionaire, is the administrative offices for the newly named Monmouth University.

DOTS and DASHES

A medium to spread cheer and carry useful and interesting items of information.

Published Weekly by the Y. M. C. A. at Camp Alfred Vail, New Jersey

Vol. 2 — **Wednesday, August 28, 1918** — **No. 10**

Boxing Ring Is Broken In.

Wednesday afternoon the outdoor boxing ring was broken in and ten lively bouts were pulled off. The timekeeper was Hallenbeck, physical director of the Y., and the referee was Kurzman, J. W. B, representative of the camp. The seconds and trainers and corps of rubbers and towel swingers were too numerous to mention—and we don't know their names anyhow.

The first bout was between Hague, 7th Battn., and Stone, of the same outfit, and was declared a draw after three rounds of milling. But No. 2, resulted in a decision in favor of Ross, 13th Service Co., over Ferris, 418th Battn. Strauss put 'em on for a few rounds with Dowling, and Dowling finally said boxing in the hot sun was too much fun for the money, and quit. Nobody was hurt and they separated good friends.

Simons, Co. E, 418, was faced by Hyde, Co. D, same outfit, and if our memory serves correctly, after a few swings and a little dancing around, one of these gladiators stopped, and began looking around on the floor, diligently. "Whatta you lookin' for?" referee asked. "D'you think this here is a four-leaf-clover party, or what?" "I'm a-lookin' for me tooth!" They all hunted for a little for the absent canine ivory without success, and after sprinkling the floor again with a mouthful of saliva, and scraping with his hobnailed feet, the boxer minus the tooth put up his dukes again and they went at it. The decision went to Hyde. Banks and Ashcroft, both of Co. F., 7th Depot, put 'em on next and chased each other around the 24foot arena through three rounds, walloping each other betimes much to the delight of the big audience. The referee gave Banks the decision. Kozenewski and Aldridge, the former of 418 and the latter of the 7th. Depot, crossed mits for three rounds of fast milling.

Helpern and Miller, the first in the 13th Service Co., and the latter of the 7th Depot Co., put on the pillows and whacked away at each other's beaks for three rounds and when it was all over and the floor had been swept again, the referee could only say, "Draw!" The two Johns came next. John Dundee and John (Jack) Britton Cirndde—unless somebody made a mistake in the spelling, put up as good a scrap as their famous namesakes could have done, and the boys who looked on, made just as much noise. One of these Johns hurt his foot—for he was without adornment on his pedal extremities, and the bout was over.

Kid Yorke, 13th Service Co., was pitted against Slugger Deach, and the bout was so funny that it had to be stopped to save the sidesof the crowd who were laughing so much. Pat Crowe—we wonder if he had a relative in Coconino Co., Arizona, and Earl Swindler, both of the 7th Depot Battalion, stepped out next, and swung for each other's beaks at the gong. They danced around the ring for three rounds and the referee called the bout a draw.

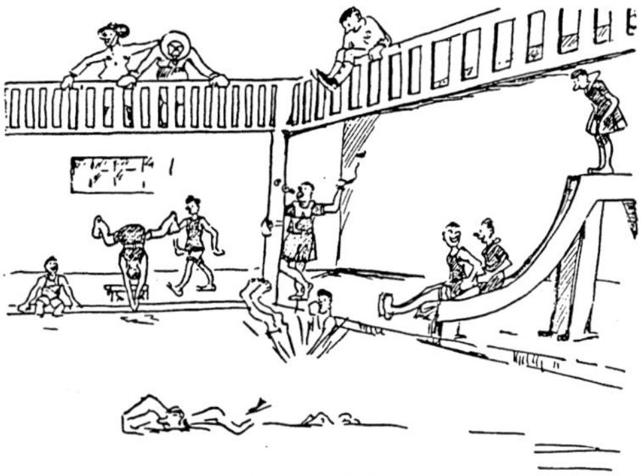

Caged Beach Nuts

Knights of Columbus Building Soon to be Built for Camp Vail.

For some time, our genial friend, Father Lacasse, who since last fall has been representing the Knights of Columbus in the camp, and teaching French, doing all sorts of odd jobs, has been expecting some announcement about a Knights of Columbus building. Wednesday afternoon, Mr. John O'Neil, State Deputy and especially interested in the Eastern District of the K. of C. work, came in and said they were soon to have a building. A site was selected, near the main gate and it is expected that the ground will soon be broken. We wonder if they will perpetuate the memory of our brother, by calling his new building, "Castle Lacasse." If they should make so bold as to ask us, we would make that suggestion.

Camp Vail will be provided with places of recreation within the camp during the winter. This new building is to be of the standard K. of C. type, usually found in camps. It will contain an auditorium, a stage—we are glad we got our's before Father Lacasse got his building, for he decorated our stage in great style—and there will be the usual activities of such places during the evenings.

"MR. LANGLY" ARRIVES.

A huge Hanley-Page airplane, driven by Captain Waller, Royal Flying Corps, of Great Brittain, landed at Camp Vail about 7 o'clock Tuesday night, after flying from the Standard aircraft factories, at Elizabeth. There were four passengers in the big plane. It has two of the great Liberty motors and immense wings. After a few days it will fly away again. Lt. Smythe piloted the big machine to the camp and looked after the comforts of the guests.

English is being taught every morning to many men who cannot read or write it, by Miss Margaret Donnan, in the Little School House, opposite the guard house. Miss Donnan is an experienced teacher, and the men have already begun to get a grip on our language.

Hearing that the boys needed music, Miss Beatrice MacCue sent a good-sized sheaf of good songs, the other day, and we will pass them along where they will do the most good.

AN UNIQUE SERVICE.

The Y. M. C. A. Building has had many kinds of services and meetings, both religious and secular, from an Officers' Meeting to a Naturalization Court, to all of which it has extended hearty welcome, but never has it had a meeting more representative of its true character than that held on Sunday morning last, when soldiers from the various organizations of the camp and of all Christian denominations joined in a union of the celebration of the Holy Communion under the leadership of ministers of different denominations. Mr. Lee, the Religious Work Director of the camp, himself a Presbyterian minister, had charge of the service. Other ministers taking part were the Rev. Charles F. McKoy, Pastor of the First Baptist Church of Long Branch, the Rev. D. L. Parsons, Pastor of the Shrewsbury Presbyterian Church, the Rev. Alfred Duncombe, Pastor of the Reformed Church of Long Branch, and the Rev. Wallace Radcliffe, D. D., Pastor of the New York Avenue Presbyterian Church of Washington, D. C., the church that Lincoln attended. Absence from town prevented ministers from other Churches from joining in the service. Dr. Radcliffe preached the sermon, which was a stirring appeal for loyalty to Christ and the full appropriation of the sacrificial spirit of His Cross. The whole service was most impressive and all who had part in it went away with a new appreciation of the truth of which we sing in our great battle hymn, "Onward, Christian Soldiers."—

"We are not divided,
All one body we,
One in charity."
One in cahrity."

A feature of the service was the singing of Miss Dorothy Linson, of Shrewsbury, who rendered very beautifully the hymn, "Just As I Am," to the music of "The Rosary."

The preacher next Sunday morning at the nine o'clock service will be the Rev. Alfred Duncombe, of Long Branch.

We want a wedding in the building. Engagements have been made in it many times, men have been naturalized in it, and many other unusual things have been done in it. Mr. Lee and Father Lacasse promise to tie the knot, and we will furnish the setting and try and corral the music. Step lively, gents, and get the first chance!

The Camp Vail YMCA published a weekly newsletter. In the August 28, 1918 edition it was reported that "a Hanely-Page airplane, driven by Captain Waller, Royal Flying Corps of Great Brittain, landed at Camp Vail about 7 o'clock Tuesday night after flying from the Standard Aircraft Factories, at Elizabeth."

Five

Fort Monmouth

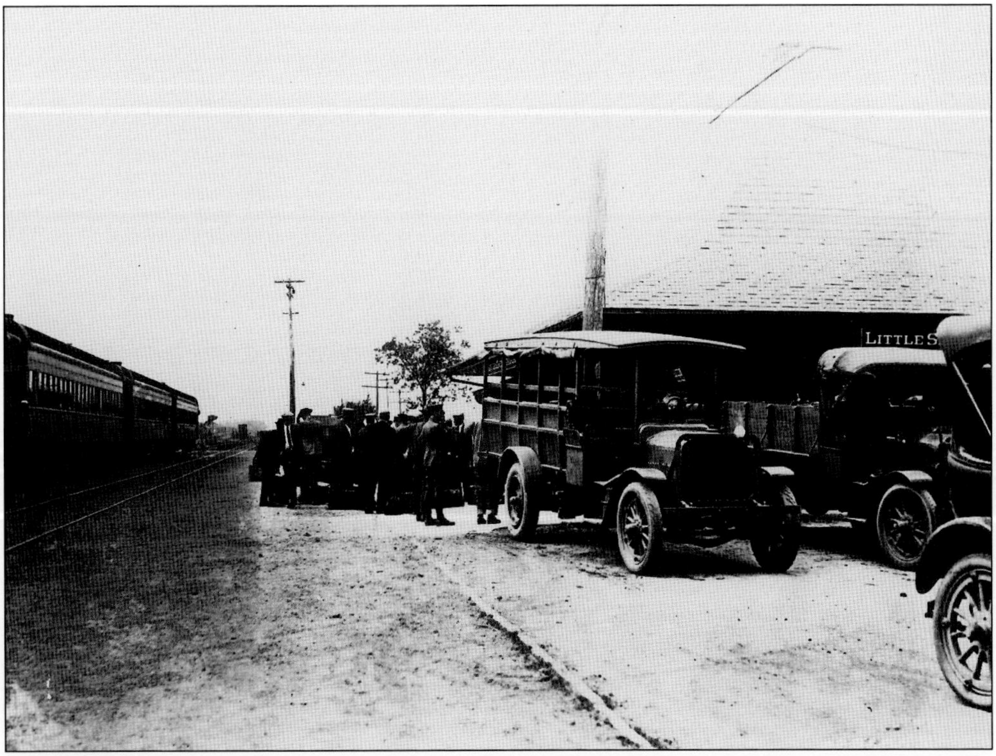

By 1917, at the outbreak of World War I, there was already a Signal Corps Camp in Little Silver when the War Department bought the abandoned Monmouth Park property for a new training camp. It was named for Alfred Vail, Samuel F.B. Morse's partner in developing the telegraph. Vail's son Theodore was a CEO of AT&T Co., and raised two volunteer battalions of telegraph and telephone operators and repairmen to serve in the European theater. In the above photograph, ROTC students are arriving at the Little Silver Train Station in 1921.

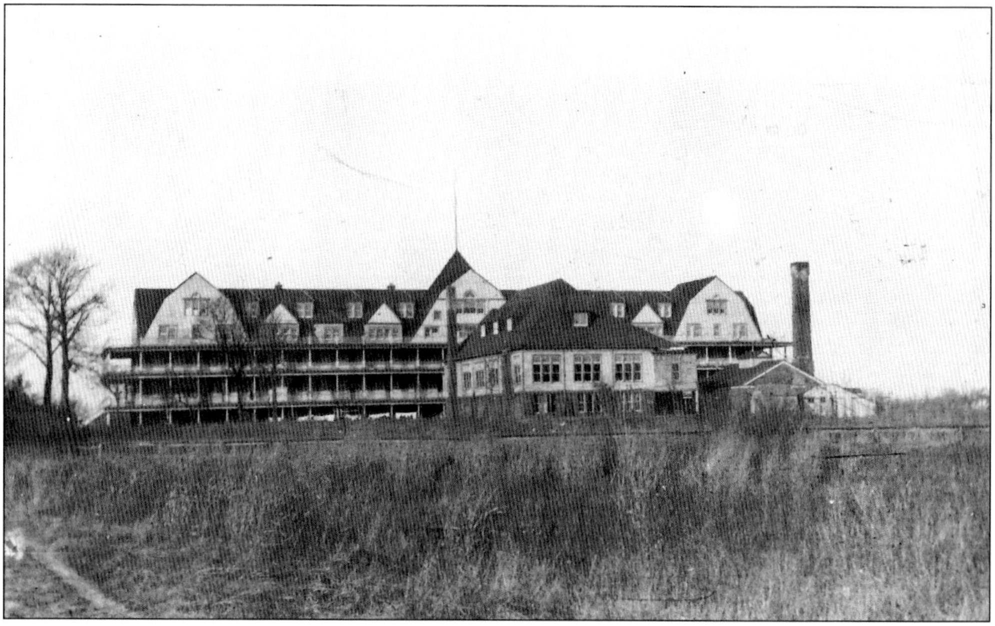

To serve the new racetrack clientele, the Monmouth Park Hotel was built in 1891 on 19 acres on the southeast side of Parker's Creek. It had 153 rooms, an electric elevator, and smoking and billiard rooms. It burned to the ground in 1915.

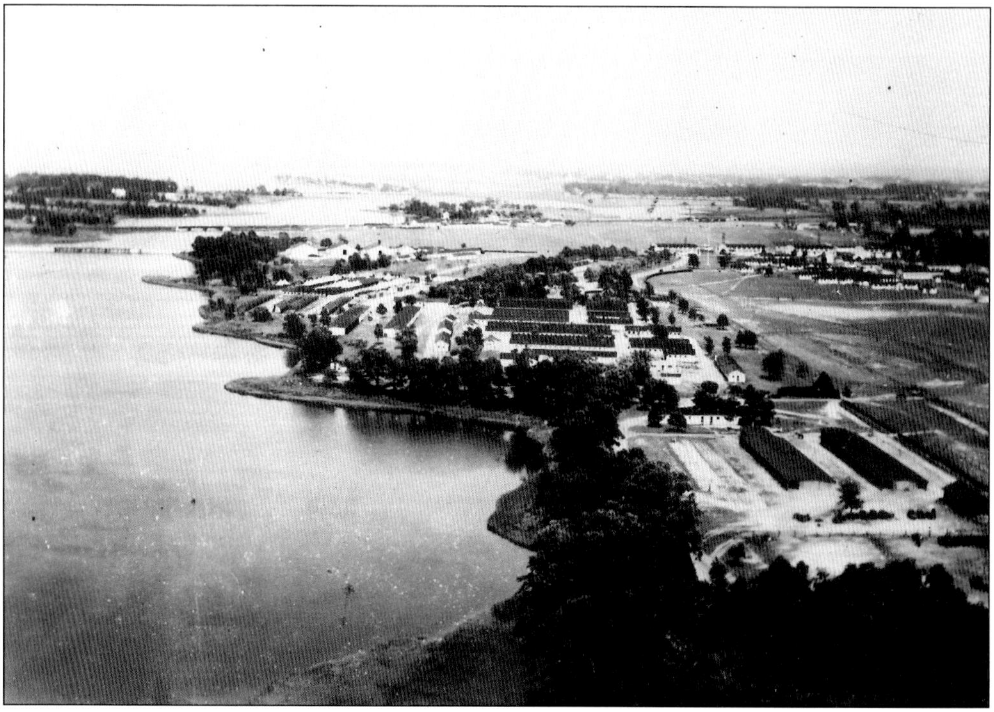

In this 1935 aerial view of Fort Monmouth, the hotel would have been located between the Oceanport Avenue bridge and the Central Jersey Railroad bridge in the top left. The aero squadron hangars can be seen in the top right in a horizontal line along Oceanport Avenue across from the entrance gate.

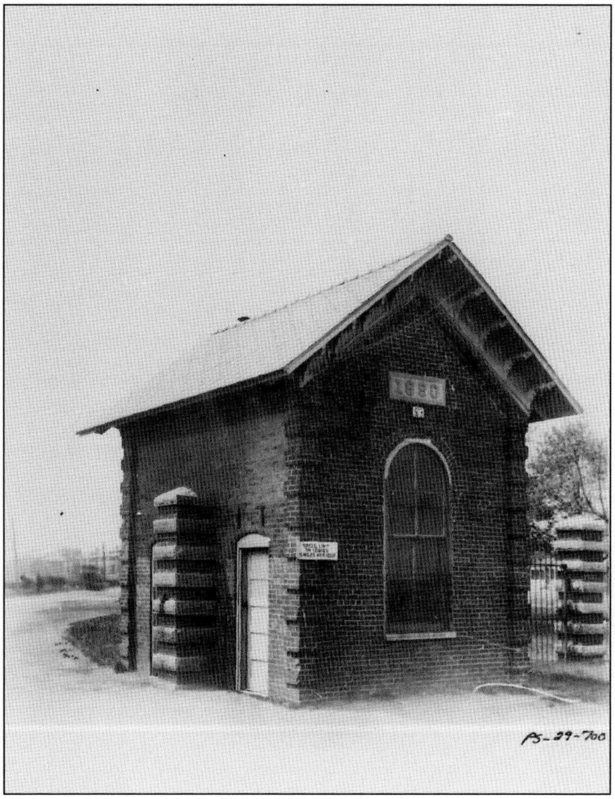

The brick 1890 ticket gatehouse to Monmouth Park off Oceanport Avenue was used as an entrance to Camp Vail, c. 1917.

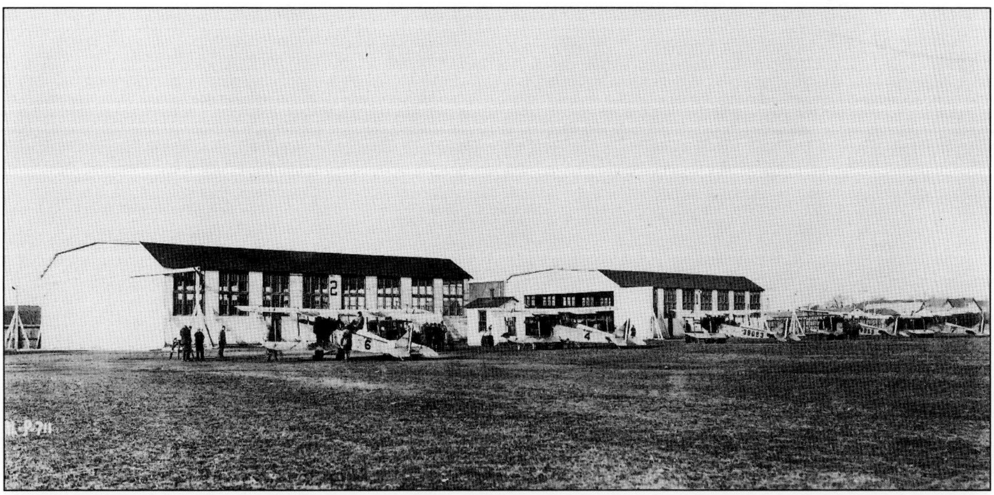

Hangars #1 and #2 at Camp Vail with aeroplanes of the 122nd Aero Squadron in front that included two DeHaviland 4s, nine Curtiss JN4-Hs, six Curtiss 4-6HOs, and three Curtiss NJ-4Ds.

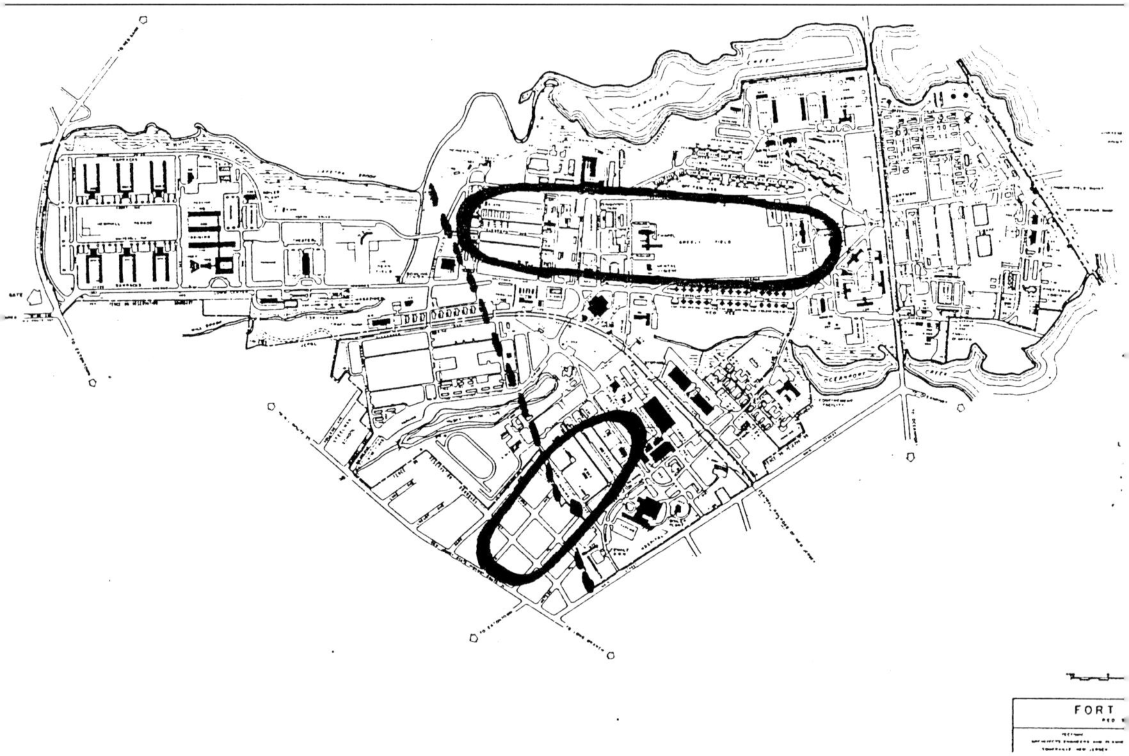

A present-day map of Fort Monmouth looking northeast. The small oval indicates the site of the first Monmouth Park track and steeplechase course; the larger oval, encompassing the post's Greely Field, indicates where the second track was built. The dotted line represents the approximate boundary between the villages of Eatontown and Oceanport.

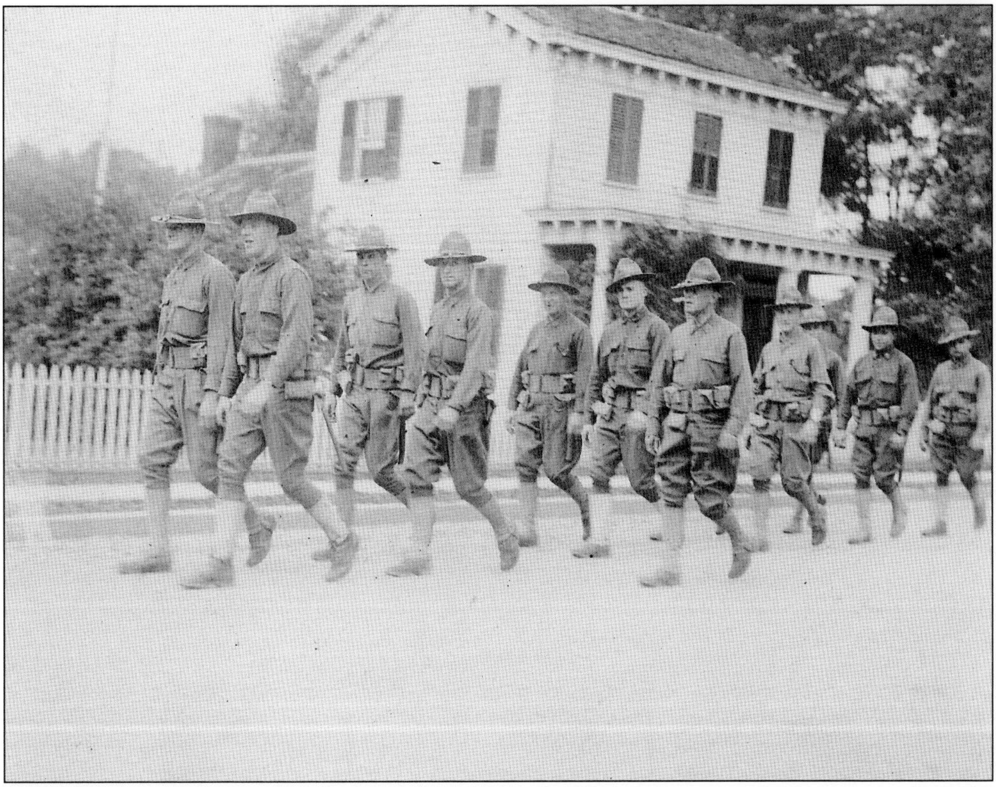

World War I soldiers marching west on Main Street in Oceanport towards Eatontown. In 1873 the house in the background was one of the properties belonging to T.T. Williams. It is located today near the intersection of Main Street and Oceanport Avenue.

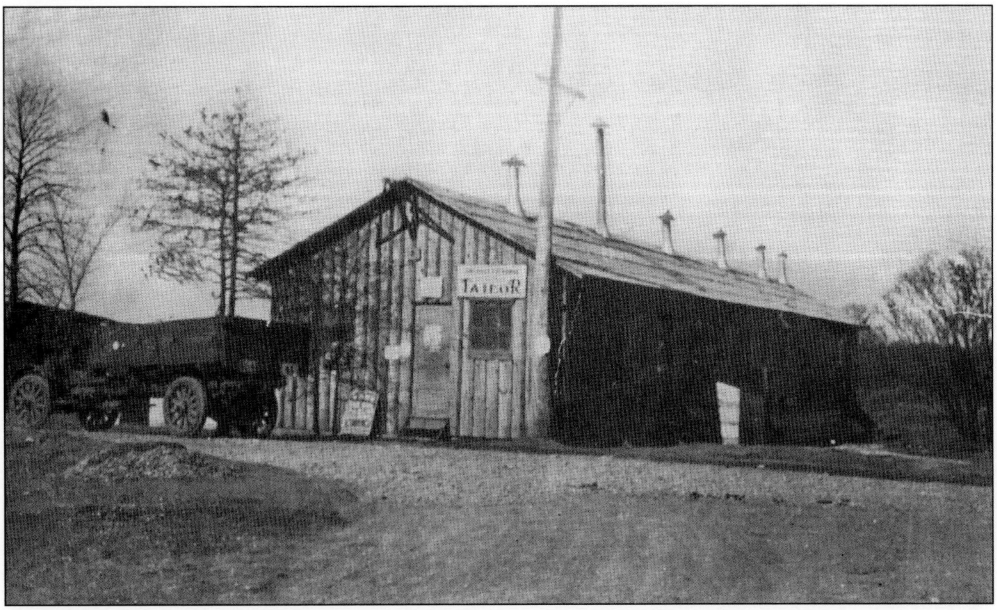

The Post Exchange in Camp Vail, *c.* 1918, where soldiers could buy toiletries, stationery, sweets, and periodicals.

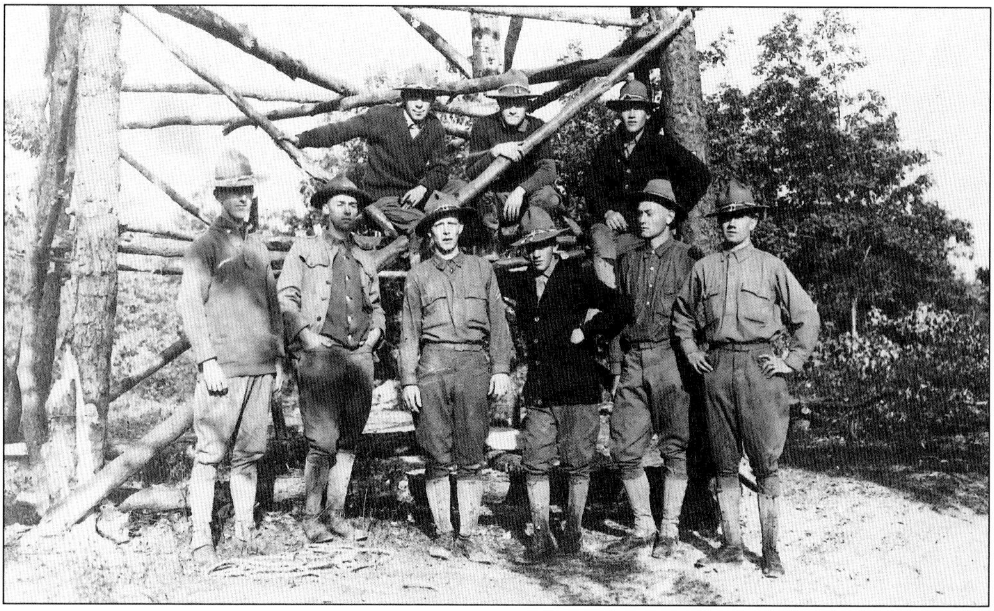

World War I soldiers posing at the base of the old racetrack viewing tower at Camp Vail. Joseph E. Carroll of Philadelphia is at the far left in the sweater.

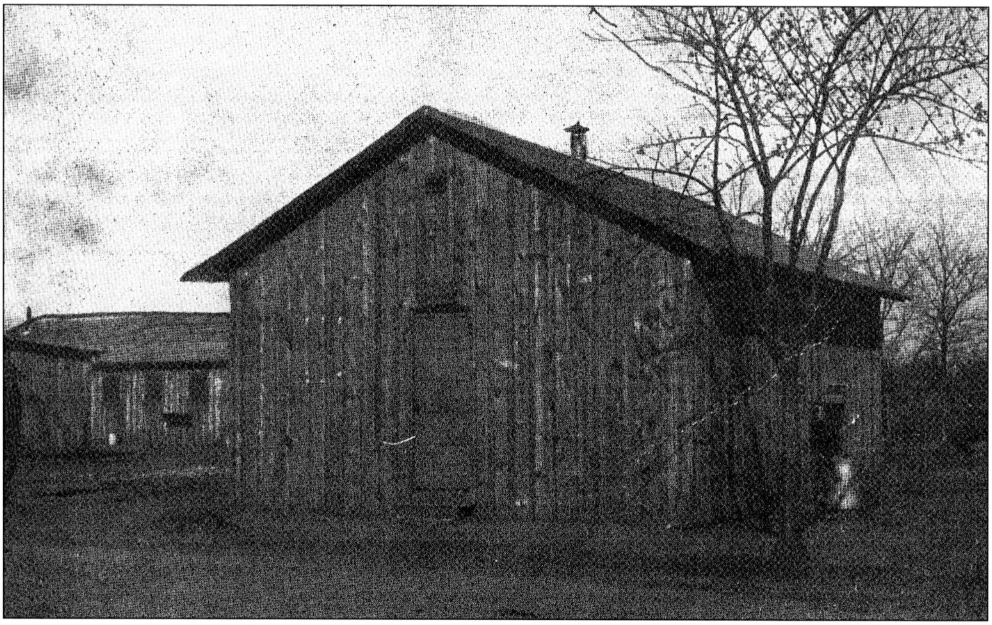

The Camp Vail Post Office.

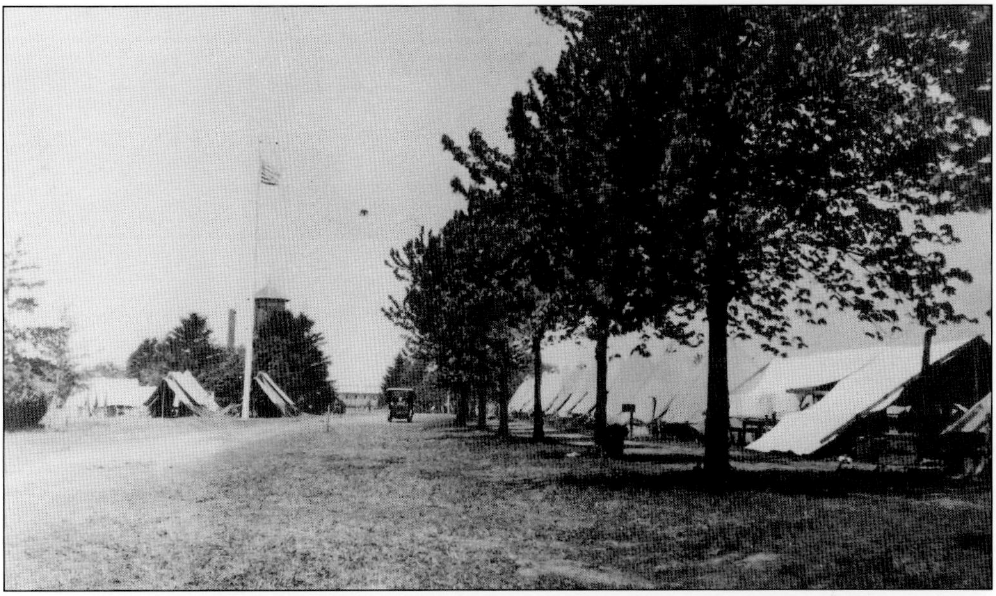

Company Street showing Company D, 2nd Telegraph Battalion, on August 2, 1917.

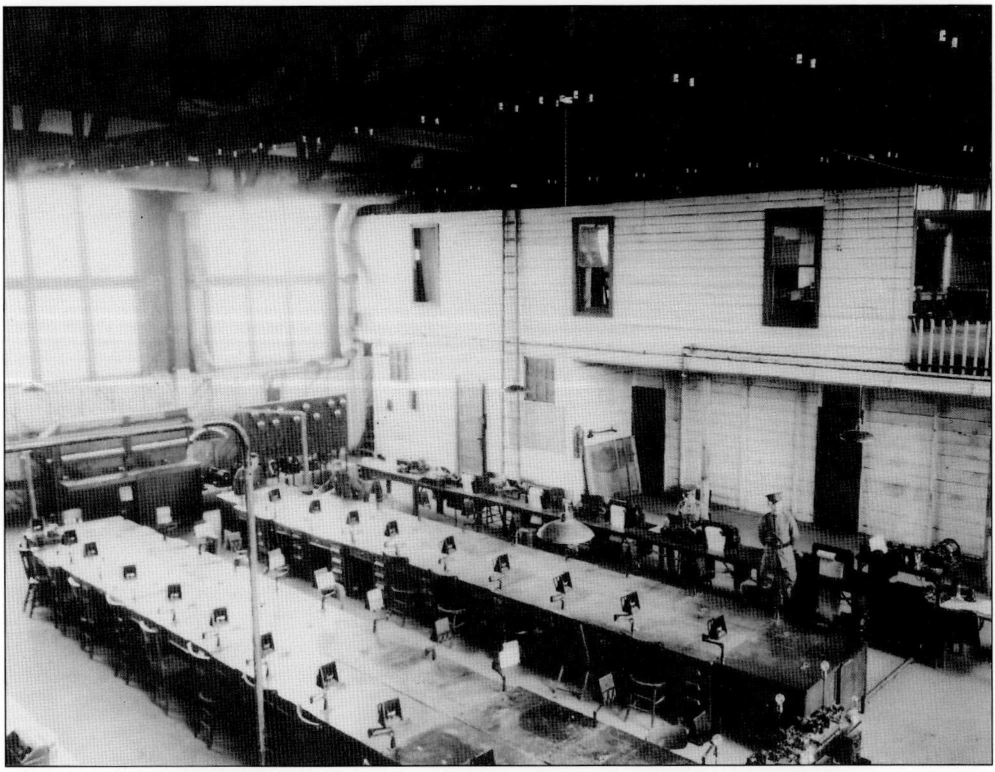

Captain John P. Ferriter stands in the telegraph classroom in Hangar 3 in 1921.

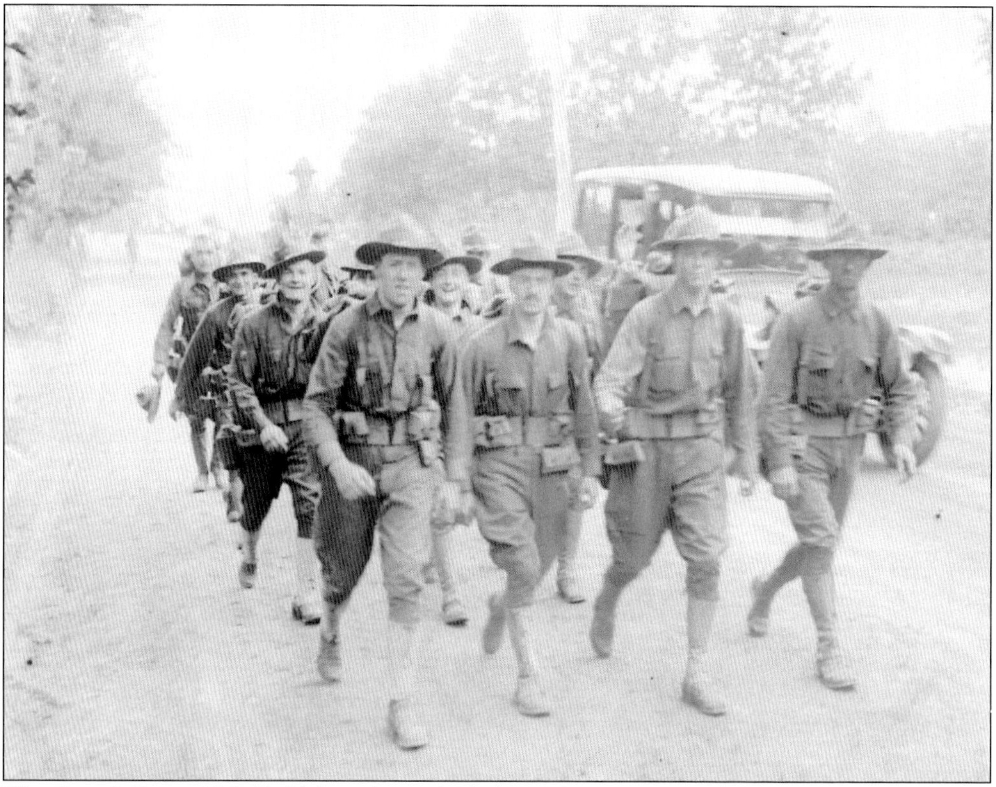

The Signal Corps 10th Field Battalion, Ambulance Division, marching north on Oceanport Avenue towards Little Silver.

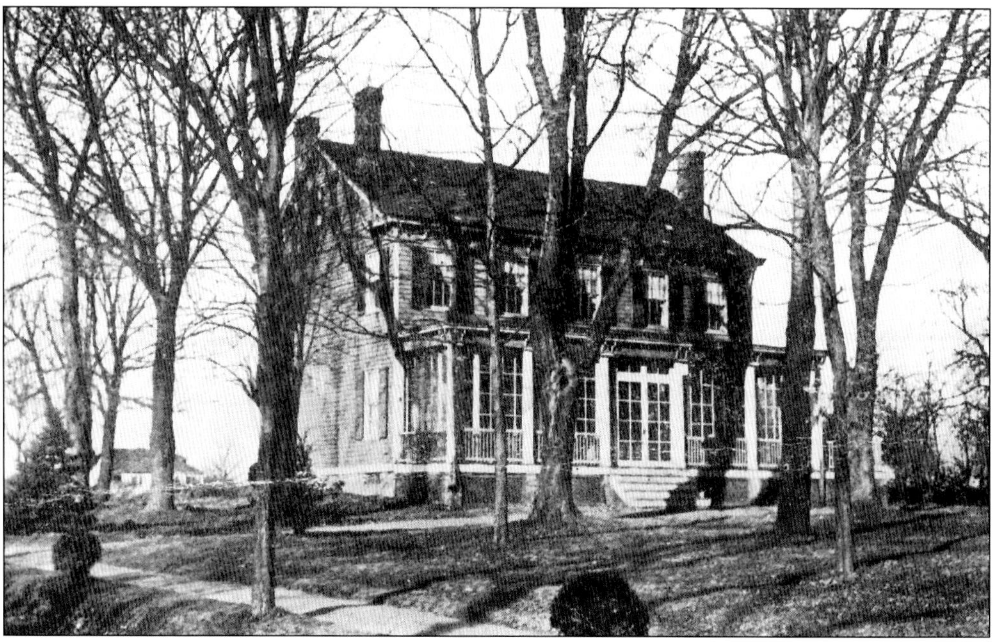

Camp Vail's Recreation House, *c*. 1917.

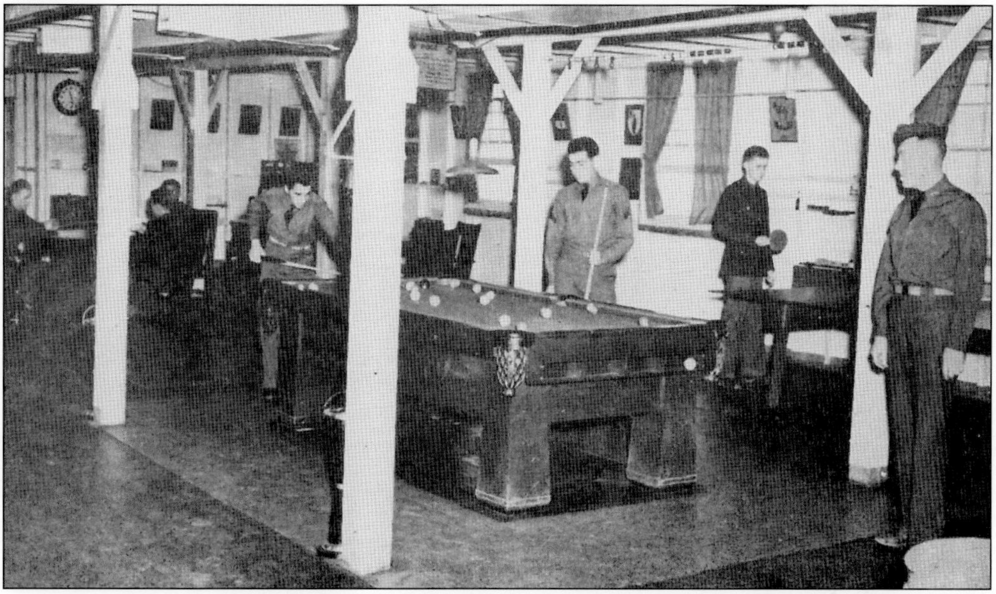

The game room inside Recreation House showing soldiers shooting billiards, playing table tennis, and cards.

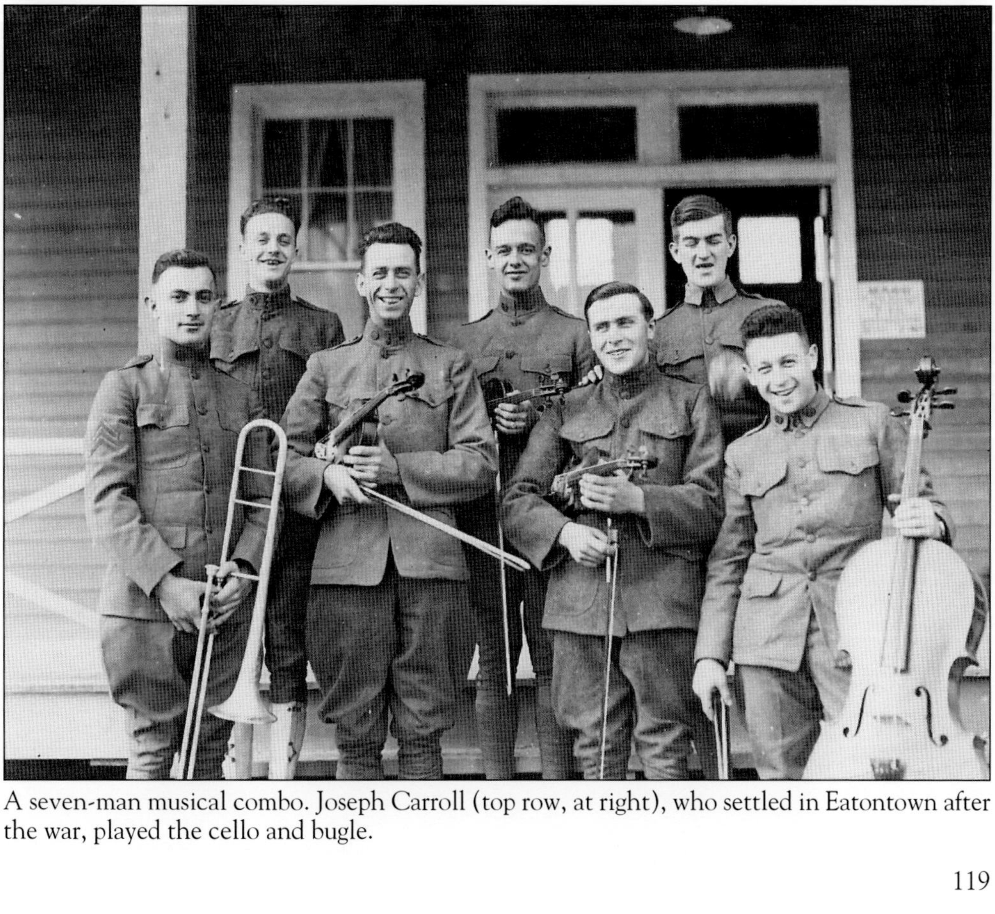

A seven-man musical combo. Joseph Carroll (top row, at right), who settled in Eatontown after the war, played the cello and bugle.

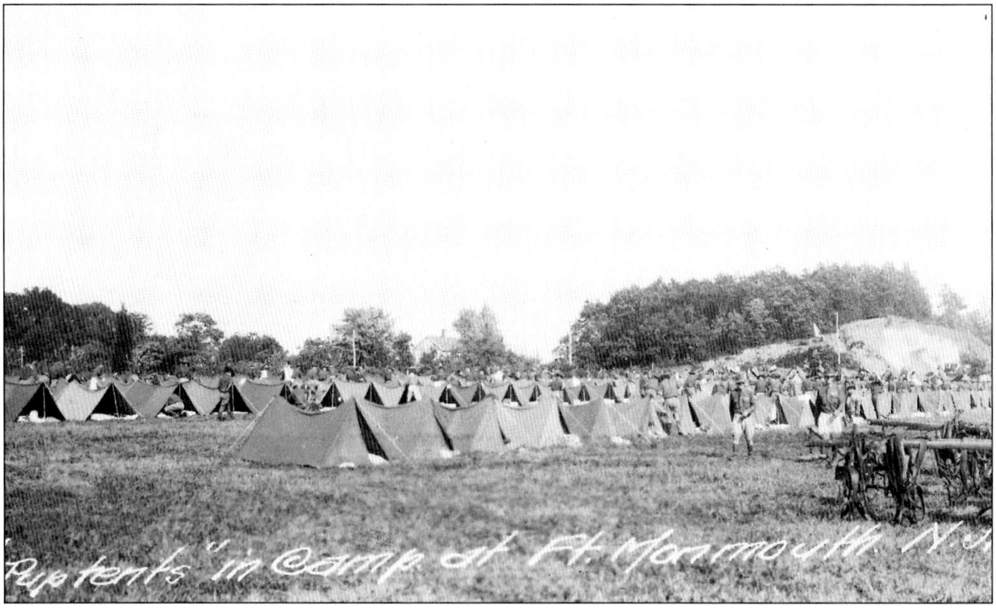

Early soldiers lived in pup tents until wooden barracks were built. In 1925, the War Department declared Camp Vail a permanent military post, naming Fort Monmouth after the pivotal American Revolutionary War battle held at Monmouth Courthouse, today the county seat of Freehold.

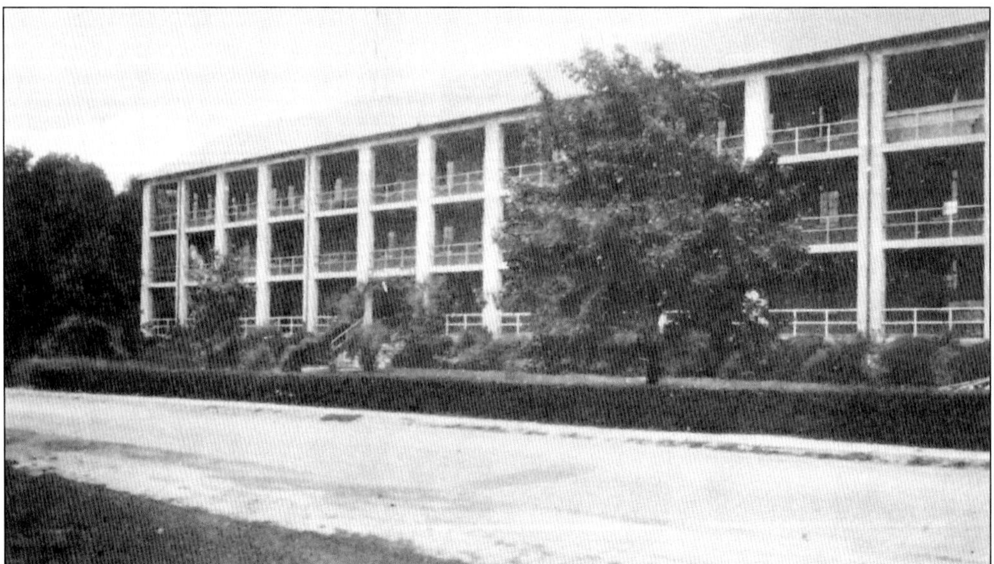
The new 51st Battalion brick barracks on Oceanport Avenue, a significant upgrade from tents and wooden army housing, c. 1930.

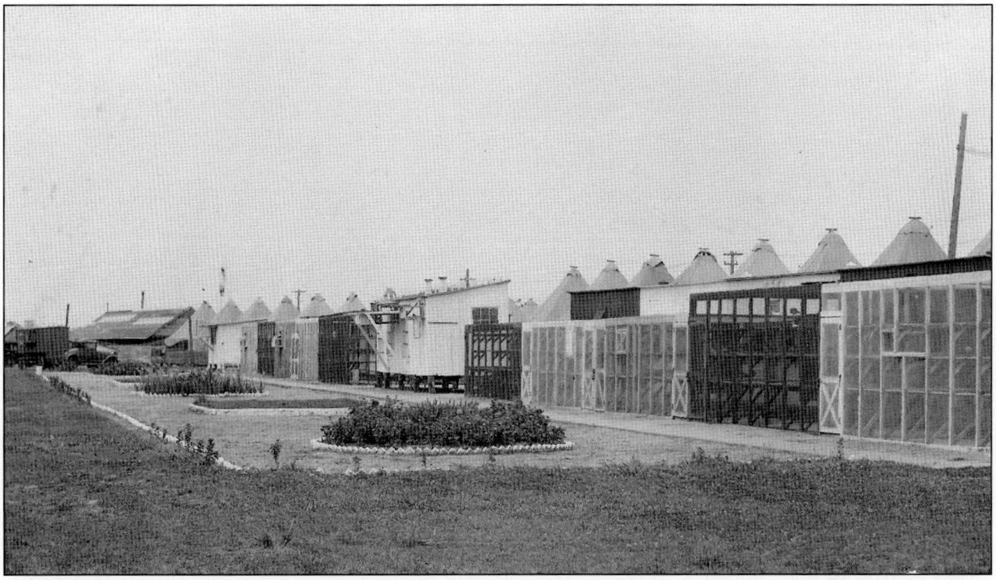

General John J. Pershing was so impressed by the Allied Forces' use of pigeons to communicate behind enemy lines that he requested a pigeon breeding and training section that eventually was set up at Camp Vail. It began operating in November 1917.

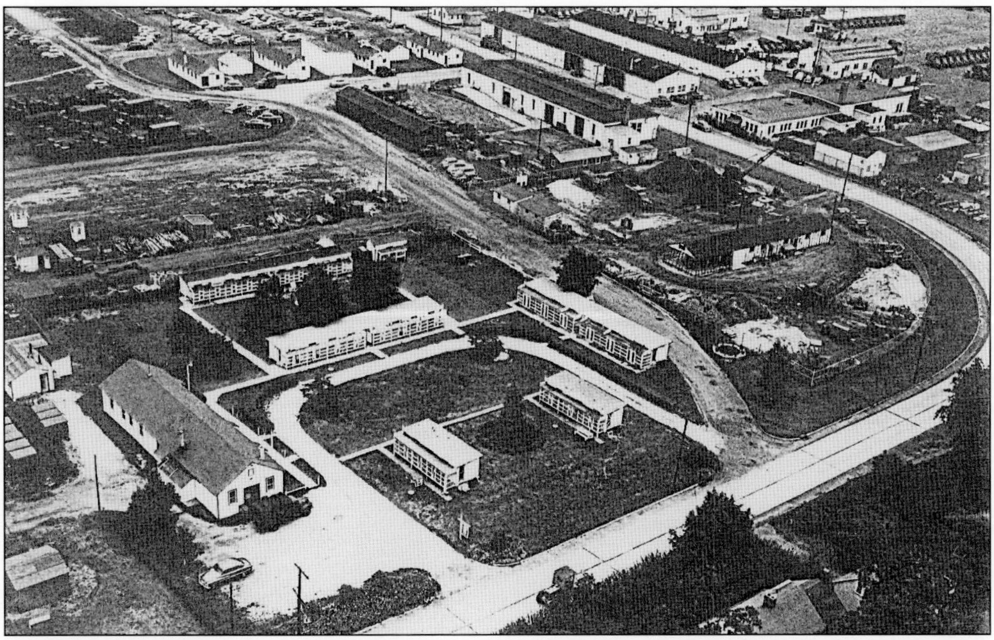

By 1925, there were seventy-five pairs of breeders, two flying lofts with one hundred birds for training and maneuvers, and a stationary loft with thirty long-distance flyers. This aerial view in 1950 also shows training lofts for two-way and night-flying pigeons.

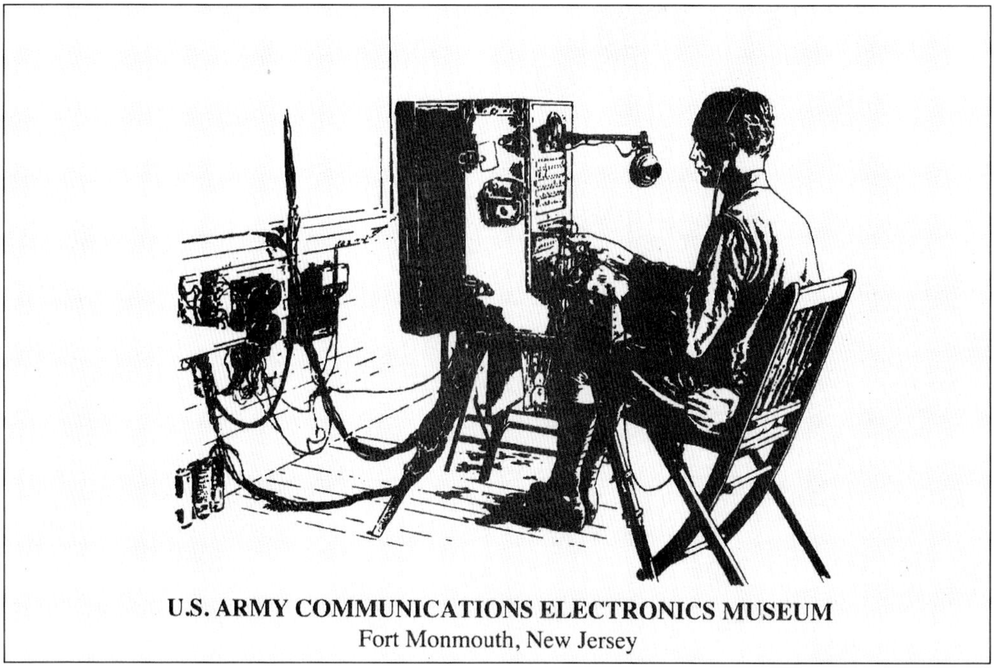

By 1935, research and development labs had gone up to handle the early work in radio detection and ranging, or RADAR, a new application for high-frequency radio. Walkie-talkies were first designed here and put to use during World War II.

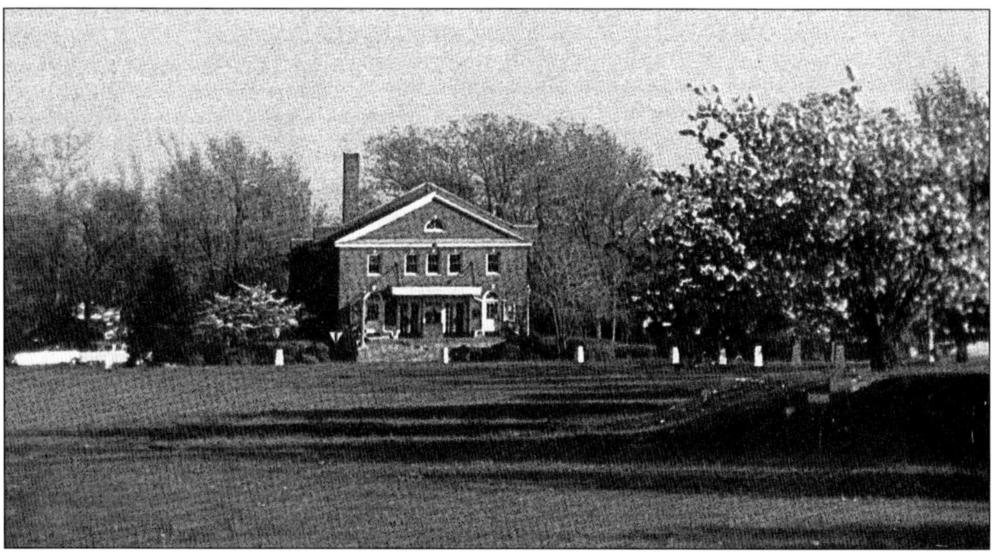

Major Benjamin Kaplan was a twenty-five year career engineer. A former theater building, Kaplan Hall is today the U.S. Army Communications Electronics Museum. Because of this army base's break-through achievements in communications research, the National Park Service has listed this museum as a maritime site on the New Jersey Coastal Heritage Trail.

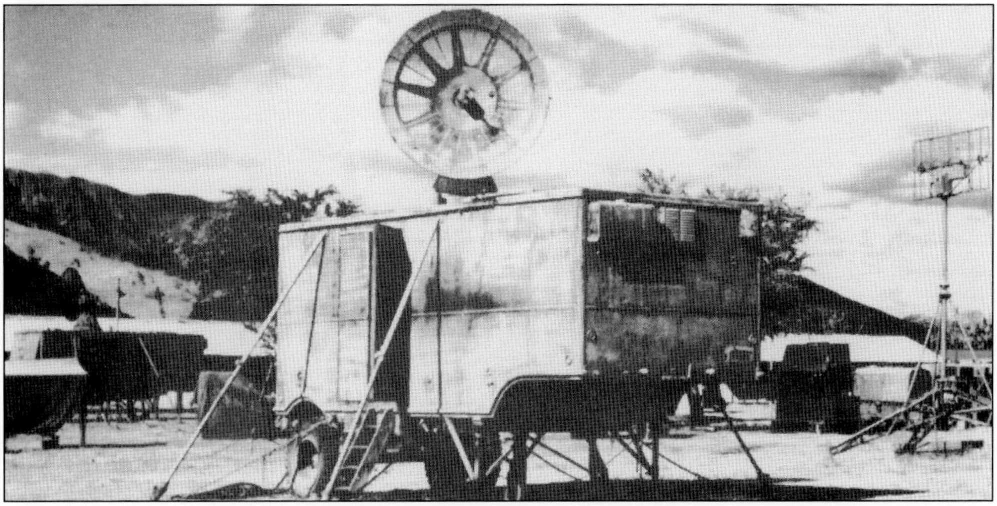

Electronics research at Fort Monmouth spawned a long list of "firsts," including: equipment used to bounce a radar signal off the moon in 1946; acoustic devices for long-range detection of nuclear explosions; radiation-resistant solar cells for outer space; weather-tracking devices in 1948; and the "talking" satellite that broadcast President Dwight D. Eisenhower's Christmas greetings to the world in 1958.

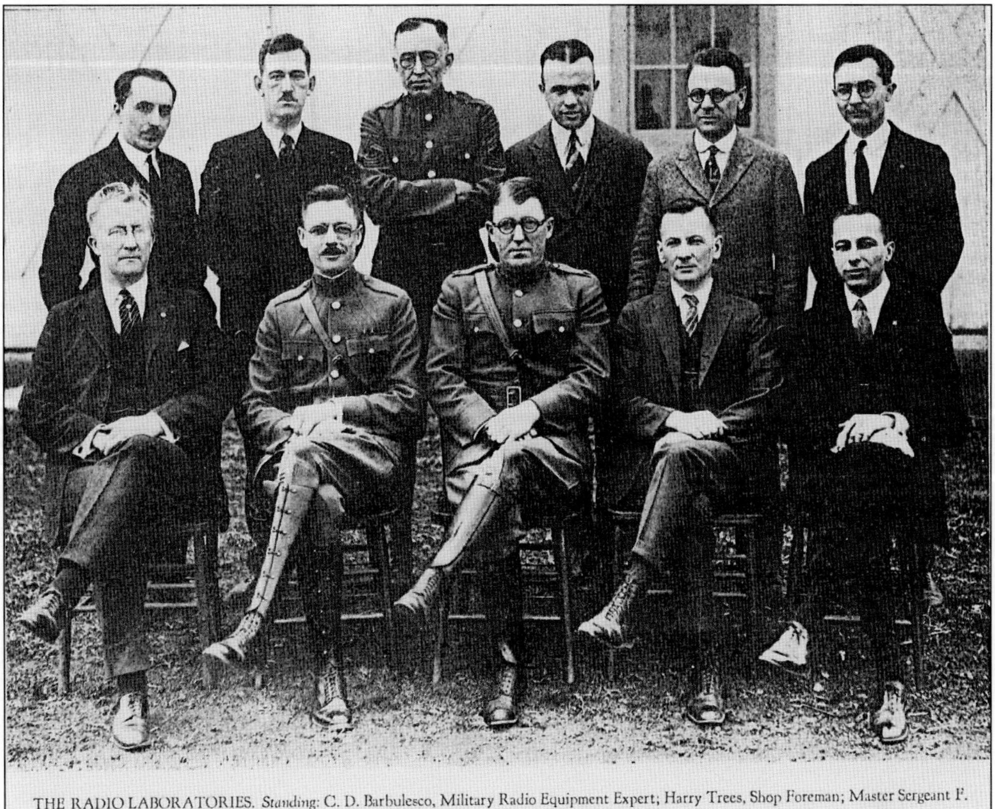

THE RADIO LABORATORIES. *Standing:* C. D. Barbulesco, Military Radio Equipment Expert; Harry Trees, Shop Foreman; Master Sergeant F. E. Stuard, S. C., Supply Sergeant; J. D. Sullivan, Chief Clerk; L. L. Millar, Chief Draftsman; W. L. Seibert, Specification Engineer.
Sitting: R. T. Kendall, Radio Engineer; 1st Lieutenant John J. Downing, S. C., Supply Officer; Major F. D. Applin, S. C. (C. A. C.), Officer in Charge; Jackson H. Pressley, Chief Engineer; Louis McC. Young, Engineer in Charge of Research Section.

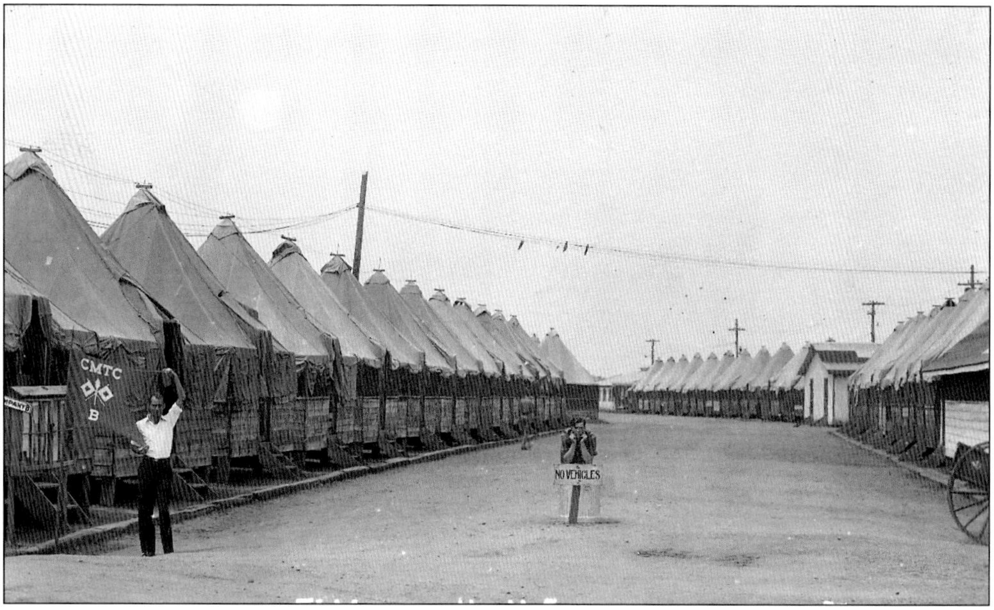

Company B was housed in tents on platforms, a definite step up from the pup tents of World War I.

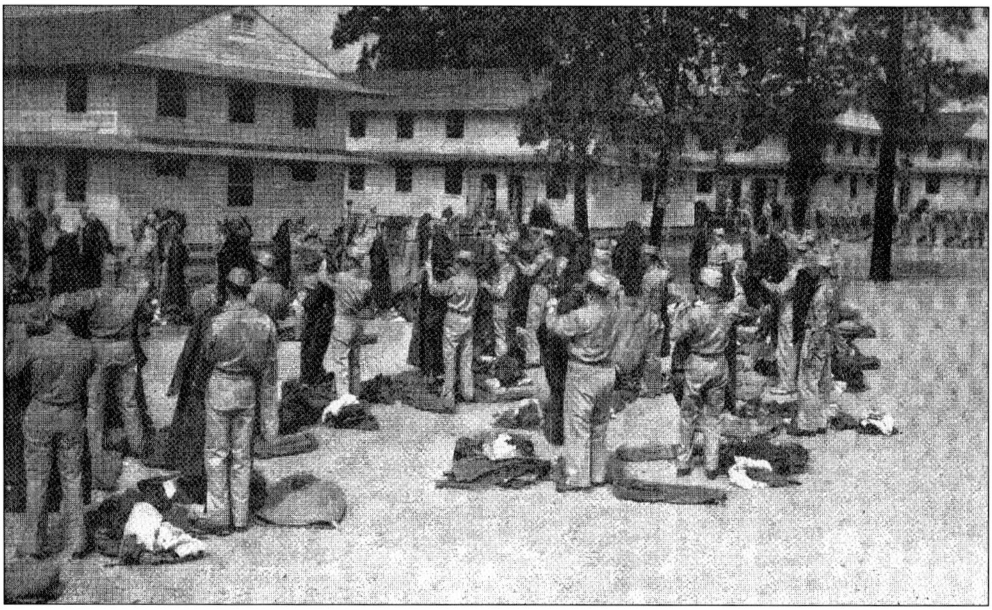
Soldiers receiving their initial clothing issuance, and being shown how to fold properly their uniforms and pack their duffel bags. In 1928 the first permanent structures (the barracks) went up.

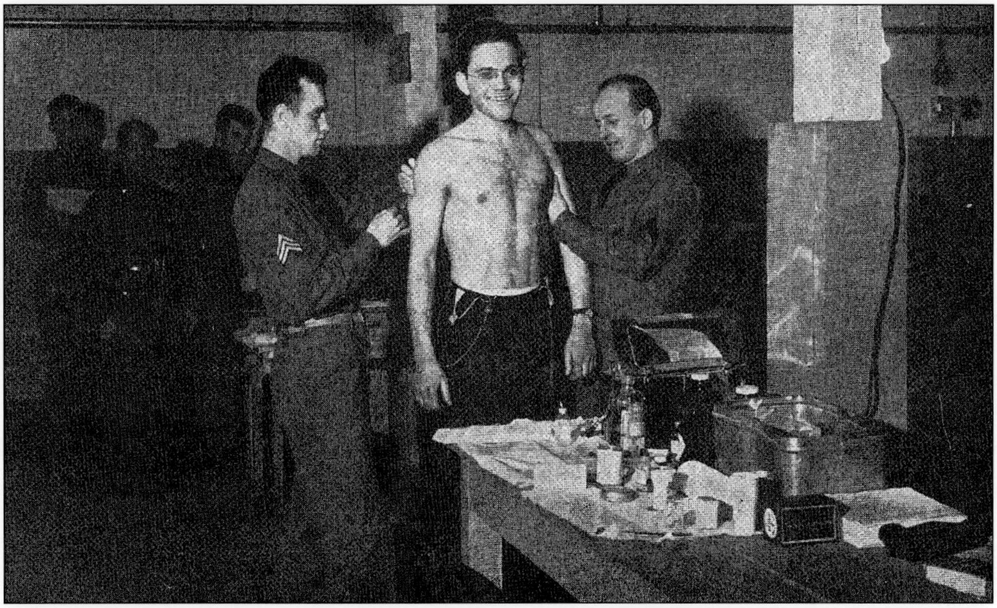

Every soldier's favorite rite-of-passage: inoculations and vaccinations.

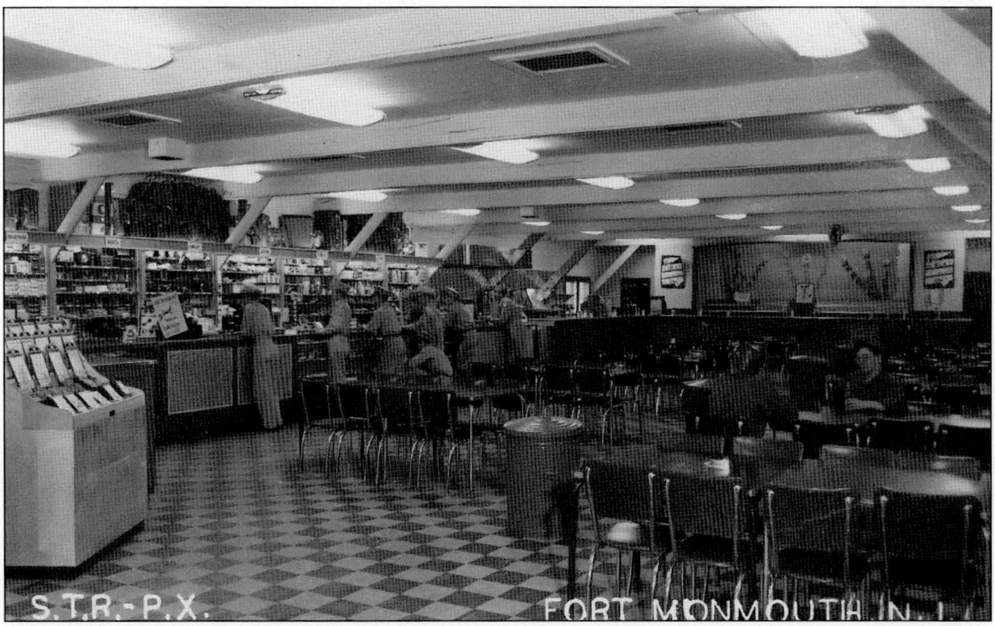

The interior of the Post Exchange (PX) where soldiers could make purchases, come and relax, and maybe order an ice cream soda, *c*. 1949.

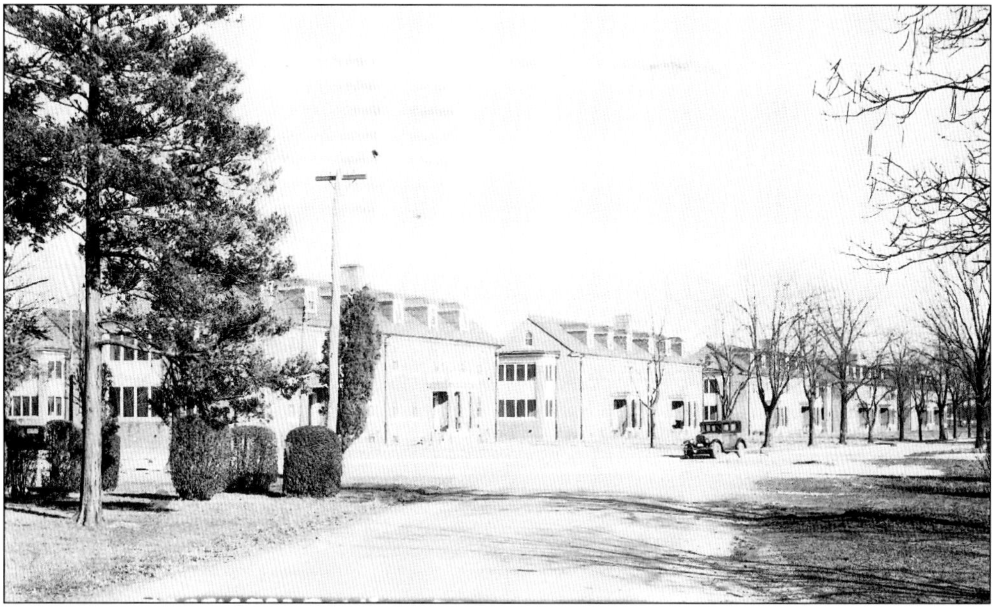

Between 1930 and 1931 brick housing for commissioned officers was built north of the flagpole at the East Gate entrance.

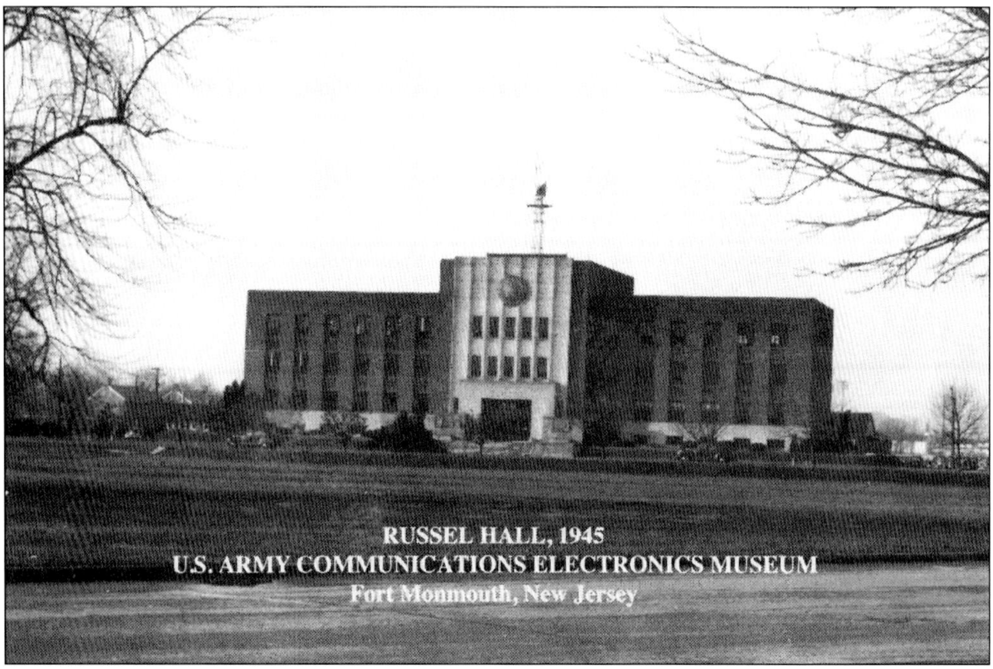

Russel Hall was built in 1936 as command headquarters.

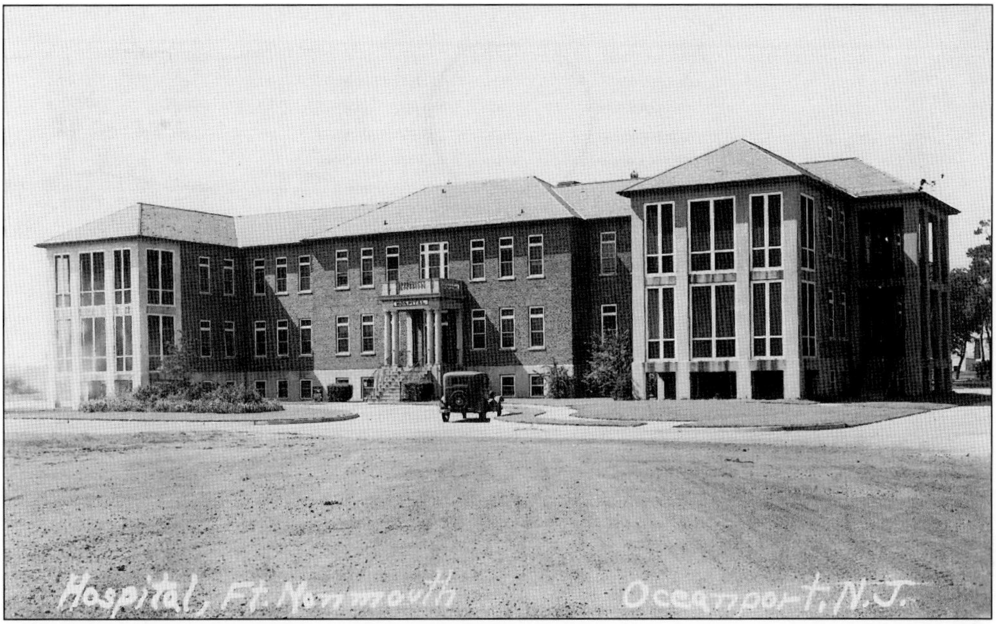

The second of three hospitals to have been built on post, this infirmary went up in 1928. The windows in the outer wings of Allison Hall had no glass to let in fresh air for healing. The hospital was named for Colonel James. B. Allison, the post's sixth commander.

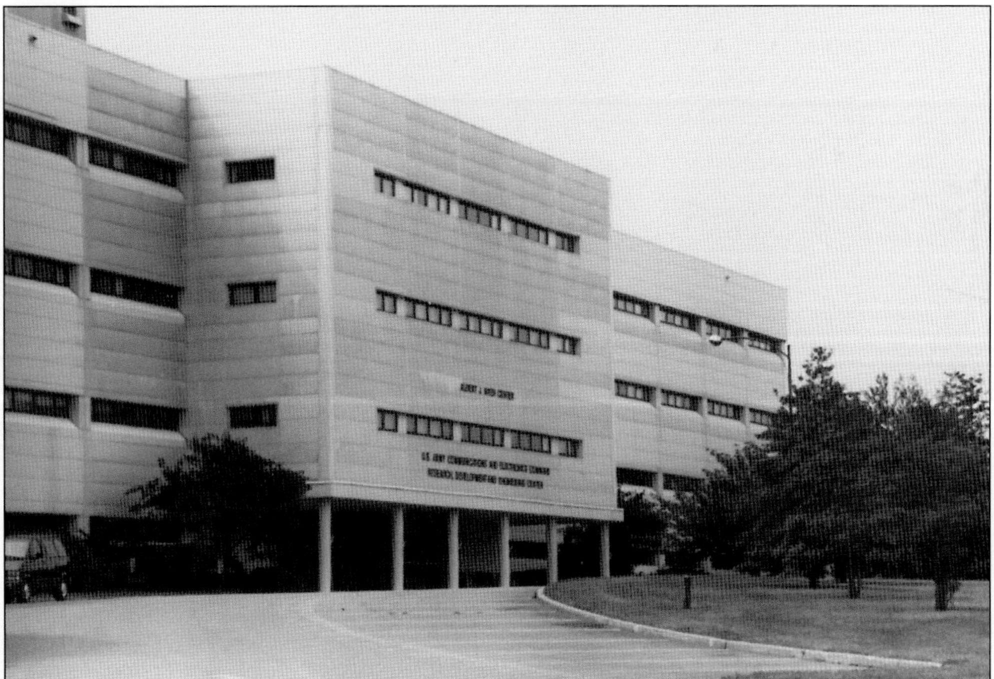

The U.S. Army Communications and Electronics Command Research, Development, and Engineering Center named for Albert J. Myers. Built in 1954, this building brought together communications research done at four separate signal laboratories: Camps Evans and Coles, Squire Labs, and the Watson Area.

Bibliography

Boyd's Monmouth County Directory 1986–1897. N.p., n.d.

A *Concise History of Fort Monmouth New Jersey*. Fort Monmouth, New Jersey: Historical Office, U.S. Army, Communications-Electronics Command, 1985.

The Early History of West Long Branch, New Jersey. West Long Branch Historical Society, 1977.

The Eatontown Advertiser. April 1877.

The Eatontown Advertiser. October 19, 1914.

The Eatontown Sentinel. October 24, 1968.

Eatontown: 300 Years of Progress. Eatontown Tricentennial Committee, 1970.

The Farm and Business Directory of Monmouth County 1914. Philadelphia: Wilmer Atkinson Co.

55th Anniversary Oceanport Hook and Ladder Co.: 1950.

The History of Monmouth County. Vols. 1 & 3. N.p., n.d.

The Monmouth County Historical Association Newsletter. No. 3.

The Monmouth County Historical Association Newsletter. No. 15.

Oceanport in Retrospect. Oceanport Historical Society, 1970.

100th Anniversary of Eatontown's Engine, Truck & Hose Co. No. 1: 1981.

Pierce, John R., and Tressler, Arthur G. *The Research State: A History of Science in New Jersey*. Princeton: D. VanNostrand Co., 1964.

Salter, Edwin. *History of Monmouth and Ocean County*. N.p., n.d.

The Story of Eatontown: 1664–1964. Eatontown Tercentenary Committee, n.d.

The Story of Eatontown. Eatontown Tricentennial Committee, 1970.

Van Benthuysen, Robert F. *Crossroads Mansions*. West Long Branch: Turtle Mill Press, 1987.

Van Benthuysen, Robert F., and Wilson, Audrey Kent. *Monmouth County: A Pictorial History*. First Jersey National Corp., 1983.